The Truth at Twenty-Four Frames per Second

An Anthology of Writings on Film History

Anthony Slide

The Truth at Twenty-Four Frames per Second:
An Anthology of Writings on Film History
© 2021 Anthony Slide. All Rights Reserved.

No part of this book may be reproduced in any form or by any means, electronic, mechanical, digital, photocopying or recording, except for the inclusion in a review, without permission in writing from the publisher.

Published in the USA by:
BearManor Media
4700 Millenia Blvd.
Suite 175 PMB 90497
Orlando, Florida 32839
www.bearmanormedia.com

Hardcover: ISBN 978-1-62933-741-8
Paperback: ISBN 978-1-62933-740-1

Printed in the United States of America.
Book design by Brian Pearce | Red Jacket Press.

Table of Contents

Introduction 7

The Truth at 24 Frames per Second 11

The Return of *Becky Sharp* 15

Beulah Bondi 22

Censored Screams! Horror Films
and the Production Code in the 1930s 34

Censored Screams! Horror Films
and the Production Code in the 1940s 47

The American Press & Public vs. Charles Spencer Chaplin 54

Russ Columbo 59

Neal Dodd 63

Geoffrey Donaldson 65

Kirk Douglas 68

Kent D. Eastin and Blackhawk Films 72

Walter Forde and *Land without Music* 74

Lillian Gish: Star of Screen, Stage — and TV 77

Filming Lillian Gish 81

Giuseppina 87

Griffith's Other Actors 89

Val Guest 96

William Haggar 109

Hull Cinemas: An Introduction 111

Hull Cinemas: William Morton 113

Bioscope Shows at Hull Fair 116

Mama's Boys	119
D.M. Marshman, Jr. and *Sunset Blvd.*	124
Mae Murray and *A Mormon Maid*	129
The Prussian Image on the American Screen	132
The Regulars	144
Wendy Richard	147
Vivienne Segal	153
Jim Sheridan	162
Sherlock Holmes and the Éclair Company	165
John Stuart	167
Thursday's Children	170
Elisabeth Welch	172
Lawrence Welk	177
Betty White: Life after Sixty	181
Norman Lloyd	185
Anthony Slide Bibliography	190
Scarecrow Press "Filmmakers Series," Edited by Anthony Slide	195
Scarecrow Press "Studies and Documentation in the History of Popular Entertainment," Edited by Anthony Slide	202
Scarecrow Press "Studies in Film Genres," Edited by Anthony Slide	203
Other Books Edited by Anthony Slide	204
Index	205

Thanks, as always, to Ben Ohmart at BearManor Media for his continued support, and Brian Pearce for the professionalism of his production and design.

1986: Anthony Slide with Lillian Gish, who has described him as "Our pre-eminent historian of the silent film."

Introduction

I wrote my first (and somewhat short) essay on film history back in the early 1960s. It was published in the June 1963 issue of a slim, and long forgotten, periodical, *Cinema Studies*, published in the U.K. by the Society for Film History Research. In a desperate effort somehow to be involved in film, I had put myself forward for the position of Honorary Secretary of the Society, and, there being no other volunteers, I was appointed. Since then, I have written or edited innumerable books (beginning in 1970 with *Early American Cinema*), and contributed articles on aspects of entertainment history to a variety of publications, some academic, some specialist, and some relatively popular.

Many of those articles have since been integrated into the body of later books. Some have never been reprinted or recycled. It is those that I am reprinting here — in large part because I believe they deserve to be preserved in a more definitive form and, equally, because I would like them to find a new readership. I have made minor revisions or corrections, but basically the pieces are reprinted as they appeared originally.

I have to confess that some of the subjects are perhaps of less interest to me today than they were when I first researched and wrote about them. However, I do not believe any are worthy of being forgotten — even if the periodicals or events to which they relate seem of little relevance or importance today.

I have deliberately not included academic essays in that I wanted as much as possible to avoid footnoting or endnoting. And I wanted the essays to be accessible and readable. They may not be academic, but I hope they might be recognized as scholarly, even if the approach is a popular one.

The individuals and subjects under discussion are primarily in the field of the motion picture, but certainly television is also represented here. The essays and articles, for whatever reason, are primarily from the 1980s. There are a few from the 1960s, 1970s and 1990s, and a small number from the 21st Century. Articles I have written in recent years have primarily been published on the Alt Film Guide website and are still accessible. I also seem to have written an extensive number of introductions to various books. Those will not be reprinted, and I cannot somehow see myself comparable to George Bernard Shaw and publishing an anthology of prefaces. There was a complaint that Shaw could write very long prefaces to very short plays. I would like to believe that I write average-length articles whose number of words is determined by what I have to say and how succinctly I can say it. (The longest book I have ever written, *The Encyclopedia of Vaudeville*, is 620 pages. The shortest, *She Could Be Chaplin*, is 134 pages. I have always regarded the latter as a monograph rather than a book, but my publisher and those criticizing the length seem to disagree.)

For the record, I have included a complete bibliography of my work, listing not only the books that I have written, but also the titles in the three series of volumes I edited for Scarecrow Press. (I might also note that I have edited a number of additional volumes that do not fall into any of those series.)

After some careful consideration (and doubts) I decided I would include my first *Cinema Studies* piece on "Hull Cinemas." I am also including two further essays relating to Hull under this same general heading. My fourth piece for *Cinema Studies* had as its subject a Welsh film pioneer, William Haggar, and that I have also decided to reprint. It stems from correspondence I had at the time with his daughter, and perhaps contains information not accessible elsewhere. Hull is a British seaport in East Yorkshire, and for those wondering as to my connection, it is that at the age of sixteen I left school, my parents moved to a village just outside of Hull and I got my first job with the Education Department of the City of Kingston upon Hull (to give Hull its full title). I was truly desperate to research and write on film history, and this seemed to be a subject that was accessible to me — far removed from the glamor of Hollywood — in a city where the smell of fish permeated the air and its most famous resident was poet Philip Larkin.

As to the title of this volume, I realize there are those who might suggest that it might, more appropriately, be called *The Truth at Sixteen Frames per Second* in that I am more frequently identified as a historian of silent film. However, and perhaps surprisingly, there are few pieces here on that subject. The sound era predominates. Hence the title. As to "The Truth," well, that is something I have always sought to embrace in whatever I have written. At times, my seeking after truth has not always pleased my readership. But I believe strongly that a historian must always be on the side of truth — no matter how controversial it may be. Obviously, I am somewhat biased in that I have determined those individuals and subjects about which I want to write. But once I decide on the individual or subject, I have never shied away from honesty in my observations and interpretations.

We are living in a dangerous age, where history (including film history) is being revised and rewritten often with little or no regard to reality. Back in the Blacklist era, academics put their careers on the line to stand up for what they believed in. There seems little enthusiasm from the academic community to take the same stand today and reject revisionism when it is nothing more than a short-sighted effort to embrace political correctness.

The first essay here, in fact, discusses issues relating to the "truth" as applied to the motion picture. It is often difficult, if not impossible, to ascertain what is the "truth" (as Pontius Pilate said). As I have already noted, I like to believe that I have always done my best to be honest and fair, but at the same time I realize there are limitations, which it is somewhat impossible to surmount. It seems that D.W. Griffith no longer deserves credit for introducing the grammar and syntax of film, or, for that matter, making a film of such monumental length, or such historical significance as *The Birth of a Nation*, which, more than 100 years after its release, still demonstrates the power of the motion picture as a tool of propagandism and preachment.

So what I am presenting here to you, the reader, is what I know and want to share on a variety of entertainment-related matters. Obviously, there is subjectivity — not in the opinions (or at least I hope not) but in the selection that I chose initially to write about, and which I choose to offer here.

The volume concludes with the only original piece to be found here — a collection of comments by veteran actor Norman Lloyd whom I have known since the 1970s and whose continuing presence reminded me so much of Jean and Dido Renoir (particularly the latter) who came into my life at the same time.

The Truth at 24 Frames per Second

McFarland Publisher Catalog, 1993, pages 14-15

"Print the legend," said John Ford — or was it Adela Rogers St. Johns? That statement, as much as the confusion as to who made it, represents the problem facing anyone writing about or studying film history. In few other disciplines is the truth so hard to ascertain, the dividing line between fantasy and reality such a cloudy one, the publicity story so indistinguishable from fact.

The primary sources for film research range from the films themselves through trade papers, personal reminiscences (oral histories or autobiographies, which may well be ghost-written) and fan magazine articles, to studio records. Only the last are relatively free from tampering and even here the suspicion remains that before such materials were handed over to a public archives many documents or items of correspondence were removed. It was, for example, obvious that all Marilyn Monroe-related items had been removed from the archives of agent Charles K. Feldman before they were handed over to the American Film Institute's Center for Advanced Film Study in Los Angeles. Many years ago, I went through every file folder in the MGM script collection after its donation to the Academy of Motion Picture Arts and Sciences, and every original Lon Chaney script was no longer present, replaced by a modern typed copy.

Literary criticism primarily demands access to the book or short story, copies of which cannot be "modified" as the years go by. Students of film must rely on the films themselves, which are subject to various forms of deterioration, censorship, artistic license, and physical abuse. Because of the instability of nitrate film stock, some productions shot prior to 1950 may not exist in any form, let alone that which its maker intended. Color film fades and so the images on screen today may be at variance with those carefully crafted by the director. It is possible for the censorious to remove a scene or a shot from a motion picture without the viewer's knowledge. There were so many local city and state censorship boards that a specific film used decades later in the preservation process may well have been subject to editing in one state, viewed in that same condition in another state and then gone on to be the only material to have survived. The wear and tear on a print each time it is run through a projector almost invariably results in the loss of a few and sometimes many frames of film at the beginning and end of each reel.

In the days of silent films, exhibitors would often cut scenes from a film they considered over-long or tedious. The preserved version of such a film may be not the one released by the studio but one "edited" by someone far removed from the creative process. Restoration is a key word in the reissue of "old" films, but how many of these restored films now contain scenes not present at the original release? What changes has the restorer been forced to make in order to make a production palatable to a modern audience? Just as most authors would welcome the opportunity to rewrite their books following publication, directors are happy to add or subtract material at the time of reissue or release in another medium. Laser discs, and later DVDs and Blu Rays, are advertised as so-called "director's cuts," meaning, in reality, the images which we see on the television screen are not the same as those seen by audience at the film's original release.

And apropos the previous comment, one must acknowledge that a considerable number — perhaps a majority — of those writing on any aspect of film history will view the film(s) under discussion on a television or computer screen. That such films were intended to be viewed by a large audience on a large screen in a theater may seem irrelevant. But it is anything but — a film was not created to be watched by an audience of one, and those produced during Hollywood's so-called "Golden Age" and even much later were never intended for viewing on anything but a full-size movie theater screen.

Films are "edited for television," dubbed into other languages, cut between a premiere and general release. Words and phrases are sometimes altered for a television airing, and, of course, imperceptibly, the films are speeded up for television in order to provide additional time for commercials.

Academics might argue that the films themselves represent the primary source in any study of the motion picture. Yet, in reality, films tell us very little about what is involved in their making. A study of the film itself will not reveal if some footage was shot not by the credited director but by an additional director without credit. A film will not reveal the editing process and what individuals were involved in addition to the credited film editor. The entire production process, from the signing of the rights to the original material, casting, the rehearsal process, the setting up of camera angles, etc. — nothing in the process is evident from a viewing of the film.

If the films themselves are unreliable documents, what of the printed sources such as trade publications and fan magazines? Here the distance between myth and reality is even greater. Industry journals, such as *Variety* and *The Hollywood Reporter*, have through the years tried to record the workings of the film community, but they are susceptible to pressure from those about whom they are writing. Trade papers have survived in large part thanks to advertising revenue — and the source of such advertising is the film industry. Journalists and reviewers are only human, and subject to the same frailties as most of us. The pressure of a deadline has in the past required that an event be reported before it takes place. One reviewer told me that, when he joined the staff of *The Hollywood Reporter* back in the 1940s, a member of the publicity department at 20th Century-Fox advised him that he would henceforth be receiving $200.00 in cash monthly. All the studio required was that its releases be treated with suitable respect. He turned down the bribe, but how many of his colleagues accepted — and from how many studios?

Was it different in the early years of the motion picture, when *Variety* was already established, but *The Hollywood Reporter* did not exist? Perhaps. While the writing style might be atrocious, the pages of early publication, such as the *Moving Picture World* and *Motion Picture News* are generally to be trusted. An exception should perhaps be made for the reviews which are almost always, without exception, positive. No point in upsetting the advertisers. Yet at the same time, one must be aware that both publications had close ties to different trade groups, representing different film producers.

One should not forget that one of the first fan magazines, *Motion Picture Story Magazine* (later *Motion Picture Magazine*) was co-founded by J. Stuart Blackton, who just happened to be co-founder of the major early producer, the Vitagraph Company of America. Vitagraph in turn was a member of the Motion Picture Trust. Little surprise that *Motion Picture Story Magazine* would feature the films and the stars of those producers who were members of the Trust.

Reviews in fan magazines are highly suspect compared to those in the trade papers. While he was reviewing for *Motion Picture Classic* in the

1910s, Frederick James Smith was also an employee of director Maurice Tourneur. In its October 1933 issue, *New Movie* reviewed ten films. Of *Dancing Lady*, it wrote, "Robert Z. Leonard has directed a fast moving show." Of *Footlight Parade*, it opined, "The songs are not so hot." Such comments would be examples of contemporary response to these films, except that they had not been completed, let alone released, at the time the periodical was published.

One must not forget that Hollywood publicists were not paid to publicize what took place on the set, but rather to conceal the truth and to disseminate to their carefully controlled outlets only what was deemed necessary for the public to know — and much of that was creative fiction. An accidental death on the set, for example, would never be reported to the press. To explain a star's absence, it was often necessary to resort to euphemisms. Appendicitis was generally used in place of abortion, and one prominent star of the 1940s had her appendix removed three times in as many years.

Not only the public, but also the subjects of these yarns began to accept them as the truth. Many former film personalities regurgitated press clippings. Blanche Sweet once told me that she was so embarrassed at her inability to answer specific questions that she had taken to visiting the Museum of Modern Art and reading current essays in an effort to appear knowledgeable.

Hollywood was a land of dreams. The producers of Hollywood's Golden Age marketed fantasy not only on screen but in all areas of promotion and publicity. Those who chronicle Hollywood history must never forget there is a difference between fantasy and reality.

[This essay has been expanded and revised since original publication.]

The Return of *Becky Sharp*

Films in Review, March 1985, pages 148-153

"A film is like a child, and when you see a print fading away, the wrong colors and out of focus, as it would hurt a parent. Suddenly you sit there, years later, and the thing comes back, and you see your child the way it was. I can't tell you how happy and most grateful it makes me." The speaker is Rouben Mamoulian, and the film about which he is talking is *Becky Sharp*, restored almost to its former self after three years of laborious and painstaking work by Robert Gitt, Preservation Officer of the UCLA Film and Television Archive, and Richard Dayton, of the Burbank-based YCM Laboratory, which specializes in archival work.

Why is *Becky Sharp* so important? Because is the first three-strip, or full color, Technicolor feature. As the *Literary Digest* (June 8, 1935) commented, there had been two phases in the history of the motion picture. The first came with *The Birth of a Nation*'s transforming entertainment into art; the second came when *The Jazz Singer* brought sound to the screen. *Becky Sharp* heralded the third phase — color. Of course, there had been earlier color processes and an early Technicolor two-color process, and, certainly, full color had been utilized for shorts such as *Flowers and Trees* (1932) and *La Cucaracha* (1934) and for sequences in a number of features — *The Cat and the Fiddle* (1934), *The House of Rothschild* (1934) and *Kid Millions* (1934). But *Becky Sharp* was the first feature to be shot entirely in full color, to utilize the full color spectrum, and the first to demonstrate the dramatic possibilities of color. (For a good succinct history of Technicolor, see Rudy Behlmer's article in the June-July 1964 issue of *Films in Review*.) To Andre Sennwald in the *New York Times* (June 14, 1935), "It produces in the spectator all the excitement of standing upon a peak in Darien and glimpsing a strange, beautiful and unexpected world. As an experiment, it is a momentous event, and it may be that in a few years it will be regarded as the equal in historical importance of the first crude and wretched talking pictures…it is a gallant and distinguished outpost in an almost uncharted domain." (Coincidentally, *Becky Sharp*'s producer Kenneth Macgowan, saw the new Technicolor process as the industry's strongest weapon against television, which in 1935 was seriously worrying studio executives; Macgowan expounded his theory in the May 31, 1935, issue of the *Technical Bulletin of the Academy of Motion Picture Arts and Sciences* and in the July 6, 1935, issue of *Commentator*.)

The two major figures behind *Becky Sharp* were Merian C. Cooper and John Hay "Jock" Whitney. Cooper, the former head of production at RKO, impressed his enthusiasm for the Technicolor process on young playboy millionaire Whitney, and the two formed Pioneer Pictures to produce Technicolor films, with Whitney also purchasing an estimated fifteen percent of the stock in Technicolor. For its first production, *La Cucaracha*, Pioneer hired the noted stage designer, Robert Edmond Jones (at $1,000.00 a week), and spent $65,000.00 on a two-reel short, with no star names, at a period when the average short cost $15,000.00.

The contribution of Robert Edmond Jones to the artistic success of three-strip Technicolor cannot be underestimated. "Color in pictures does not mean that the screen will be deluged with brilliant hues," he explained. "Color is rather the 'tone' of the picture, or the underlying harmony of all tones. Each square inch of the picture must be related to every other square inch." He experimented by filming a scene of John Barrymore in *Hamlet*, and he tried shooting various scenes of actress Nan Sunderland with "mood lights" played upon her. Andrew R. Boone reported on Jones' work in the May 1935 issue of *Popular Science*:

"Twenty boys, each manning a 'gelatin' or colored spot light, stood offstage when the cameras began to grind again. Jones called for first one combination of lights, then another. At first the actress was enveloped in cold, tragic blue. This drab color literally painted her in gloom as she contemplated the loss of her lover. Then she heard footsteps and turned expectantly, hoping for his return. As she smiled the screen changed to the colors of dawn, her face flooded with rose and yellow."

These tests still survive and are exactly as reported.

Pioneer considered a number of projects for its first feature-length production, including *Peacock's Feather* (to star Ann Harding), *The Last Days of Pompeii* (which Cooper was scheduled to produce to wind up his RKO contract) and *The Miracle*. However, the ultimate choice was *Becky Sharp*, an adaptation of Langdon Mitchell's 1899 play (which had starred Mrs. Minnie Maddern Fiske), and which, in turn, was adapted from William Makepeace Thackeray's novel, *Vanity Fair*. Helen Gardner first played Becky Sharp on the screen in 1911; Mrs. Fiske made a film version in 1915; Mabel Ballin played the character in a 1923 version; and in 1932 Myra Loy starred in an atrocious modern-dress version, directed by Chester Franklin.

As *Becky Sharp*'s producer, Whitney and Cooper selected Kenneth Macgowan, whose work on the stage with Eugene O'Neill was exemplary and who had co-authored a 1922 book — *Continental Stagecraft* — with Robert Edmond Jones. The latter shot a variety of screen tests with various performers, including Mrs. Leslie Carter (who was presumably to have played the role eventually portrayed by Alison Skipworth), Elsie Ferguson (who was, perhaps, considered for the part of the Duchess of Richmond), and Zita Johann (in the Frances Dee role). The Hays Office gave its approval to the script on November 19, 1934, at which time Joseph I. Breen wrote Macgowan that "We believe it vitally important that the heroine should be played as a Nineteenth Century golddigger but in no sense, at no time, should there be any suggestion that she is a loose woman sexually." The film was shot at the RKO-Pathe Studios in Culver City, later known as the Selznick Studios and Laird International.

Miriam Hopkins was the company's choice for Becky Sharp, and Lowell Sherman was signed to direct. Production officially began on December 3, 1934 — although Jones had been shooting tests since November 28 — and continued without problems until Sherman developed a severe cold. He continued filming with a nurse on the set until December 27, when he was taken to Cedars of Lebanon Hospital. He died the following day of pneumonia, the same day as Universal was scheduled to preview what was to be his last production, *Night Life of the Gods*.

Production was temporarily halted until January 7, 1935, when John Hay Whitney's choice as Sherman's successor, Rouben Mamoulian, took over production. It was initially announced that he would retain the footage that Sherman had shot, but on January 19, *Daily Variety*, reported that following a meeting between Mamoulian, Macgowan and Whitney, it was decided to remake the earlier sequences.

According to Mamoulian, he demanded certain changes to the script by Francis Edwards Faragoh, and also questioned Jones' contract which gave him responsibility for the color coordination. Mamoulian recalls, "I said, 'Look, if he's in charge of colors what do you want me for? My only interest in this would be to work with colors. I've worked with them on stage all my life.' Well, Mr. Jones — he was an exceedingly nice man — said to me, 'I've watched your productions on Broadway and I think in this case I would be quite willing to give up my right to be in charge of color, and I'll just do whatever you want me to do as a set designer.'"

With the use of colors such a crucial reason for *Becky Sharp*'s appeal, it is unfortunate that one must act almost as a judge and jury with regard to whether the credit goes to Mamoulian or Jones. Certainly, according to an interview in the June 1935 issue of *New Theatre*, Jones worked for four months prior to shooting, making color sketches of key scenes, planning the dominant colors to be used in each sequence, and even the transitions from one scene to the next. "He worked out a plot for the progression of color throughout the entire film: beginning with low values so that the color is almost unperceived in the opening shots, and building climatically to bright posteresque color harmonies in the scenes of dramatic action."

The most impressive use of color occurs at the Duchess of Richmond's ball, which reaches its climax with news of Napoleon's proximity to Waterloo. Mamoulian recalls in great detail devising the color coordination for that sequence, building up to red as the climactic color. Certainly there is a dramatic intensity to the sequence not apparent in the extant tests of the ball scenes shot by Jones. It was Mamoulian also who claims to have cast William Faversham for the small, but dramatically important role of the Duke of Wellington, and who also requested Doris Lloyd for the part of the Duchess — she had also been in his first play, *The Beating on the Door* (1922).

Mamoulian had two heroes — Napoleon and Buffalo Bill — and when it came to showing the former in *Becky Sharp*, the director decided to use only a shadow. "I thought I don't want to make him that real," says Mamoulian. "I thought I'd do it with a shadow, and, therefore, I needed a real Napoleonic profile. And there was one extra, a short, little man, very shy, but he had a good profile, and I said, 'I'd like you to play Napoleon.' I told my assistants and everybody connected with the picture, from now on, address this fellow as Your Majesty. And gradually, from day to day, this fellow is getting more and more Napoleonic until finally he thought it enough, and we did this shot. Sometimes a shadow is better than reality."

If Mamoulian had no problems working with Jones, the same is not true of the best known member of the Technicolor family. "I came on the set the first day and I saw this lady, telling the electricians how to light it. I said, 'Pardon me, what are you doing?' She said, 'I'm Mrs. Kalmus. I'm in charge of color.' Everybody's in charge of color! So I went to Jock Whitney and Kenneth Macgowan and said, 'Look, tomorrow, either she is not there or I am not there.'"

Miriam Hopkins added to the production's delays by also being taken ill with pneumonia, and spending ten days — January 18 through January 28 — off the set. As an actress, she gave Mamoulian few problems — he liked her and enjoyed working with her once he had established who was in charge. She did give Nigel Bruce problems by constantly upstaging him and even, once, reducing the actor to tears.

Becky Sharp must surely be one of the most ill-ridden productions in the history of the cinema, Aside from the death of its first director and the illness of the star, there were problems with the sound, so much so that some of the dialogue was unintelligible, and the entire soundtrack had to be electronically re-recorded. Also, the work print of the Duchess of Richmond's ball sequence caught fire in the projection room, and it took weeks for the editor to reconstruct the reel from whatever written notes had been retained.

With an eventual cost estimated at one million dollars, *Becky Sharp* received its world premiere at Radio City Music Hall on June 13, 1935. Critical reception was mixed, ranging from the *New York Herald Tribune*'s pronouncement that *Becky Sharp* was "the most important cinematic experiment since moving shadows first became articulate" to the *New York Mirror*'s view — which seemed to be the general consensus — that "its pictorial beauty compensates for its lack of action, depth and suspense." The only negative comment concerning the color came from George Lewis in *New Theatre* (August 1935), who wrote, "In many respects the new color has the appearance of an animated colored photograph of the kind now adorning magazine back covers in the interests of cigarettes. It has that brash, noisy overemphasis, which, while necessary to capture attention in an advertisement, is hardly a recommendation for the development of an art form."

In 1943, the rights to *Becky Sharp* were acquired by Film Classics, which reissued the film in the inferior, but far cheaper, Cinecolor process. At the same time, Film Classics cut all the 35mm release prints from eighty-four minutes to sixty-six minutes. By the late 1950s, the film had been acquired for television by National Telefilm Associates (NTA), which made it available only in 16mm black-and-white, cut versions. (Columbia also planned a remake in 1946.)

Of the 448 prints originally made of *Becky Sharp* by Technicolor none are believed to have survived, and the Technicolor Company retained only a 35mm nitrate print of the first reel. Working with this one reel as a color guide, Robert Gitt and Richard Dayton have restored the film to its original three-color look for sixty-four minutes of its length, to good quality two-color for a further ten minutes and to acceptable two-color for the remaining ten minutes. Their task is an extraordinary one, fully documented in the November 1984 issue of *American Cinematographer*, involving working with incomplete negatives, protection masters, and 16mm negatives and prints. Registration of the three colors — yellow, cyan and magenta — was a major problem due to shrinkage of original nitrate materials, and an even greater problem when some elements were missing altogether.

The result of Gitt and Dayton's work has been widely praised at screenings at the 1984 New York Film Festival — where *Becky Sharp* was the first film to sell out — and at the West Coast re-premiere in Los Angeles. What exactly can a contemporary audience appreciate in *Becky Sharp*?

Certainly, the colors are lush and beautiful, and salvage a feature which has little dramatic intensity. Miriam Hopkins' performance is played on one, very strident level, but she is also very much the character of Becky Sharp, delivering devastating one-liners and artificial platitudes with a delightful fervor. Alan Mowbray is acceptable, and does his best with some atrocious dialogue, notably the comment, "I worship you from your little toes up." Cedric Hardwicke dominates all his scenes, with remarks such as "poor innocent lamb," to Becky's pleading that he is not such a bad wolf, or his final rejoinder to Becky's husband, "Why squabble about something that you don't own and I don't want."

To a large extent the film relies on the ensemble playing of a distinguished cast, many members of which have exceedingly small roles. Billie Burke, for example, has little more than two lines of dialogue in one scene. Tempe Piggett, whose name appears way down in the cast list, has a far bigger part. William Stack is ingratiatingly slimy as the elder brother, breathing lustful, religious platitudes to Becky. Nigel Bruce is full of good humor and steals every scene even if his performance lacks depth and can hardly have taxed his acting ability. And, yes, Mrs. Richard Nixon is also in the film — as an extra at the Duchess of Richmond's ball.

Becky Sharp is also a film which plays very well with a big audience. It does not work on viewing in an isolated environment, but it has the strength and vitality to carry an audience along with it. The film never takes itself too seriously — it is a comedy of manners, a flawed 18th Century screwball comedy. Perhaps because audiences are a little uncertain as to whether they really should be laughing, *Becky Sharp* has come in for a little too serious analysis and criticism.

One major flaw in *Becky Sharp*, and one of which critics appear to be unaware, is a lapse in continuity in the last reel, which takes place in

Becky's lodgings in Bath. As is apparent from the opening of the sequence, when Nigel Bruce and Frances Dee climb up a flight of stairs to Becky's room and from the closing sequence when Becky opens the window of her room and throws the book at William Stack, her lodgings are quite definitely on the second floor of the building. And yet, throughout the scene, couples can clearly be viewed walking by outside her window, which must be a good fourteen feet above street level!

Whatever one's feelings towards the film, praise is due Robert Gitt and Richard Dayton for having restored it so closely to its original form. A dubbed print of *Becky Sharp* has recently been discovered in Italy, and it could be that the last reel of the film of this print will help restore full color to the last reel of the restored *Becky Sharp*, which is the most inadequate as far as color quality is concerned.

"Everything that is beautiful to the eye is a great gift to humanity," wrote Rouben Mamoulian in 1935. "Color on the screen is such a gift." The restoration of *Becky Sharp* was kept to a minimum of around $30,000.00. If film preservation is to continue — and Gitt and Dayton are about to start work on restoring the first two-color Technicolor film, *The Toll of the Sea* — there must be great gifts forthcoming not only from the private sector but from the government through the National Endowment for the Arts.

[Robert Gitt and Richard Dayton did restore The Toll of the Sea. *In 2019, Paramount Pictures, under the leadership of Andrea Kalas, produced a digital restoration of* Becky Sharp.*]*

Beulah Bondi

Focus on Film, April 1980, pages 31-43

Veteran character actor Fritz Feld recently hailed Beulah Bondi as the character actress who never relied on gimmicks. It was a fitting tribute to a woman whose performances in more than sixty motion picture over the last forty-five years have undoubtedly gained for her the title of doyenne of the character actress, a performer, who, with the aid of subtle make-up and a tremendous ability to act and characterize, has played everything from tender mothers to hateful harridans, from domineering country women, to regal society matrons.

Beulah Bondi was — and still is a performer who could understand the need to get completely into the part she was playing; to become the character she had to understand the personality of the figure she was creating. As she explained to me, "I always felt if I was going to play a role, I had to know the character from the time she was young until she was what I meant as a character, so at times it was my imagination, but I usually tried to dress from the skin out, whatever the character was. If it was an aristocrat or some royalty, or if it was a beggar woman, I felt I had to know her from the inside out, so I studied people. I studied walks. I studied voices. I studied tempos. I studied inflections. I studied gestures. It's like having many, many picture drawers I can draw from. But I don't think I ever repeated a character, because my whole philosophy and belief is that everyone has a different mentality and a different physicality. That is why when a character is handed to me it's a completely new person — like meeting a friend for the first time. Then it's by analyzing, with imagination, what she is, why she is, when I meet here. She's the result of all her yesterdays. I don't think I've ever duplicated my characters."

As Fritz Feld's remarks indicate, character actors can be split into two basic groups. There are those with a gimmick which never wearied an audience and could be repeated in film after film: Franklin Pangborn and his flustered, mincing demeanor; Herman Bing and his inimitable splutterings; Arthur Treacher and Eric Blore perennially butling; fluttery ZaSu Pitts; ever-old and vaguely sinister Maria Ouspenskaya; Fritz Feld with the popping sound made by his hand and mouth; and those whose gimmicks are less easily definable, such as Billy Gilbert, Erik Rhodes and Ned Sparks. The other group of character actors — the adaptables — might include Dub Taylor, Sam Jaffe, Spring Byington, and Una O'Connor (whose screams in many horror films of the 1930s almost became a gimmick). John Ford built up an entire stock company of such adaptable character players, many of whom had known stardom in the silent era, including Mae Marsh, Ruth Clifford, Olive Carey, Frank Baker, Francis Ford, and Hank Worden.

Of the adaptables, it is no exaggeration to state that Beulah Bondi has been the most adaptable and the most enduring. Her face is as well known today as it was to moviegoers forty years ago. She has survived in popularity many of the stars she once supported. Paradoxically, Beulah Bondi looks younger today, or at least no older, than she did in the 1930s, for so many of her screen roles back then demanded that she portray elderly women. In fact her Broadway career began with such a characterization.

She was born Beulah Bondy in Chicago on May 3, 1889. Her mother taught her elocution and encouraged her theatrical aspirations, and Beulah made her stage debut at the age of nine as Cedric Erroll in *Little Lord Fauntleroy* at the Memorial Opera House in Valparaiso, Indiana. In 1907, she graduated from the Frances Shriner Academy — now Shriner College — for which she holds a particular affection, and to which she has returned many times. In 1967, she received the Alumni Award for Distinction in the Humanities, at which time she noted, "It was here I first learned the meaning of cooperation. I learned to live and get along with others, something that has helped me profoundly in my work on the stage and in films."

From Shriner, she went to Valparaiso University, where she received her master's degree in oratory. In 1919, after much amateur theatrical work, Beulah joined the Stuart Walker Stock Company in Indianapolis, and remained there for two years before leaving to play stock elsewhere. Beulah Bondi believes these years spent in a working and training atmosphere were tremendously important to her. "I've always felt we character actresses had wonderful training, very different training from that actors get now. Because, as you know, many young actor get one role and they can tell you how to act. Any profession — medicine, the law or acting — I thought ten years was nothing to learn it. I had two years as an amateur, and then I had four years of professional stock training, and I was just fortunate that, when I went to New York, the day I arrived I met a director. He said, 'I'm just going to start a new play. They want a woman, sixty to seventy years old. They won't believe you can do it, but I've worked with you in stock and I know that you can.' That's luck! You come out of the subway, meet your former director, and he's starting a play, and he takes you over and fights the battle for you." The date was December 21, 1925, when Kenneth Webb's *One of the Family* opened on Broadway at the 49th Street Theatre. Beulah Bondi — the "y" in her surname had by now been replaced by an "i" — portrayed Maggie, the elderly servant, in a cast which included Grant Mitchell, Kay Johnson, and Louise Closser Hale.

Miss Bondi embarked on a highly successful Broadway career, appearing in *Saturday's Children* (1926) and *Cock Robin* (1928), among others. In the former, she played a tight-lipped, self-pitying landlady and stole scene after scene from the play's star, Ruth Gordon; not scene-stealing by design but by talent. She was to steal many more scenes in the future.

On January 10, 1929, *Street Scene* opened at New York's Playhouse Theatre with a cast which included John Qualen as Carl Olsen, Erin O'Brien-Moore as Rose and Beulah Bondi as the hard-bitten and dour Emma Jones. Its author, the Pulitzer Prize-winning Elmer Rice, was responsible for the play's direction and also for its casting. Rice's success is indicated by the play's 601 performances on Broadway.

King Vidor saw the play in New York, and chose it to be his first film for Goldwyn after a six-year sojourn at MGM. He was particularly impressed by the character players in the stage production, and asked eight of them to participate in the film: Eleanor Wesselhoeft, Beulah Bondi, Conway Washburne, T.H. Manning, John Qualen, Anna Konstant, George Humbert, and Matthew McHugh. They were to provide excellent support to principals Sylvia Sidney, William Collier, Jr. and Estelle Taylor. Vidor described Beulah and John Qualen as "two of the best actors I have ever had the pleasure of directing." Of course, Qualen was to go on from *Street Scene* to a film career which was as illustrious as Miss Bondi's and encompassed many more film appearances.

Beulah Bondi could not have asked for a better introduction to the cinema than *Street Scene*. The director remained faithful to the play, not attempting to "open up" the production but keeping the action confined to the play's brownstone tenement on a block in Manhattan's West 60s — a block that might just as well have been on any street in any American city. To escape from the necessary restrictions of the stage play, King Vidor used an ever-changing number of camera set-ups — not one set-up is repeated — and then had composer Alfred Newman synchronize his score to the rhythm of the camera movement.

"As I remember, we were tested in the winter of 1930, and we came out to Los Angeles in May, and made *Street Scene* here in a month," says Miss Bondi. "It was, of course, my first picture, and I felt very comfortable in it. Fortunately King Vidor agreed with Elmer Rice to rehearse as we had rehearsed in New York. One week was devoted exclusively to rehearsals, and actual shooting took a mere twenty-one days. It was a completely new technique for me. I had been taught to project, to let the person in the last row of the balcony hear me, so the microphone was a completely new instrument to me. When I first heard some of the actors, well, I could barely hear them. I did not realize the power of the microphone. But I think by observing the experienced actors with me, it didn't take very long before I realized there was modulation in voice and certainly restriction in action. I was learning a completely new technique, and I loved it."

Released by United Artists, *Street Scene* opened at New York's Rivoli Theatre on August 26, 1931, to almost totally favorable reviews, with most critics singling out Beulah Bondi's performance for praise. "Rush" in *Variety* (September 1, 1931) commented, "In purely acting sense the honors go to Beulah Bondi as the malicious scandal monger of the tenement, playing the part she created on the stage and playing it to the hilt." The critic in *International Photographer* (October 1931), after comparing *Street Scene* in its simplicity and humanistic approach to the early Biograph productions of D.W. Griffith, described Beulah Bondi's performance as the best in the production, stating, "She follows not the prescribed routine of overemphasis; rather she rests her work on restraint and deliberation."

It was small wonder that following the release of *Street Scene*, Sam Goldwyn, together with Irving Thalberg, offered Miss Bondi an exclusive, seven-year contract with Goldwyn and MGM. "Mr. Goldwyn was very enthusiastic," recalls Miss Bondi. "I thanked him, and told him I was going back to New York, and that my attorney would look at the contract. And a very nice gentleman in the office said, 'You don't seem very eager to sign this.' I said, 'I'm eager to sign and go in pictures, but I haven't read the contract, and so I must go back and see my attorney.' When my attorney called Mr. Goldwyn long distance from New York, he said, 'I understand you think Miss Bondi has talent, and you want to sign her to a seven-year contract. Well, if you think she's worth anything, why don't you give her a good contract?' Evidently that didn't please Mr. Goldwyn, because he said, 'If she doesn't want the contract, let her tear it up.' My agent turned to me, and he said, 'Can you live without this contract, Beulah?' And I said, 'I have lived a long time before I met Mr. Goldwyn and Mr. Thalberg, I think I can live without them. Let's tear it up.'" The contract would have guaranteed Beulah Bondi a weekly salary of $500.00, the salary which she received for her role in *Street Scene*, both on stage and in the film."

Beulah Bondi's career as a screen character actress began immediately after *Street Scene*, even without the aid of a contract from Goldwyn and Thalberg, with her averaging three film roles a year from 1931 to 1940. She could be as impressive in a fairly major role, such as the minister's wife, Mrs. Davidson, in *Rain* (1932) as she is in the minor character of the naïve head of an orphanage, who is very vague about sexual matters, in William Wyler's delightful *The Good Fairy* (1935). Of course, there were occasional films for which even Beulah Bondi could do nothing. One such was Universal's *The Invisible Ray* (1936), with Boris Karloff and Bela Lugosi in a ridiculous story of a man whose touch means death. The director was Lambert Hillyer, who had been responsible for many of William S. Hart's films, and Beulah has never forgiven him for forcing her to wear trousers in the production — "I couldn't believe my character or myself in pants."

Her film appearances did not prevent Beulah Bondi from performing on the New York stage. There were unfortunate failures such as Dan Totheroh and George O'Neil's *Mother Lode*, which opened on December 22, 1934, and ran for a mere nine performances. Beulah played Mrs. Kate Hawkins, under the direction of the play's star, Melvyn Douglas. Also in the cast was a young actor named Tex Ritter, who was to find his own peculiar niche in films. Far more successful a play was Sidney Howard's comedy, *The Late Christopher Bean*, which opened on October 31, 1932, with Beulah Bondi as the nagging wife, Mrs. Haggerty. The play was such a hit that it was less than a year before MGM filmed it as *Christopher Bean* with Miss Bondi recreating her original role and providing excellent support to the film's star, Marie Dressler. Also in the film, in the role he essayed on stage, was George Coulouris, whom Orson Welles truly introduced to cinema audiences with *Citizen Kane*.

Beulah Bondi continued to commute between New York and Los Angeles for many years. "I'd been a New York actress, and I felt New York was the place. However, after the third picture that I was brought out for — I believe it was *Rain* — I found myself singing as I walked down the red carpet at Grand Central, and I thought, 'Well, you're happier going back to California.'" Miss Bondi moved permanently to Los Angeles at the outbreak of World War Two, and in 1944 purchased the beautiful Spanish-style house where she still lives in the Whitley Heights neighborhood of Los Angeles. With its simple dignity and charm, the house makes a perfect setting for its owner.

Despite her move to Los Angeles, Miss Bondi continued to appear sporadically on the stage. In 1940, she played *Mrs. Wiggs of the Cabbage Patch* at the Mohawk Drama Festival at the request of her close friend Charles Coburn, who was directing the festival.[1] Broadway saw Beulah Bondi again in 1950 when she co-starred with Jessica Tandy in Samson Raphaelson's *Hilda Crane*. In the summer of 1957, she was actress-in-residence at the University of Denver, playing Mistress Kearney, a picturesque mountain woman, in *Traipsin' Women*, a play especially written for her by Dan Totheroh, a playwright for whom Beulah Bondi had first acted as far back as the early 1920s, when she appeared in the off-Broadway production of *Wild Birds*.

For most film *aficionados*, the high spot in Beulah Bondi's screen career came in 1937 when she portrayed Lucy Cooper in Leo McCarey's *Make Way for Tomorrow*. An unabashed tear-jerker, *Make Way for Tomorrow* illustrates the barriers which exist between the old and the young, between parents and children. It was one of the few early films to deal with the problem of growing old, in the tradition of, and far more sophisticated than, *Over the Hill* and a forerunner to *I Never Sang for My Father*.

The opening two titles set the theme of the production: "life flies past us so swiftly that few of us pause to consider those who have lost the tempo of today, Their laughter and their tears we do not understand for there is no magic that will draw together in perfect understanding the aged and the young. There is a canyon between us, and the painful gap is only bridged by the ancient words of a very wise man — 'Honor thy father and thy mother.'"

Victor Moore, a comedian with a long record of stage and screen successes behind him, gives one of the few straight performances of his career, a fine characterization only slightly marred by occasional lapses into comic mannerisms. In an article in the January 11, 1947, issue of the *Saturday Evening Post*, Moore named Barkley Cooper in *Make Way for Tomorrow* as "my favorite role," and wrote, "The theme made a deep impression both on us at the studio and on the public. We became so absorbed in our parts that we never knew or cared when quitting time came. I felt my role so keenly that sometimes I couldn't prevent tears from coming to my eyes. 'Barkley mustn't feel sorry for himself,' Leo would say. 'Let the audience do the crying.' The extras, grips, cameramen and

---

1. Because Beulah Bondi was still alive when this article was published, I did not mention that she and Charles Coburn were rumored to be more than just friends.

propmen were so moved that several of them told Beulah Bondi, who played the mother so well, that they had just written long-delayed letters to their parents. One old lady, after hanging up the extras' clothes on a line, said to me, 'You and Beulah are acting the story, I'm living it.'"

Despite the presence of such fine players as Fay Bainter, Thomas Mitchell and Barbara Reid (fresh from a triumphant success in Deanna Durbin's *Three Smart Girls*), Beulah Bondi has no trouble in walking away with the acting honors. Modestly, she recalls, "I loved doing it, but I don't think it was my most difficult role." The scene in which she talks over the telephone to Victor Moore at her daughter-in-law's bridge party must surely qualify as one of the most moving soliloquies ever recorded on film.

There are many who will agree with Leo McCarey that it was the saddest story he has ever filmed; McCarey much preferred it to his screwball comedies, such as *The Awful Truth*. Beulah Bondi describes it as "my favorite of all," and I, for one, heartily concur.

Two actors have worked with Beulah Bondi on five separate occasions: Lionel Barrymore, who like Miss Bondi seemed to specialize in portraying characters older than his real age, and James Stewart. But Stewart has had the distinction of playing Miss Bondi's son in all five productions. It is little wonder the actress describes him as "one of my own."

Stewart and Miss Bondi first worked together on Clarence Brown's 1936 production of *The Gorgeous Hussy*, in which the actress portrays Mrs. Andrew Jackson. "Wear" in *Variety* (September 19, 1936) described her performance as "a particularly clever impersonation." Playing opposite Beulah Bondi, as Andrew Jackson, was Lionel Barrymore, and together the couple play what she laughingly describes as her only risqué scene. For the film she was required to appear getting into a double bed with Barrymore, and that particularly day also happened to be the first time Miss Bondi's mother visited a film set. Miss Bondi believes *The Gorgeous Hussy* was probably the last time a couple was allowed by the Production Code to appear in bed together; from then on, as she recalls, "I played an old woman getting into a single bed. Now in films they can do anything in any kind of bed."

1936 was the first year an Academy Award was given for Best Supporting Actress, and Beulah Bondi was nominated for her performance in *The Gorgeous Hussy*, but the award went to Gale Sondergaard for her role in *Anthony Adverse*. Miss Bondi was nominated only one other time in 1938 for an Academy Award for her supporting role in *Of Human Hearts*, but again she lost out, this time to Fay Bainter in *Jezebel*.

Beulah Bondi worked again with James Stewart and Clarence Brown in 1938, when she portrayed the wife of a frontier preacher (Walter Huston) in *Of Human Hearts*. Based on Honore Morrow's novel, *Benefits Forgot*, *Of Human Hearts* tells of a mother — Miss Bondi — who suffers the hardships and privations of life on the Ohio River and sacrifices everything for the career as a surgeon of her ungrateful son. When Abraham Lincoln (played by another fine character actor, John Carradine) learns of the poverty the mother faces while her son, dressed in the finest of uniforms and lacking nothing, serves at the front in the Civil War, the president, in probably one of the most ridiculous plot contrivances ever perpetrated on film, practically halts the War to enable James Stewart to return home and make amends to Mother Bondi.

Of Human Hearts offered Beulah Bondi an opportunity to portray a woman in three stages of life: as a young mother, a middle-aged woman and an old lady. She seems perfectly at ease in all three characterizations, handling the transitions of age with dexterity, and one must fully agree with the comment in *Photoplay* (April 1938): "Easily the finest performance in what amounts to an orgy of great portrayals is that of the mother played by Beulah Bondi."[2]

As Mrs. Smith in Frank Capra's *Mr. Smith Goes to Washington* (1939), Miss Bondi was required to do little except look concerned, which she does very well. Five years later, she was back with Capra and James Stewart in *It's a Wonderful Life*, and here she was given more of an opportunity to display her acting talents, playing both Stewart's loving mother and the hard-bitten woman she might have been had he not been born. Beulah Bondi's last performance as James Stewart's mother was in *The Identity Crisis* episode of *The Jimmy Stewart Show* on NBC in the fall of 1971. Only Stewart appeared to have got any older!

Thornton Wilder's 1938 Pulitzer Prize-winning play *Our Town* was brought to the screen in 1940 with immaculate good taste by producer Sol Lesser. To direct, Lesser chose Sam Wood, responsible for such MGM classics as *A Night at the Opera* and *Goodbye, Mr. Chips*; for the music, Lesser approached the distinguished American composer Aaron Copland, here contributing one of his few film scores; and to play Mrs. Webb opposite Guy Kibbee, Lesser selected Beulah Bondi.

[In the course of preparing *Our Town* for the screen, Sol Lesser and Thornton Wilder exchanged more than sixty letters, some of which were

---

2. As an item of trivia, it should be recorded that a Greenville, South Carolina, high school student, Ray Harris, won a prize of $5,000.00 from MGM for suggesting the title *Of Human Hearts* for the film.

reprinted in the November 1941 issue of *Theatre Arts Monthly*. Much of the correspondence concerned the ending. Lesser originally adhered strictly to the play, and closed his film with Emily's death. At a preview screening, such an ending proved too strong for the audience, and new scenes were shot with a happy ending. After seeing this new ending, Thornton Wilder wrote Lesser, "Sure I see what you mean. In the first place, I think Emily should live. I've always thought so. In a movie you see the people so close to that a different relationship is established. In the theatre they are half-way abstractions in an allegory; in the movie they are very concrete. So, insofar as the play is a generalized allegory, she dies — we die — they die; insofar as it's a concrete happening it's not important that she die; it's even disproportionally cruel that she die. Let her live — the idea will have been imparted anyway." It is interesting to note that in the same correspondence, on January 15, 1940, Wilder wrote to Lesser, "How splendid Fay Bainter and Beulah Bondi will be."

When I discussed *Our Town* with Sol Lesser recently, he told me that he had originally wanted the film to close with the stage manager (Frank Craven) completing a jigsaw puzzle of a map of the United States, with the last piece being Grover's Corner, New Hampshire, but Sam Wood strongly disagreed with him on this point. Lesser also remembered that Sam Wood had little faith in the production, and was both surprised and delighted when the first preview indicated they had a success on their hands.

The film has stood the test of time well, for unlike other of Thornton Wilder's plays, such as *The Skin of Our Teeth*, *Our Town* has not dated. The comings and goings of the people of Grover's Corner, New Hampshire, make as compelling viewing today as they did forty years ago. Writing of the play, Sol Lesser said, "Thornton Wilder has transmuted the simple events of human life into universal reverie. He has achieved a profound, strange, significant drama, brimming over with compassion. The same might be said of Sol Lesser's film production of *Our Town*.]

It would be wrong to single out Beulah Bondi's playing for there is not a faultless performance in the entire production. Two of the principals, Frank Craven and Martha Scott, were repeating their roles from the original New York production, as were Arthur Allen and Doro Merande in minor roles. William Holden, in one of his first screen appearances, shows promise of the fine actor he was to become.[3]

---

3. Beulah Bondi told me that she did not care for Sam Wood or his direction. He seemed incapable of providing any direction to the actors, so much so that she and her fellow actors would rehearse scenes on their own prior to shooting.

The 1940s brought no slowdown in the film career of Beulah Bondi, with her appearing in at least two films a year. There were new stars to support: Bette Davis in *Watch on the Rhine* (1943), John Wayne in *Back to Bataan* (1945), Veronica Lake in *The Sainted Sisters* (1948), to name a few. She was Charles Coburn's wife in *The Captain Is a Lady* (1940), and Rosalind Russell's mother in *Sister Kenny* (1946). Miss Bondi even played the lead in the totally forgotten *She's a Soldier, Too* (1944). However, by the 1940s, one thing became very apparent: Beulah Bondi was regarded by the film industry as suited to playing old ladies — not necessarily nice old ladies, but old ladies nevertheless — and it says much for Miss Bondi's acting talents that she was able to imbue each of them with a unique character and personality.

One film which illustrates the scope of Beulah Bondi's characterizations is *The Southerner*, the third American film directed, in 1945, by Jean Renoir. Here she is required to portray a decidedly crabby old granny, light years removed, say, from the whimsical old Mrs. Northrup who gracefully embraces death in *On Borrowed Time* (1939).

In his autobiography, *My Life and My Films*, Renoir explained his decision to take on the direction of a film which dealt with Southern life, so far removed from his French background as the son of the celebrated impressionist painter. "What attracted me in the story was precisely the fact that there was really no story, nothing but a series of strong impressions — the vast landscape, the simple aspiration of the hero, the heat and the hunger. Being forced to live a life restricted to their daily material needs, the characters attain a level of spirituality of which they themselves are unaware." The production was besot with problems. Renoir was unable to shoot on location in Texas, and, eventually, the exterior scenes were photographed near the town of Madera on the banks of the San Joaquin River. Joel McCrea and his wife Frances Dee were originally slated for the leading roles, but had to be replaced at the last minute by Zachary Scott and Betty Field.

Beulah Bondi was well aware of the director's reputation, and recalls: "I was delighted to be in *The Southerner*, and he was a joy to work with. There was such empathy between us." However, both the film and Miss Bondi's performance in it came in for mixed criticism; Renoir's stark realism bored audiences eager for light entertainment. "Kahn" in *Variety* (May 2, 1945) commented, "It may be trenchant realism, but these are times when there is a greater need. Escapism is the word." Needless to say, *The Southerner* was unpopular in the South, and, indeed, banned in Memphis, Tennessee. Some critics found Miss Bondi's performance too theatrical. James Agee wrote, "Beulah Bondi, an actress I generally admire, demonstrates merely how massively misguided, and how smarmed with unconscious patronage, the whole attitude of the theatre has always been towards peasants." Others were delighted. The English critic Richard Winnington wrote, "I cannot let pass this short review of a fine and beautifully acted film without referring to the superb playing of the grandmother by Beulah Bondi. It merits at least a couple of dozen Oscars at current rates."[4]

Another complex Beulah Bondi characterization was evident in a little-known William Wellman production of 1954, *Track of the Cat*, whose chief claim to fame is its use of color to reproduce black-and-white. It was a commercial flop when released, despite its director's comment that "never have I seen such beauty, a naked kind of beauty," with the only color basically being the flesh tones of the characters. All else was in tones of black-and-white.

Miss Bondi portrays Ma Bridges, a bigoted, iron-willed figure with a warped mind. Playing her three sons are William Hopper, Robert Mitchum and Tab Hunter. Beulah Bondi feels the character role she plays was perhaps the most difficult she has ever had to "hang on" to. "She was a very bitter person," says Beulah. "She has a drunken husband, her children are a disappointment. She's a Bible-reading woman, but she's bitter. And I was working with a man, Bill Wellman, who was said to be very difficult. But, no, I found he was wonderful to work with, and we became great friends before the picture was over. Sometimes you get a part to study, and psychologically you've got to know what has caused this rancor and suspicion and ugliness. To go home at night for dinner, and hang on to that thing! My mother used to say once in a while when I was playing these roles, 'I'll be so glad when you finish this character, so you can be yourself again at the dinner table.' On the set, working with people, I don't socialize. I don't really think I got acquainted with all the stars I loved working with, because of playing something so completely. I had to have an inner hold on what she was."

Beulah Bondi's screen appearances became fewer and fewer in the 1950s, possibly because the cinema had forgotten how to use its character actors. In fact, with one or two exceptions — in particular, the films of Mel Brooks and Gene Wilder — the cinema today has totally ignored the need for good character players. However, there was always television, and

---

4. For the last couple of years of his life, Robert Gitt and I would visit Jean Renoir on Sundays and screen films for him. One Sunday, we took along Beulah Bondi who had not seen Jean in many years. Unfortunately, neither seemed to have much to say to each other, and the meeting was disappointing.

Miss Bondi was far from inactive, appearing in many television series, not to mention a year of commercials advertising Oxydol. She played her last film role in 1963 in the far from distinguished *Tammy and the Doctor*. Miss Bondi is still interested in returning to the screen, but all the scripts she has been sent, and continues to be sent, are, she feels, unsuitable for her.

As her screen roles have diminished, Miss Bondi has taken to extensive traveling, and she has been around the world four times. Three years ago, at the age of eighty-three, she traveled by boat to South Africa, and returned to America, via Europe, by air.

On March 20, 1975, she was seen on TV's *The Waltons* for the first time as Aunt Martha Corinne Walton. So successful was her appearance that a second *Waltons* episode, *The Pony Cart*, was written by Jack Miller to feature Martha Corinne. As directed by Ralph Serensky and broadcast over the CBS network on December 2, 1976, the episode proved to be a moving experience, with Beulah Bondi portraying a kindly but meddlesome ninety-year-old lady, whose death teaches tolerance to the entire Walton family, and makes them realize how much she meant to them. It was a great tribute to her acting that Beulah Bondi was nominated for an Emmy for her performance, and an even greater tribute when her colleagues within the industry gave her a standing ovation on September 11, 1977, when she won that Emmy against stiff competition from a number of players in *Roots*, for the Best Actress in a Single Appearance on a Drama or Comedy series.

Today, Beulah Bondi stands alone as the last great character actress of the cinema, a woman who has brought her own special brand of characterization to fims. She vigorously denies that she has ever wanted to be a star, adding, "I think we — the character actresses — were sort of the mortar between the bricks. I never had any idea of stealing a scene or being better than anyone else. The idea was to make the whole thing perfect — cooperation! Work with, not against, to make the play. The play or the film is the thing, and I still believe that!"

[Beulah Bondi died at the Motion Picture Country Hospital in Woodland Hills, California, on January 11, 1981.]

Censored Screams!
Horror Films and the Production Code in the 1930s

Filmfax, April/May 1999, pages 38-43, 80

The Production Code Administration (PCA) was established in 1933 by Will Hays as a division of the Motion Picture Producers and Distributors of America (later the Motion Picture Association). It was a desperate attempt by the film industry to self-censor its productions rather than run the risk of the introduction of Federal screen censorship. To head the new organization, Will Hays hired Joseph I. Breen, and he and his staff became the arbiters of what was acceptable in the content of all films screened in the United States, using as a basis for their judgment, the Production Code, which was occasionally revised through the years, and copies of which can be found in the annual *International Motion Picture Almanac.*

The Production Code was a "moral document," which encompassed three general principles:

> *No picture shall be produced which will lower the moral standards of those who see it. Hence the sympathy of the audience shall never be thrown to the side of crime, wrongdoing, evil, or sin*

> *Correct standards of life, subject only to the requirements of drama and entertainment, shall be presented.*

> *Law, natural or human, shall not be ridiculed nor shall sympathy be created for its violation.*

The files of the Production Code Administration (which is often described as the Hays Office or, more correctly, the Breen Office) provide a wealth of documentation on how films were "censored" in the United

States, but also provide insight on working titles, production schedules, and foreign censorship decisions. Being "working files" rather than archival entities, they contain only what a PCA staffer involved with the film chose to keep. Some of the files contain a minimal amount of material. Some of the files — for example that for *Freaks* — are missing or may never have existed.

Following are fifteen of the most prominent horror films of the 1930s, and below each a summary of what the files reveal as to their censorship, both in this country and abroad. These findings are not a condemnation of the work of Joseph I. Breen and his staff. What they reveal is the incredible efficiency of the PCA staff, who could read a script in less than two hours, or a novel in less than a day, and immediately document its failings under the Production Code. Their efforts were not directed toward the emasculation of a script or storyline, but rather to making it more palatable both to American audiences and, equally important, to foreign audiences and foreign censoring agencies. They were neither naïve or hypocritical. They were sophisticated enough to recognize lesbian undertones in, say, *Dracula's Daughter*, and as politically correct (by modern standards) to oppose the use of racist terms and animal cruelty.

The Black Cat (1934)

After an initial reading of the script, the PCA staff met on February 26, 1934, with Universal's Efe Asher, Peter Ruric and director Edgar G. Ulmer, to discuss the "gruesomeness" suggested by a script involving the skinning of a man alive and the killing of a cat. The PCA's primary concern was over the latter. Among the more than a dozen changes required, it was agreed that a photographer — in the opening wedding sequence — would not be portrayed as homosexual, that a derogatory reference to Czech Slovakians (sic) as devourers of the young be changed, that there be no indecent exposure of Joan in the shower, and that the guests not be identified as German. When a second script was submitted two days later, there were no changes except for the elimination of the Czech Slovakians. However, when the PCA viewed a rough cut on April 2, 1934, it conformed with the provisions of the Code. Although the file contains no evidence to that effect, it is assumed that a Certificate was issued. A reissue Certificate No. 4601-R was issued on August 12, 1938.

Bride of Frankenstein (1935)

On July 28, 1933, PCA's James Wingate wrote to Universal that the initial script for a film titled *The Return of Frankenstein* had been read.

There were only minor problems; primarily three references to God, and the tag line of a baby wetting its diaper. After submission of a new script, also titled *The Return of Frankenstein*, Breen wrote to Universal on July 24, 1934 that references to and by Frankenstein, comparing him to God, should be deleted or changed to "creator." Other minor problems included the monster's use of the word "mate," suggesting his desire for a sexual companion. The next script elicited a strong response from Breen on December 5, 1934:

> *We counted ten separate scenes in which the monster ether strangles or tramples people to death — this, in addition to some other murders by subsidiary characters. In a picture as basically gruesome as this one, we believe that such a great amount of slaughter is unwise, and we recommend, very earnestly, that you do something about toning this down.*
>
> *Care must also be used to avoid any suggestion of irreverence, particularly with the use of the name of God.*
>
> *Your studio is, of course, only too well aware of the difficulty which attended the release of the first Frankenstein picture in a great many parts of the world. The criticism at that time, directed at the picture, seemed to be based primarily on two elements of undue gruesomeness, and an alleged irreverence on the part of some of the characters, particularly wherever they even suggested that their actions were paralleling those of the creator. It is our belief that the ending should carry a sufficient moral message to obviate this latter criticism, provided you take the greatest care with your dialog.*

On December 7, 1934, director James Whale met with the PCA's Geoffrey Shurlock and Islin Auster. It was agreed, among other things, that the killings be minimized, an owl or bat be substituted for a rat, the mermaid would have "impossibly long" hair enveloping her body, and the figure of Jesus on the cross be eliminated. Whale assured everyone that his intention was to shoot a film "with the utmost care and good taste,"

Once the film was completed, it was viewed by the PCA on March 20 and 21, 1935. Twelve cuts were required, including shots of the monster in the pool drowning Hans, the monster actually pushing Hans' wife into the cistern, the mother carrying her dead baby in her arms, the idiot nephew strangling his uncle, the murder of the woman by the halfwit, a shot of a heart being taken from a jar with forceps, and the monster throwing a man over the roof. Universal was loath to make all the cuts, and a meeting between Universal's Junior Laemmle (the son of Carl Laemmle and the studio's production chief) and Breen was organized on March 25, 1935. At this time, the studio agreed to six cuts, including "offensive breast shots" in reel one, the monster actually drowning Hans, and partial deletion of the halfwit's murder of the woman.

Universal made additional changes to the print, lengthening the scene between the monster and the girl to maintain suspense, lengthening the scene in the jail where the monster is chained to the floor, and a new scene of the monster stalking Frankenstein's wife. These were approved by the PCA on April 8, 1935. On April 11, the PCA viewed what was to be the final cut of the film, and Certificate No. 768 was issued on April 15. Two days later, Universal advised that a "happy ending" had been added. On May 21, 1935, Universal thanked Breen for his help, noting the film has been passed by the British Board of Film Censors with only one minor cut.

Bride of Frankenstein was banned in Hungary, Palestine and Trinidad. Heavy cuts were required in Japan and Sweden.

The Crime of Dr. Crespi (1935)

Film Daily (September 24, 1935) described *The Crime of Dr. Crespi* as "a sordid tale almost unrelieved by any touches of refinement, character, humor, or situations." The Production Code Administration was inclined to agree. On January 15, 1935, Breen wrote to Will Hays, "My confidential information is to the effect that this picture is probably the most revolting and nauseating picture which has ever been photographed." The next day, Breen wrote to Vincent Hart in the PCA's New York office, "We have an inside tip here that the film is most revolting and offensive. If any attempt is made to submit the picture to you for approval, you will, of course, refer it to this office.

The film was submitted and, after a private screening, rejected by the PCA on February 7, 1935. Producer John H. Auer viewed a print with Geoffrey Shurlock on March 7, 1935. The film was reviewed on March 14, with Breen present, and it was agreed that the following cuts would be made:

> The scene of the operation on Dr. Ross's skull to be reedited to eliminate the sounds of cutting and scraping and the close shots of the efforts necessary to cut the skull, the horrified reaction of the assistant, and those shots "which tend to accentuate the horrible and gruesome quality of the scene."

The scene in the hospital morgue to be cut to eliminate shots of the 'stiffs.'

The shots of Ross's head to be cut to the absolute minimum.

The shot of the injection of the hypodermic needle to be eliminated.

The second scene in the morgue with the embalmer to be deleted.

The close shots of Crespi's hands around the man's neck to be deleted.

All shots of the dead man at the funeral to be deleted.

The shot of Ross's wife and child at the side of the coffin to be deleted.

All shots of Ross in the graveyard to be deleted.

The autopsy scene to be edited to reduce shots of Ross to an absolute minimum.

Shots showing the cutting of Ross's body and the reaction of the doctors to be deleted.

As much as possible of the shot showing the enormous surgical dressing on the back of Ross's head to eliminated. (The producer was unable to cut this sequence because he had no alternate shots available.)

The shot of Crespi after he has shot himself, with blood running from a wound in his head, to be eliminated.

The film was again viewed on March 29 and April 2, 1935, and still further cuts were required. Eventually, after a final PCA viewing on April 17, 1935, Certificate No. 789 was issued.

The film was banned in British Columbia, India, Malaya, Quebec, and Ohio (where it was subsequently released in 1942 with substantial cuts).

Dracula's Daughter (1936)

"Off the record," on September 5, 1935, Junior Laemmle sent Joseph Breen a copy of the initial script for *Dracula's Daughter*. It was read by Geoffrey Shurlock, and Breen informed Junior that it contained "countless offensive stuff," making it "utterly impossible" for Code approval. Junior advised Breen that R.C. Sheriff was rewriting the script, and that revised version was submitted on October 21, 1935. Two days later, Breen responded with a six-page letter, noting the script was "not quite acceptable," and raising a number of points, including:

> When Dracula's soldiers bring a group of young women to the castle, it should be clear that they were only to be dancing partners for the Count's guests.
>
> It should be established at the outset that the beautiful girl whom John meets is a vampire bat, and that the doctor should make it "definitely and frankly" clear that vampire bats must consume human blood to survive. (This was presumably to make clear that there was no potential sexual relationship between John and the girl.)

Other changes included elimination of excessive drunkenness — "jollity but not debauchery" — that the lover become the husband, that the peasants not be seen crossing themselves, that there be no sexual connotation in the shot of Dracula crushing the girl, and that the rats, "huge or otherwise," be eliminated.

On January 14, 1936, Universal informed Breen that the entire first script had been discarded, and that a new script was being prepared, with shooting to commence of January 15, 1936. On that same date, Breen wrote that the basic story met the requirements of the Production Code. He warned that the British Board of Film Censors might well reject the film, and advised against the showing of gruesome or horrifying details of mutilation. On March 23, 1936, a partial script was submitted, and Breen asked that the cross should be placed reverently and not flung into the flames, and that the cremation of Dracula's body not be shown in detail. He asked that the character of Lili not be shown in the nude, that there be no suggestion of a sexual attack on her by Countess Marya, and that all dialog suggesting a sexual relationship between her and Sandor be eliminated. It was very obvious to the PCA that the character of Countess Marya was presented as a bisexual vampire with a strong suggestion that she was lesbian.

Certificate No. 2100 was issued on April 16, 1935, in time for a preview of the film at Universal on April 30, 1936. *Dracula's Daughter* was banned in Austria and China, and heavily censored in Sweden.

The Invisible Ray (1936)

On September 5, 1935, Universal submitted a script, and the following day Breen reported that it met the basic requirements of the Production

Code. He asked for care in the scene in which the doctor gives an injection, removal of a castor oil gag, deletion of a running gag of the cook spitting on a waiter's posterior, avoidance of "undue intimacy" between Diane and Drake, and deletion of some suggestive dialog. "In conclusion, we recommend care throughout this picture, to avoid injecting any undue gruesomeness into it. As you know, there seems to be a growing feeling of resentment against the over-emphasis of horror pictures, and we recommend that you take great care to see that this particular picture escapes that danger."

A final script was submitted on September 17, 1935, concurrent with the start of production, and that same day, Breen asked for minor changes involving Dr. Felix injecting a Negro baby, the baby feeding at its mother's breast, omission of the phrase "Good Lord," removal of the actual phraseology of the marriage service, and that the six statues not be identifiable Saints. The finished film was viewed on December 17, 1935, and the following day Certificate No. 1746 was issued.

Island of Lost Souls (1933)

Island of Lost Souls was produced prior to creation of the Production Code administration, but, on June 1, 1932, Paramount did submit a copy of the H.G. Wells novel, *Island of Dr. Moreau*, to the PCA's predecessor organization, the Studio Relations Office (created in 1927 by Will Hays as an advisory body). The book was read by Lamar Trotti, and on June 3, 1932, his boss, Jason S. Joy, the head of the Studio Relations Office, wrote to Paramount's B.P. Schulberg:

> ...*frankly, I do not see in the story as it now stands, enough of the unusual or plausible, to make it worthwhile following the other pseudo-scientific or horror pictures...I assume that some thought has been given to the possibility of injecting the idea of crossing animals with humans. If this is the case, it is my opinion that all such thought should be abandoned, for I am sure you would never be permitted to suggest that sort of thing on the screen.*

Paramount ignored Joy's opinion and, on September 22, 1932, the final shooting script was submitted, with the production scheduled to begin shooting four days later. All that Joy asked, after a reading of the script, was the deletion of the line, "Do you know how it seems to feel like God?" Paramount stressed the importance of the question and, with Joy unable to provide an alternative line, went ahead and used it.

The film was previewed on December 2, 1932, and seven days later, James Wingate confided to Will Hays that it was "one of the best of the horror stories that have been brought to the screen." Joseph I. Breen did not concur and, when Paramount submitted the film to the PCA for a reissue Code Certificate in September 1935, it was rejected. Paramount tried again in March 1941 with the same effect but, after cuts in twenty-one scenes in reels three, four, five, six, and seven, Certificate No, 7210-R was issued on March 17, 1941.

Island of Lost Souls was banned in Germany, Hungary, India, Italy, Latvia, the Netherlands, New Zealand, Singapore, South Africa, Tasmania, and the United Kingdom (where it was resubmitted in July 1958, and approved for screening with cuts in reels three, four and eight).

Mad Love (1935)

A script dated April 18, 1935, was read by the PCA and, on April 22, Breen wrote to MGM that the basic story met the provisions of the Production Code. Among changes in thirteen scenes, he asked that the railroad wreck be merely suggested, that the knife embedded in the body should not be shocking or horrifying, and, most importantly, that there be no suggestion of perversion between the professor and the wax figure, no fondling, and no spraying of perfume. Because of Breen's concern over horrific elements in the playlet at the film's opening, MGM agreed that it would be played as a burlesque. Through the end of May 1935, script changes were submitted and approved. *Mad Love* was viewed by the PCA on July 3, 1935 and, two days later, Certificate No. 1034 was issued. *Mad Love* was banned in Austria, Finland, Hungary, and Palestine, and in the United Kingdom, twenty-two scenes were eliminated and nine scenes modified.

Mark of the Vampire (1935)

Under the title *The Vampires of Prague*, a script dated November 12, 1934, was submitted by MGM. On December 18, 1934, Breen wrote that it was "fundamentally satisfactory. We presume that the ghost and horror sequences will be done with due delicacy." A revised script was submitted and, on December 28, 1934, Breen asked for deletion of the word "digitalis" from Dr. Doskil's line, deletion of "of course they'll want bedding if they're going to be married" from the deaf man's speech, substitution of "Heaven" for "Lord," keeping of the corpse out of site as much as possible, and that there be no suggestion that the Baron guard against leaving fingerprints. (The last related to a Production Code requirement that the specifics of a criminal act could not be shown.) The film was viewed on March 25, 1935, and, two days later, Certificate No. 725 was issued. *The Mark of the Vampire* was banned in Hungary, Italy and Poland.

After approval of the film, the PCA was disturbed by a letter from Dr. William J. Robinson that appeared in the July 28, 1935, edition of the *New York Times*. "There is a good deal of criticism of obscene and vulgar movies. Many of them are bad enough. But a dozen of the worst obscene pictures cannot equal the damage that is done by such films as *The Mark of the Vampire*,

"I do not refer to the utter senselessness of the picture. I do not even refer to its effect in spreading and fostering the most obnoxious superstitions. I refer to the horrible effect that it has on the mental and nervous systems of not only unstable, but even normal men, women and children,

"I am not speaking in the abstract. I am basing myself upon facts. Several people have come to my notice who, after seeing that horrible picture, suffered nervous shock, were attacked with insomnia, and those who did fall asleep were tortured by most horrible nightmares.

"In my opinion, it is a crime to produce and to present such films. We must guard not only our people's morals, we must be as careful of their physical and mental health."

Mystery of the Wax Museum (1933)

Produced prior to implementation of the Production Code, the script for *Mystery of the Wax Museum* was submitted to Jason Joy at the Studio Relations Office, who wrote to Darryl F. Zanuck at Warner Bros. on September 27, 1932, that one possible danger was a leaning towards "too great gruesomeness in certain scenes." Joy asked deletion of all profanity, suggested consultation with a lawyer in reference to a derogatory remark about physical health guru Bernard McFadden, caution in handling the drug element, and deletion of the line, "He made Frankenstein look like a pansy."

The film was viewed on December 22, 1932, and James Wingate wrote to Zanuck that it was "free from elements to which official censorship could take serious objection." He was wrong. On February 9, 1933, B.O. Skinner, director of the state censorship board in Ohio, wrote to Warner Bros. that "it contains so many elements we find objectionable, as setting fire to the museum to obtain insurance, naming a poison and telling how it could be taken to produce death, using of dope, and also the general theme of horror. I feel it would be much better for us if the production of this type of film would be discontinued." *Mystery of the Wax Museum* was, however, approved by the PCA on reissue, with Certificate No. 2641-R being issued on September 3, 1935.

The film was banned in Australia, Spain (but later passed in both with cuts) and Malaya ("gruesome and revolting theme"). It was initially rejected by the British Board of film Censors in that the location was London and the only wax museum there was Madame Tussaud's. The Board's objection was overcome by the simple removal of the introductory title, "London 1921." The Board also asked for other deletions, including a hypodermic syringe and a close-up of Igor.

The Raven (1935)

After submission of the script, the PCA organized a conference on March 14, 1935, with studio executives and director Louis Friedlander. They agreed that no detail of the operation on Bateman would be shown, Bateman's appearance would never be "unhumanly repulsive," instruments of torture would be passed in review as if in a museum, blood would not be shown except in a flash, the pendulum knife would not touch Thatcher's body, and there would be no improper dress or contact in the bedroom scenes. On March 16, 1935, the PCA looked at various shots of Boris Karloff as Bateman to determine their suitability. Four days later, the PCA had read the final shooting script, dated March 9, 1935, and Breen wrote, "We...deem it necessary to remind you that, because of the stark realism of numerous elements in your story, you are running the risk of excessive horror." *The Raven* was viewed on April 15, 1935, and, the following day, Certificate No. 790 was issued.

The Raven was banned in British Columbia, China, the Netherlands ("because of degrading effect on the public"), and Ontario ("Featuring horror and shuddering melodrama, full of fiendish and diabolical doings"). An Associated Press story, dated August 23, 1935, stated that *The Raven* would be the last horror film passed by the British Board of Film Censors. The Board's president, Edward Short warned that such films were "unfortunate and undesirable."

Revolt of the Zombies (1936)

A treatment dated January 11, 1936, was submitted by Academy Pictures Corp., and on January 22, 1936, Breen wrote to producer Edward Halperin that the basic plot was satisfactory. He asked that the characterizations of the French officials be handled carefully to avoid all possible objection, that material reflecting unfavorably upon "yellow races" be dropped, and that the scene in Claire's bedroom on her wedding night be eliminated. The film was viewed on May 8, 1936, and Certificate No. 2161 was issued that day, subject to elimination of six frames showing a man wiping fingerprints off a knife.

Son of Frankenstein (1939)

After reading a script, dated October 20, 1938, Breen wrote to Universal on October 27, 1938, pointing out sequences that would probably be rejected by the British Board of Film Censors. These included avoiding anything gruesome in the showing of skeletons and Fritz's corpse, and the scene of the monster operating on a child. On November 3, 1938, Breen cabled J. Brooke Wilkinson at the British Board of Film Censors for his opinion. The latter responded by cable and letter the next day: "Strongly advise you to use every possible endeavor to prevent production of any further pictures of this type intended for exhibition in this country." Wilkinson provided fascinating documentation on the number of films approved by his Board in the "horrific" category: 1933 — five, 1934 — five, 1935 — six, 1936 — two, 1937 — one, 1938 — one.

"The sole reason of this falling off," he wrote, "is due entirely to the difficulties experienced by the trade, in handling such films in this country."

While sympathetic to Wilkinson's concerns, Breen was relatively impressed by *Son of Frankenstein*. On January 9, 1939, he wrote to his colleague, Francis S. Harmon, "While the present picture follows the Frankenstein story, it is a vast improvement on its numerous predecessors. For one thing, it is less shocking — less horrific, as our British friends have it — and it is infinitely better made. It is splendidly cast, with a number of good actors: Basil Rathbone, Lionel Atwill, Josephine Hutchinson, et al., and very excellently directed by the top-flight director, Roland Lee. The story, too, is a better constructed story, and the dialog much above the 'Frankenstein' level."

Certificate No. 4987 was issued on January 14, 1939. The film was banned in Denmark and Finland.

Tower of London (1939)

After reading a first draft script, dated July 24, 1939, Breen wrote to Universal on July 27, 1939. Among the problems he raised were the gruesomeness in the torturing of two men in Scene 2, the appearance of the "repulsive beggar" in Scene 46, the execution in Scenes 65-69, the boy's scream of pain in Scene 137, and the appearance of the fourth beggar in Scene 179. Breen asked for deletion of the reference to Henry VI as an "imbecile," "Hell," and the business of Edward's rubbing the humpback of Richard III (as "apt to give offense to people suffering from physical deformities"). "Burps" were to be eliminated, and drinking minimized. The problems in the script remained through subsequent submissions and, when the film was viewed on November 4, 1939, it contained nine problems:

The Torture scene in the tower.

The executioner lifting the axe, and the sound of its descent.

Richard shoving a sword through the body of Wales.

Latin prayers (unacceptable in the United Kingdom).

The lashing of Wyatt.

Undue exposure of breasts.

Scenes of falling horses and a horse lying dead on the ground (unacceptable in the United Kingdom).

A man pulling a sword out of a body.

Certificate No. 5819 was issued November 13, 1939, and it is uncertain that all the above problems had been addressed by that time.

The Werewolf of London (1935)

After a reading of the initial script, a conference was organized on January 15, 1935, between Universal executives and members of the PCA staff. Universal agreed that a soliciting prostitute be modified to a beggar, a morality note be introduced in the first scenes through an aging missionary in Tibet stating that violation of beliefs or superstitions always brings trouble, the transformation of Glendon from man to wolf would eliminate all physical details, and, at the conclusion, Glendon would make a dying confession to his wife that he knew he had violated the laws of God and man, and that his death was a deserved one.

Universal's Stanley Bergerman tried to persuade the PCA on February 7, 1935, to allow the transformation scene showing Henry Hull lengthening his nose, ears, teeth, etc, and increasing the growth of hair. The PCA advised it would reserve judgment until a viewing of the finished film. At that time, on March 22, 1935, it asked for elimination of some gruesome shots in the fight between Hull (Dr. Glendon) and Warner Oland (Dr. Yogami). Certificate No. 714 was issued on March 23, 1935, subject to three cuts. The film was banned in the Netherlands ("Because of degrading effect on the public").

White Zombie (1932)

After a viewing of the film on July 28, 1932, the Studio Relations Office described it as "A good idea gone wrong, due mainly to poor acting." Apparently, the only local censorship problem encountered by *White Zombie* was in Pasadena, where a permit for its screening was refused, in January 1933. Internationally, it was banned in China ("too suggestive of superstitious and too full of scenes depicting brutality and murder") and Malaya. On reissue, *White Zombie* was submitted to the PCA by United Artists and, after a viewing on June 18, 1935, Certificate No. 509 was issued, subject to the following deletions:

> *Close shot of tyrant "grave man" with camera panning from feet to hairy chest.*
>
> *All shots of girl in step-ins.*
>
> *All shots of girl in coffin.*
>
> *Close shot of Bela Lugosi with bullet hole in cheek.*
>
> *Close shot of enlarged eyes of Bela Lugosi focused on the screen.*

Censored Screams!
Horror Films and the Production Code in the 1940s

Filmfax, June/July 1999, pages 46-49, 88

Last issue, we discussed the beginnings of the Production Code Administration in 1933, and its effects on the Horror films of the 1930s. By the 1940s, the PCA had become a routine part of the production process.

Scripts were submitted to the PCA's Joseph I. Breen and his staff for evaluation and approval, and fewer changes were demanded as studios became familiar with the workings of the PCA and basic tenets of the moral document known as the Production Code. At the same time, producers were aware that, regardless of whether or not the script was approved, as Breen always pointed out, "Our final judgment will be based on the finished film."

As the documentation on the following fifteen films indicates, Joseph I. Breen and his staff were as much a part of the creative process as the directors and producers of these horror films.

The Beast with Five Fingers (1946)

A temporary script, dated September 5, 1945, was submitted to the PCA, on November 8, 1945, Breen responded that the basic story met the requirements of the Production Code. He noted that Hilary's driving a nail through the hand was too gruesome to approve, and that the hand burning in the fire should be more suggested than shown. After a reading of a revised final script, Breen expressed concern that the new characterization of Conrad should establish that he was not cheating tourists, and that the business of his selling phony cameos was unacceptable. (In the final film, the character of Conrad is renamed Bruce Ryler and played by Robert Alda.) Production Code Certificate No. 11334 was issued on February 27, 1946. *The Beast with Five Fingers* was banned in Sweden ("because of whole atmosphere") and in British Columbia (but passed by the Board of Appeal).

Bedlam (1946)

A script for *Chamber of Horrors — A Tale of Bedlam*, dated June 15, 1946, was submitted to Breen, who responded on June 26, 1946, that it was "completely unacceptable" because of the illicit relationship between Lord Mortimer and Nell, and between Lord Mortimer and Kitty Sims. He continued, "To attempt to dramatize on the motion picture screen a story which is concerned with idiocy and idiots, with malformed and deformed monstrosities, with maniacal human beings — who suggest in their appearance common brutes, like dogs and pigs — seems to us to suggest a kind of story which is completely unsuited for public exhibition in theaters before mixed audiences.

"When there is added to this basic dramatic treatment, the mounting suggestions of gross brutality and gruesomeness and maniacal shrieks and cries of horror, you have what we think is a thoroughly unacceptable screen document, and one which is certain to prove to be outrageously shocking to normal people everywhere."

After a discussion with RKO, it was agreed that any indication of illicit sex would be removed, and that scenes with "insane people" would be rewritten to avoid the suggestion that a Quaker was obstructing justice.

A final script for *Bedlam* (a.k.a. *Chamber of Horrors*), dated June 30, 1945 was read by the PCA, and on July 13, 1945, Breen wrote to RKO that it contained twenty pages with problems, including the grinding of a man's hand under the heel, cruelty to a parrot, and the burying alive of Sims. Certificate No. 11077 was issued on November 9, 1945.

The Body Snatcher (1945)

On September 27, 1944, Breen wrote to RKO that the story was unacceptable "because of repellent nature of such matter, which has to do with grave-robbing, dissecting bodies, and pickling bodies." After an October 3, 1944, meeting with RKO, it was agreed that the story would be rewritten to avoid gruesome scenes such as those in the anatomy room. A final script, dated October 16, 1944, was read and met the requirements of the Production Code, but on October 19, 1944, Breen asked for changes on five pages. The changed pages were submitted and, on October 26, 1944, Breen pointed out it was unacceptable to show the method of "Burkeing" (or strangling) a man because it might easily be imitated. When the PCA viewed the finished film, it still contained flashes indicating this method of strangulation, but the PCA decided there was insufficient detail for it to have further concern. Certificate No. 10563 was issued on January 4, 1945. *The Body Snatcher* was banned in British Columbia (but passed by the Board of Appeal) and Kansas, New York, Ohio, and Pennsylvania all required cuts to be made.

Dead of Night (1945)

Although a British film, *Dead of Night* was still subject to PCA approval in that it was released by an American company, Universal, a member of the Motion Picture Association of America (MPAA), and that without a Production Code Certificate or Seal, it could not be screened in any theaters owned by members of the MPAA.

Universal screened the production for the PCA, which, on February 4, 1946, asked for deletion of various expressions of profanity: "Good Lord" (twice), "To hell with it" in reel six and "Get the hell out of here," "like hell" and "hell of a job" in reel seven. The PCA did not cut any of the original stories but that same month, Universal decided to delete "The Christmas Story" with Sally Ann Howes and the phantom child and "The Golfing Story" with Basil Radford and Naunton Wayne. As a result, the film was cut from 104 to 75 minutes. Certificate No.11506 was issued on February 26, 1946.

The Devil Bat (1941)

After reading an initial script, Breen wrote to produced Sigmund Neufeld on September 3, 1940, that the basic story met the requirements of the Production Code. He stressed it was important to avoid gruesomeness and excessive horror at all times. The insanity of Dr. Carruthers (Bela Lugosi) should not be overemphasized. The legs of Maxine (Yolande Mallott) should not be exposed above the knees at any time. Other points raised included the need to avoid offense to the newspaper profession and the exercise of care in the honeymoon dialog. A second and third script were submitted in October and November 1940, and they contained the same problems. Certificate No. 6897 was issued on December 6, 1940.

Frankenstein Meets the Wolf Man (1943)

A script titled *Wolf-Man Meets Frankenstein*, dated October 7, 1942, was submitted to the PCA, and, on October 9, 1942, Breen wrote Universal that the basic story could not be approved because of its unacceptable attitude towards "mercy killings." Breen also advised Universal that the British Board of Film Censors had decided not to approve "horrific pictures" until conclusion of the present war. Further, he asked the avoidance of unnecessary gruesomeness, that drinking be held to a minimum, that there be no suggestion that Rudi and his wife were leaving the dance for a sexual purpose, and that there be no suggestion of cruelty to animals. Certificate No. 9024 was issued on December 12, 1942.

The Ghost of Frankenstein (1942)

A script for *There's Always Tomorrow*, dated October 25, 1941, was submitted to the PCA and on October 29, 1941, Breen wrote to Universal that the basic story met the requirements of the Production Code. He noted it was important that all scenes with the monster be handled carefully to avoid brutality or gruesomeness; that the number of killings be held to a minimum; and pointed out that scenes in the operating room and in the insane ward of Dr. Frankenstein's house would be deleted in the United Kingdom. Various script changes were submitted to the PCA through December 16, 1941, all for a film titled *There's Always Tomorrow*. Certificate No. 8192 was issued on February 20, 1942, by which time *There's Always Tomorrow* had become *The Ghost of Frankenstein*. When Universal tried in 1948 to release the film in Denmark, it was banned.

I Walked with a Zombie (1943)

A script, dated October 12, 1942, was read by the PCA and, on October 15, 1942, Breen wrote to RKO that the basic story met the requirements of the Production Code. He suggested a change in locale from the West Indies to Africa, because of a possible negative reaction to the films from the countries of the West Indies. He also hoped that thought had been given by RKO to the reaction to such a story by Negroes in the United States.

Changes were required on seventeen pages, including omission of a snake ("The showing of snakes has always produced a bad audience reaction"), the masking of the killing of chickens, and that there be no apparent cruelty to animals.

Script changes were submitted through November 14, 1942. The PCA asked elimination of a scene showing Rand (James Ellison), a married man, hugging and kissing Betsy (Frances Dee), and that Rand not commit suicide after killing Jessica (Christine Gordon); the death should be suggested as accidental in that "criminals" might not escape justice under the Production Code through the expediency of suicide. Certificate No. 8949 was issued on December 21, 1942.

The Mask of Dijon (1946)

A first draft script was read, and on October 22, 1945, Breen wrote to producer Alfred Stern that the major difficulty with the storyline was the suicide of Dijon. As with *I Walked with a Zombie*, it could not be approved, and would have to be changed to accidental death. He also pointed out that there could be no lovemaking between Vicky, a married woman, and Tony. After a further reading of the script on November 1, 1945, it was asked that the wounding of a policeman be eliminated.

Certificate No. 11331 was issued on December 8, 1945. The ending — showing Erich von Stroheim being accidentally guillotined — was cut in Alberta and British Columbia. The National Legion of Decency placed the film in Class B (Objectionable in Part), noting, "The free will of others is usurped for the accomplishment of evil."

Phantom of the Opera (1943)

Phantom of the Opera presented virtually no problems in script form. On January 18, 1943, Breen asked that the scene of the falling chandelier and resulting panic in the theater be cut down "to avoid any possibility of an adverse effect on audiences viewing the picture in a theater." Four days later, he noted that Jeanne's line, "I don't care for etchings after nightfall," was unacceptable as "sex suggestive."

However, after viewing the film, the PCA informed Universal's Maurice Pivar that *Phantom of the Opera* could not be granted a Certificate because of the "number of unacceptable breast shots." Too much of Susanna Foster's cleavage was visible. As a result, Universal substituted a number of long shots for close-ups, eliminated some close-ups, trimmed medium shots, and eliminated an entire cadenza from reel six. Certificate No. 9388 was issued on June 3, 1943.

The Picture of Dorian Gray (1945)

On September 13, 1943, Breen advised MGM that the basic story met the Provisions of the Production Code, but continued, "For obvious reasons, it will be absolutely essential that there will be no possibility of any inference of sex perversion, anywhere in the story, otherwise, the finished picture could not be approved. Therefore, we have gone through the script very carefully."

Among the lines cut were "doing what was improbable," "He was always searching for new sensations." "for as sure as there's a God in Heaven," "Pleasure subtle and secret," and "an insatiable madness for pleasure, which stops at nothing." Breen asked that an Oriental dance not be offensive to Buddhists, and that great care be taken in the casting of subsidiary characters throughout; specifically Dorian's cronies.

Two further scripts were submitted and changes made. On February 23, 1944, Breen asked that Dorian not stab Basil several times, that the women in the dives not be characterized as prostitutes, and that there be no inference of perversion in Dorian's cronies. Along similar lines, on March 6, 1944, he asked deletion of the line, "strange rumors about his mode of life."

Certificate No. 10351 was issued on October 24, 1944. The film was classified A-2 (Unobjectionable for Adults) by the National Legion of Decency, but the Legion's Very Reverend Monsignor John J. McClafferty pointed out to Breen that "There were portions in the film which could be interpreted as conveying implications of homosexuality." His comments were based not on a viewing of the film but on reports in various trade papers.

The Return of the Vampire (1943)

A script dated July 21, 1943, was read and, on July 26, 1943, Breen wrote to Columbia that the basic story was acceptable under the provisions of the Production Code. He asked avoidance of gruesomeness and the actual drinking of blood, care in the costuming of Helen, and pointed out it was essential to consult a competent Catholic authority in regard to the story. Various scripts were submitted through August 24, 1943, and Certificate No. 9643 was issued on October 15, 1943. The film was banned in the United Kingdom and British Columbia for the same reason: "Because it is a horror picture."

The Uninvited (1944)

An incomplete script, dated March 27, 1943, was submitted, and, on March 30, 1943, Breen wrote to Paramount that all profanities needed deletion, together with a reference to an ill-mannered little dog as of the "female variety." Various scripts were submitted through June 1943, and Breen asked deletion of "dearest" in the dialog to avoid inference of an "unacceptable relationship" (i.e. a lesbian one) between Miss Holloway and Mary Meredith (later renamed Stella), and that there be no glorification of Carmel as an adulterer.

Certificate No. 9337 was issued on August 10, 1943. *The Uninvited* was classified "B" by the National Legion of Decency: "The spiritistic séance sequence is so constructed as to convey impressions of credence and possible invitation to spiritistic practices." The Legion's Reverend

Brandon Larnen wrote to Breen on May 10, 1944, that "In certain theaters large audiences of questionable types attended this film at unusual hours," drawn by erotic and esoteric elements in the production. He also noted a lesbian connection to the Holloway-Meredith relationship.

Breen found Larnen's response "rather curious," while Paramount's Luigi Luraschi commented, "a figment of their own imagination may have led them to believe they saw things which did not exist (after all, it was a ghost picture, you know)."

The Vampire's Ghost (1945)

A preliminary script dated July 25, 1944, was read, and on August 29, 1944, Breen wrote to Republic that the basic story was in compliance with the Production Code. He asked avoidance of gruesomeness, that the costumes of the natives at all times be adequate to cover the intimate parts of their bodies, and that competent technical advice be sought in the characterization of Father Gilchrist (Grant Withers). An estimating script, dated September 9, 1944, was later submitted, and, on September 19, 1944, Breen asked that a bottle not be broken and used as a cutting weapon, and that a fade-out be avoided in one scene because it would be sex-suggestive. Certificate No. 10530 was issued on December 26, 1944.

The Wolf Man (1941)

A script for *Destiny*, dated October 9, 1941, was submitted, and, on October 10, 1941, the PCA wrote to Universal asking it minimize the many gruesome angles, and that there be no apparent cruelty to animals in regard to the wolf and the gypsy bear. Certificate No. 7973 was issued on December 4, 1941.

The American Press & Public
vs.
Charles Spencer Chaplin

Cineaste, Vol. XIII. No. 4, 1984, pages 6-9

"He loves the world he lives in, and despises it," wrote Waldo Salt in his 1928 *Scribner's* magazine portrait of Charles Chaplin. The same comment might well summarize the world's attitude towards the comedian. From a popular hero of the 1910s, the undisputed funniest man in the world, the first genius discovered by the film industry, Charles Spencer Chaplin saw his popular reputation gradually erode away. As he experimented with using the motion picture for social comment and as his personal scandals became more entertaining than his films — indeed his personal scandals were more frequent than his features — the general public grew tired of the Little Tramp's screen persona. "Charlie is no longer the sweet misfit," lamented one reviewer. "Charlie, in fact, is no longer Charlie." Yes, as if to emphasize his distance from the masses that had brought him fame and wealth, Charlie Chaplin had ostentatiously become Charles Chaplin.

Chaplin's popularity peaked in 1931 with the release of *City Lights*. It was the last Chaplin feature to have both popular and intellectual appeal. The reaction to his next film, *Modern Times*, illustrates the rift that was forming between Chaplin and his public: the popular critics were quick to deny any social significance in the feature, while the liberal press noted the comedian's social criticism and leftist slant. "I'm not a Republican or a Democrat, I'm a clown," explained Chaplin. But to much of the public, he was slowly perceived as none of the above — he was, at best, a left winger and, at worst, a Communist. By April of 1947, Hedda Hopper was writing to J. Edgar Hoover: "I'd like to run every one of those [Communist] rats out of the country and start with Charlie Chaplin...It's about time we stood up and be counted."

The Great Dictator did little to enthuse the public or their Hollywood commentators, represented by the likes of Hedda Hopper and Louella Parsons, After all, what did it matter if Chaplin chose this method to fight Nazism, when throughout World War Two, he never entertained the troops, never visited the Hollywood or Stage Door Canteens, and did nothing for British War Relief? There is a certain truth to Jim Tully's comment that "Chaplin pities the poor in the parlors of the rich." *Monsieur Verdoux*'s release in 1947 made it very plain that Chaplin was totally out of touch with the popular audience. "It was Fascism before," complained *Motion Picture Herald*, "now it's the atom bomb."

The 1950 reissue of *City Lights* — the first and last in a planned series — should have restored Chaplin to his rightful place in the popular opinion as the greatest of all screen comedians. *Life* magazine unhesitatingly named the feature the best of 1950 and during the first week of the its rerelease it was one of the top grossing films in New York, The anti-Chaplin forces were in full reign, and it was too late to halt their progress. The city of Memphis, finding the story totally innocuous, announced that it was banning *City Lights* because its maker was "an enemy of Godliness in all its forms."

If Chaplin's popularity with the masses had long waned, his favor among the intelligentsia remained high and, indeed, that support has never diminished. Critics such as John T. McManus of the liberal New York newspaper, *PM*, saw Chaplin as "A victim of the Fascist clique." The difference in attitudes between the two groups can easily be understood by comparing a 1950 *New Yorker* "Talk of the Town" piece, which treats Chaplin's visit to New York with almost semi-reverence, to an article by Adela Rogers St. Johns, which appeared at approximately the same time in *The American Weekly*. The long-time Hollywood journalist opened her piece with the comment, "Women were his prey and his scourge. While gold rolled in, he was penny-pinching and poor-mouthed."

The 1951 publication of Theodore Huff's definitive critical biography was well received by the reviewers, but the book counts for little when one recalls that a year later *Limelight* opened in America to only mixed reviews, and was the subject of a concerted boycott effort by such unlikely colleagues as the American Federation of Labor and the American Legion. Even Howard Hughes, the head of RKO, urged the independently-owned RKO theatre chain not to exhibit the film.

[And as has been pointed out since I first wrote this essay, the Theodore Huff Biography was published only by a small, relatively insignificant publisher. The major publishers had no interest it its subject or profitability.]

Chaplin's popularity in the United States reached an all=time low in 1952. Two days after Chaplin had left for an extended vacation in Europe, on September 19, 1952, Attorney General James P. McGranery barred the comedian's return until a hearing to establish his fitness under the immigration laws. McGranery saw reasons to bar Chaplin for both his moral turpitude (the 1944 Joan Barry paternity suit was widely rehashed) and his political affiliations. The popular columnists were delighted with McGranery's decision; Westbrook Pegler wrote of Chaplin as "a menace to young girls"; Hedda Hopper without too much originality commented, "Good riddance to bad rubbish"; Florabel Muir wrote "Maybe you'll miss us but I don't think we'll miss you." Dorothy Thompson was the only columnist to defend Chaplin, urging, "Judge him in the only way an artist can be judged — by his art — and he emerges as one of the most effective anti-Communists alive."

On the surface, Chaplin remained as popular as ever in Europe. The British newspapers all denounced the U.S. action, and the comedian was received by the Queen of England and the Presidents of France and Italy. One British critic did, however, see in *Limelight* — the European premieres of which constituted one reason for Chaplin's decision to make the fateful trip — the end of an era. C.A. Lejeune, writing in *The Observer* (October 19, 1952), commented, "The fire still glows, but now it seems the fire of winter; as though the old Chaplin had turned his back for the last time on the people who laughed with him, and, in a gentle mockery of the Chaplin fade-out, softly and silently faded away."

Curiously, despite Chaplin's exile in Europe, he remained a fascinating figure to American newspaper and magazine writers, but the appeal was for the man, not his works. The films were generally unavailable for reassessment. Students of Chaplin's screen career were limited in their study to his primitive Keystone comedies, along with the Essanay and Mutual shorts, usually in poor quality prints. The titles of Chaplin's features might still be remembered, but the films themselves were forgotten.

Chaplin attempted a heavy-handed act of revenge against America — he called it "a positive service to the United States" — with his 1957 production of *A King in New York*, filmed in England and parodying the work of the House UnAmerican Activities Committee. The film was a sad, unhappy satire, so obviously the work of an aging, bitter filmmaker, and it garnered even worse reviews on its initial British release as on its eventual 1974 U.S. release. Douglas Gomery, writing in the *London Daily Express* (September 7, 1957), noted, "Chaplin attacks the American for using a child for political purposes, Yet in the film he is using his own child — too attack America." The British suddenly began aping their American counterparts, complaining that Chaplin was a resident of Switzerland, had paid no British taxes and yet had used British Eady Funds to partially finance the film. One of the few Englishmen willing to praise the production was J.B. Priestley, who wrote, "There is not a hint of Communist savagery and inhumanity in the satire." *A King in New York* is important only in that it demonstrates the full evolution of Chaplin, the pseudo-philosopher. "As political satire it's feeble," wrote Stanley Kaufmann in *The New Republic* (December 29, 1973), "as cultural satire it's moderately keen; as self-revelation by Chaplin, it's an essential work."

There was one last chance for a Chaplin revival and that came in the mid-1960s, first with publication of *My Autobiography* in 1964, and then with Chaplin's direction of *The Countess from Hong Kong* in 1966. The autobiography proved a disappointing romanticized view of a stormy career. One important bonus provided by the book's publication was Chaplin's decision to allow a complete retrospective of his features at New York's Plaza Theatre, beginning in November of 1963, which gave a new generation of film critics (including Stanley Kaufmann and Andrew Sarris) an opportunity to reappraise Chaplin's work. *The Countess from Hong Kong* could have restored Chaplin to greatness — photographs of his directing the feature made the covers of *Look*, *Life* and *Newsweek* — but the film was both a critical and a popular disaster. Rumor had it that Chaplin was his old, inventive self on the set, but the cameras were not recording Chaplin's directorial efforts, only the sulking, wooden performance of Marlon Brando.

Something else happened in the 1960s to further hurt Chaplin's reputation and that was the extraordinary revival of interest in Buster Keaton. Aside from the intelligentsia and the popular audience, a new viewing group had appeared on the scene — film buffs — and they adopted Buster Keaton as their favorite screen comedian. This same group even rediscovered Harold Lloyd and Harry Langdon, and it was almost as if there was perverse satisfaction to be found hailing Harry Langdon as a superior comedian to Chaplin in his use of pathos and childlike innocence. United Artists tried to revive commercial interest in Chaplin with the 1969 reissue of *The Circus*, but the audience, yet again, was not there. What audience was left to the comedian was only interested in the scandalous and the sleazy, and not coincidentally 1966 saw the publication of both Lita Gray Chaplin's *My Life with Chaplin* and Michael Chaplin's *I Couldn't Smoke the Grass on My Father's Lawn*.[5]

5. Lita Gray Chaplin was not happy with the original "memoirs," which was primarily the work of her collaborator. In 1998, I had the pleasure of publishing a new version of the memoirs, titled *Wife of the Life of the Party*.

The film industry had long distanced itself from Chaplin, but in 1972 attempted to make amends for its tacit support of his ostracism with the presentation of a Honorary Academy Award "for the incalculable effect he has had in making motion pictures the art form of this century." Chaplin came home to Hollywood, but for him it was too late, and, equally, all was not forgiven as became apparent when a storm of controversy arose as to whether he should have a star in the Hollywood Boulevard Walk of Fame. A more dignified final tribute to the living Chaplin came in 1975 with Richard Patterson's affectionate and well-considered documentary feature, *The Gentleman Tramp*.

Chaplin has never been forgotten the way that, say, Buster Keaton was once forgotten. He has been the subject of more books than any other screen personality — there is even a book about the books on Chaplin. But fame is not necessarily akin to popularity. A popular performer needs an audience; he needs the generation that grew up with him to *want* the next generation to like him. James Agee had that desire and acutely put it across in his classic 1949 *Life* magazine essay, "Comedy's Greatest Era."

That same sense of concern that Chaplin's genius be understood is present in the new television documentary series, *The Unknown Chaplin*, created by Kevin Brownlow and David Gill. If — and it is a big if — *The Unknown Chaplin* finds a major television audience in the United States, will Chaplin capture a fresh group of disciples for his comedy? Will a new generation of filmgoers see a modernity to Chaplin's techniques, comparable to the working methods of such diverse filmmakers as Jerry Lewis and Francis Ford Coppola? Will older audiences that laughed at the Chaplin features discover new and intact sequences to enjoy? I supect the answer is No. Rather like many of Chaplin's own features, *The Unknown Chaplin* is a work for the critics rather than the popular audience.

Certainly, Chaplin is not going to be restored to popularity overnight. This is the age of the punk rock and the new wave generation, to whom the degenerate comedic style of the Three Stooges is more closely allied, Chaplin is a little too gentle, too much akin to ballet or pantomime than to Boy George or Benny Hill. But punk rock, Boy George, and even the Three Stooges are fads, while Chaplin has been around and survived for most of this century. Perhaps what cartoonist Al Capp wrote back in 1950 will eventually become reality:

"When the history of art in our time is written, and when the ideological passions of our time are laughable curios, the great artist that our time has produced will be recognized as Charlie Chaplin.

Russ Columbo

Brochure Accompanying Take 2 CD release, TT409CD

There is both an irony and a poignancy to Russ Columbo's 1931 recording of "Save the Last Dance for Me." *[The title of this CD release.]* Not only did he dedicate the song to the love of his life, actress Carole Lombard, but also it highlights the tragedy of his early and pointless death at the age of twenty-six.

There is a certain fatalistic mockery attached to the deaths of stars at the height of their fame. They cease to be remembered for what they have accomplished in their lives, but rather for the manner in which they left the world. It happened to Rudolph Valentino in 1926, and it was also Russ Columbo's destiny. The singer was at the height of his recording career and on the brink of a major screen career when, on the evening of Sunday, September 2, 1934, he visited his friend Lansing Brown, a well-known Hollywood portrait photographer. As far as can be ascertained, Brown struck a match against the barrel of a Civil War dueling pistol, sitting on his desk. A charge exploded and a bullet from the gun ricocheted off a piece of furniture and bounced back, hitting Columbo in the left eye. The singer collapsed and two hours later died at Los Angeles' Good Samaritan Hospital.

Russ Columbo was buried at Forest Lawn Memorial Park in Glendale. The pallbearers included Bing Crosby, Zeppo Marx and director Lowell Sherman, and among the mourners were Ann Sothern, Sally Blane (who was with him at the hospital when he died) and Carole Lombard (who collapsed during the service). Lansing Brown was also present; a jury at Columbo's inquest found that "Russ Columbo came to his death by a gun wound accidentally inflicted by Lansing Brown."

The death was certainly strange, and what happened afterwards was positively weird. Just prior to Columbo's death, his mother suffered a heart attack, and for the remaining ten years of her life, she was never informed that her son was dead. At Carole Lombard's suggestion, she was told that Russ had gone on an extended trip abroad. Weekly letters supposedly written by Columbo were read to the nearly-blind woman. To further add to the mystery of Russ Columbo's death is the murder by gangsters of his brother Alberto in March 1954.

Russ Columbo was born Ruggiero Eugenio de Rudolpho Colombo in Philadelphia on January 14, 1908, the youngest of twelve children. Somewhat of a child prodigy, the young Columbo performed on the violin at the age of five at Atlantic City's Steel Pier. In order to permit Columbo to study violin under Alexander Bevan, the family moved to Calistoga, California, and later San Francisco (where it is often erroneously claimed that he was born), and then Los Angeles. Columbo was first violinist in the Belmont High School Band, and while still at school in Los Angeles, he began playing background music for silent films. In the mid-1920s, supposedly he met for the first time silent screen legend Pola Negri; a highly publicized lover of Rudolph Valentino, Negri was struck by the resemblance between Valentino and the young violinist, who around the same period changed his name to Russ Columbo. In 1932, Columbo was invited to sing the theme song, "Paradise," at the premiere of Negri's first American talkie, *A Woman Commands*.

It was as a violinist rather than a singer that Columbo began appearing with professional bands, first with George Eckhart and His Orchestra, and then, in 1927, with Professor Moore and His Orchestra at the newly-opened Roosevelt Hotel in Hollywood. When the featured violinist failed to appear on the opening night of the engagement, Columbo deputized for him. His extreme good looks were particularly appealing to the public, and a year later, Columbo was signed to sing with the Gus Arnheim Orchestra at the Cocoanut Grove at Los Angeles' Ambassador Hotel, succeeding Bing Crosby.

Columbo was first heard on radio in 1927, but it was not until he left for New York to form his own band that he became a regular performer on the medium. In 1933, he and his band moved to Los Angeles, and Columbo was heard coast-to-coast on NBC. His romantic style of singing coupled with his highly-publicized good looks and supposed relationship with actresses such as Greta Garbo and Dorothy Dell let to his being dubbed "The Romeo of Radio" and "The Valentino of the Air." While playing at the Silver Slipper nightclub in Los Angeles, Russ Columbo met composer Con Conrad ("Margie," "Ma, He's Making Eyes at Me," etc.) and the two collaborated on Russ Columbo's radio theme song, "You Call It Madness, I Call it Love." Columbo and Conrad collaborated on more than a dozen songs, including "Too Beautiful for Words," "When You're in Love" and "Let's Pretend There's a Moon."

From the late 1920s through the early 1930s, there was a substantial change in Russ Columbo's vocal style. "Back in Your Old Back Yard" from April 1928 boasts a snappy tempo and speedy delivery virtually indistinguishable from other band singers of the period. It is totally different from the phrasing of "I Don't Know Why I Just Do" from September 1931, whose slow pacing is almost numbing. The influence of Bing Crosby is also very apparent in the early recordings, most noticeably in "Sweet and Lovely." After 1931, the style is both romantic and sophisticated; the typical band vocalist technique is gone and the listener is very much aware that here is an individual and original artiste. As Columbo sings in the August 1934 recording of "Too Beautiful for Words," as a composer, he "can't compare with Berlin or Gershwin," but here, despite the passing years is "a perfect rhapsody."

Russ Columbo's screen career is somewhat more extensive than is generally recognized. He made his screen debut in 1928 for Paramount in the Gary Cooper-Lupe Velez vehicle, *Wolf Song*. It was followed by *Wonder of Women*, (1929), *Dynamite* (1929, in which he sang the theme song, "How Am I to Know"), *Street Girl* (1929), and *Hello Sister* (1930, in which he did not appear but for which he composed the musical score). At that time, the singer was billed on screen as Russ Colombo.

In 1931, Columbo wrote both the words and music for *Hell Bound*. He had been in both *Broadway thru a Keyhole* (1933) and *Moulin Rouge* (1934). There was talk that Columbo would star in the 1934 Warner Bros. musical, *Twenty Million Sweethearts*, which had a radio theme and was supposedly very loosely based on Columbo's life. Instead the latter embarked on an extensive tour of the United States with a newly-formed orchestra, and the leading role in the film was played by Dick Powell.

Universal's Carl Laemmle signed Columbo to a contract in 1934, and the singer's first and, as it transpired, only feature under the agreement was *Wake Up and Dream* (1934), directed by Kurt Neumann, filmed in August of 1934 and released in October of the same year. Laemmle did plan to star the singer in the first all-sound version of *Show Boat*, to be directed by Frank Borzage. Following Columbo's death, the project was shelved until 1936, when Allan Jones played the Columbo-intended role of Gaylord Ravenal under the direction of James Whale.

There is no doubt that Universal intended to "build" Russ Columbo as a major Hollywood star, a worthy rival to Dick Powell or Allan Jones, a singer who would have none of the dull personality of Nelson Eddy or the non-looks of a contemporary radio singer such as Arthur Tracy. Paradoxically, it was Columbo's brother, Alberto, who embarked on an exclusive film career in 1934, which while never permitting him to appear in anything but supporting roles did last through the early 1950s.

The recordings included here help the listener not only to appreciate Columbo's uniquely romantic style, but also to study the development of his approach to lyric and melody. We will never know what Russ Columbo might have been, but from this compact disc, we can comprehend what he was as a foremost entertainer of his day on the band circuit and on radio. It was a mid-19th Century element that robbed the world of Russ Columbo, but by one of the many curious twists of fate that governed his career, it is thanks to a 20th Century invention, the phonograph record, that Ross Columbo will never die.

Neal Dodd

Films in Review, April 1977, page 254

The "unidentified player" in the still from *Strange Wives* (*FIR*, February 1977) is the Rev. Neal Dodd, who had an extraordinary career in Hollywood, in and out of films.

Born September 6, 1878, in Port Madison, Iowa, Dodd was ordained at the Nashota House Seminary in Wisconsin on July 25, 1907. He came to Los Angeles in 1918, and founded St. Mary of the Angels Episcopal Church at 1743 North New Hampshire Avenue in Hollywood. It was this building which for seven years housed the first offices of the Motion Picture Relief Fund of which Father Dodd was one of the founders and its first secretary. The church later moved to 4510 Finley Avenue, Hollywood. To raise money for Dodd's church, Rob Wagner and Rupert Hughes published a slim volume in 1936 titled *Two Decades, "The Story of a Man of God" — Hollywood's Own Padre.* Hughes wrote, "Reverend Neal Dodd not only mingled with moving picture people and spoke to them, but he spoke well of them and their work publicly. He had even the sublime courage to appear on the screen as an actor of clergymen when there was occasion for such impersonation."

Apparently Father Dodd made his first screen appearance in a 1920 Pathé newsreel. He went on to appear in 300 films; his favorite roles were those of the clergyman in *It Happened One Night* and the Senate Chaplain in *Mr. Smith Goes to Washington.* Other appearances by the only clergyman holding a Screen Actors Guild card include *The Only Woman* (1924), *Lost at Sea* (1926), *Tillie's Punctured Romance* (1927), *Anna Christie* (1930), *Merrily We Go to Hell* (1932), *The Secret Life of Walter Mitty* (1947), *Sorry Wrong Number* (1948), *Louisa* (1950), and *Here Comes the Groom* (1951). As director Nick Grinde once remarked to me, "You could always rely on Father Dodd never to forget his lines, and he didn't cost as much as an actor because he supplied his own Bible."

Father Dodd took his screen work very seriously, as an interview with him in the *New York Times* of September 3, 1950 reveals. He would not marry a divorced character in a film. Nick Grinde recalled that when scriptwriter F. Hugh Herbert decided one day to avail himself of Father Dodd's presence on the set and get married, Dodd refused to go through with the ceremony until he had removed his make-up.

Throughout his life, Father Dodd defended the stars with whom he worked and whom he married — including Jack Pickford and Marilyn Miller and William S. Hart and Winnifred Westover. "They have to live with their window shades up," he said, "The rest of us have the privilege of living with the shades down." Father Dodd retired in 1952 and died, May 26, 1966.

Geoffrey Donaldson

Classic Images, November 1997, page 50;
Revised for publication in a brochure for opening
of the Geoffrey Donaldson Institute

Those of us who have been around for a few years will be familiar with the name Geoffrey Donaldson. He was an Australian living in the Netherlands who contributed articles on various European film festivals to *Films and Filming*, and provided valuable information on film history in his letters to *Films in Review*, when the publication was in its heyday. Geoffrey Donaldson was also the leading authority on the history of Dutch Cinema, and for many, many years, he collected minutiae on silent films from the Netherlands from obscure trade publications and interviewed the pioneers of that country's cinema.

Thanks to the efforts of Hoos Blotkamp-De Roos and the Nederlands Filmmuseum (now known as the Eye Institute), Geoffrey Donaldson's life-long dedication to the cinema of his adopted country is shared with a wider audience in *Of Joy and Sorrow: A Filmography of Dutch Silent Fiction*. In chronological order, Geoffrey Donaldson provides complete documentation on early fictional Dutch films from the silent era. Included in each entry is a synopsis, both the original Dutch title and its English translation, complete player and technical credits, a bibliography of both contemporary and modern references, the length, the first known screening, and information as to the preservation status of the film.

Rather than present this extraordinary work of reference in catalog form, the Nederlands Filmmuseum has chosen to publish it as a coffee table volume of over 300 pages with more than 360 photographs, of which thirty-two are frame enlargements reproduced in their original tints or tones. An overview of Dutch cinema from 1896-1933 is provided by Peter Delpeut, and the book also includes indexes by film, individuals, companies, and characters, and a bibliography. The title was chosen because the earliest Dutch films are concerned either with intense joy or deep sorrow. And did I mention that the book is in English rather than Dutch, and, therefore, accessible, without problem, to a majority of film buffs, students and scholars?

Just as Denis Gifford's *British Film Catalog* is the definitive source for documentation on British productions, so is *Joy and Sorrow* the consummate reference source on Dutch silent cinema. There is nothing that could or should be added. The work is complete and beyond reproach. It does not merely enhance our knowledge of Dutch silent films, but rather, because so little is known of the subject outside of the Netherlands, the book opens up a whole new area in film history. It is a reminder of just how prolific Dutch filmmakers were in the silent era, and, as one turns its pages, the reader discovers that Dutch films — such as *Carmen of the North* from 1919, starring two of the most popular of Dutch performers, Annie Bos and Adelqui Migliar — even found their way to the United States. About the only thing *Joy and Sorrow* does not tell us is whether Dutch films of the 1910s and 1920s were as good as the somewhat smaller output of the modern Dutch film industry. Based on a limited viewing of some of the films of producer Alfred Machin, I suspect that perhaps they were.

As the Nederlands Filmmuseum notes, the intriguing saga of Dutch cinema is a story to be proud of. The Dutch film archives should also be proud of this book, and, above all, of its author, Geoffrey Donaldson, who, if he was not already a naturalized Dutchhman, I would recommend be named an honorary Dutch citizen. On a personal note, I am honored to be listed among the individuals who assisted Geoffrey Donaldson in some small way, but how depressing to note that the acknowledgements to the dead outnumber those to the living. The pioneering research spirit of the 1960s and 1970s seems long gone, as dead and forgotten as those incredible resource letters that once filled the back pages of *Films in Review*. Thank goodness that Geoffrey Donaldson is still with us *[as of 1997]* and that a film archive has the enthusiasm and the good sense to publish his work.

Rereading my review, I am pleased that I was able to give Geoff Donaldson the credit he so richly deserved. At the same time, I am aware that the piece is somewhat impersonal and does not reflect my deep friendship with Geoff from the 1960s until his death. We communicated mostly by letter and I first met him in London. I am particularly pleased that I was able to introduce him to Elsie Cohen, the founder of London's Academy Cinema and a lady involved in early Dutch cinema.

In later years, my partner, Robert Gitt, and I would stay with Geoff at his Rotterdam apartment, and my last memory of him is his watching and waving from the balcony as Robert and I waited outside the apartment building for the tram to take us to the station — it was the last time I saw him. Geoff would often tell me that I looked somewhat like his lifetime companion, Harry, and that we both bore a striking resemblance to comedian Benny Hill. I am not certain how I feel about such comparison, but I am very much aware how deeply fond I was of Geoff Donaldson and how much I, and the world of film history research, miss him.

[Geoffrey Donaldson was born in Newcastle, Australia, on November 29, 1929. He died on May 9, 2002 in Rotterdam, the Netherlands. The Geoffrey Donaldson Institute was founded by Egbert Barton on November 29, 2013.]

Kirk Douglas

Program Note for 2009 Britannia Awards,
hosted by BAFTA/LA

It requires no Hollywood hyperbole to describe Kirk Douglas both as an American film legend and as a unique worldwide figure in screen entertainment. The characters that he has portrayed circle the globe in equal measure to his audience appeal and critical praise for his work. In the ancient world, he has been a Roman slave in *Spartacus*, a Greek hero in *Ulysses* and a Scandinavian invader in *The Vikings*. He has been as American as General Patton in *Is Paris Burning?* and Doc Holliday in *Gunfight at the OK Corral*. He has been a French officer in *Paths of Glory* and a Dutch painter in *Lust for Life*, a title that might well describe the healthy philosophy of its star.

Kirk Douglas is a unique screen performer, one of a fast disappearing, special kind of Hollywood star, who is as much a personality as a great actor, and yet one who never allows Kirk Douglas, the name above the title, to interfere with or overwhelm Kirk Douglas the lead player. One doesn't generally consider him as a stage performer, despite his graduation from the American Academy of Dramatic Arts and his early years on Broadway, and, yet, he has shown himself to be a consummate professional when it comes to appearing in film adaptations of some of the greatest of classic plays such as Eugene O'Neill's *Mourning Becomes Electra*, Tennessee Williams' *The Glass Menagerie* and George Bernard Shaw's *The Devil's Disciple*. On television, he has played Dr. Jekyll and Mr. Hyde in a 1973 British musical production (in which he sang in the manner of Rex Harrison, somewhat to his chagrin) and he starred in a 1988 American production of *Inherit the Wind*.

An argument might be made that the early Kirk Douglas roles generally fall into the category of anti-social hero, a type of character generally associated with the Richard Widmark school of acting. This is certainly true of Douglas' first film, *The Strange Love of Martha Ivers*, in which he is featured as the weak, alcoholic husband of a wealthy businesswoman, played by the formidable Barbara Stanwyck.

It is with *Champion* in 1949, playing boxer Midge Kelly, that Kirk Douglas found his métier. Here he is a realistic, uncompromising anti-hero, vicious and selfish and yet demonstrating the strength and vulnerability of which the actor is uniquely capable. To a large extent, Midge Kelly is guilty of the same urges that affect everyone, but, unlike the average Jane or Joe, he gives in to them. Only a brilliant and dedicated actor could portray such a character, someone with whom audiences can empathize and can hate to equal degree. It must also be acknowledged that his shirtless appearance in much of *Champion* gave Douglas the opportunity to display the physique, of which he was justifiably proud and which would be seen quite frequently in films to come, to the obvious delight of female moviegoers.

Midge Kelly identifies himself in *Champion* as a "hey-you." It is very obvious that after *Champion*, Kirk Douglas would never fall into that category of irrelevancy. "I can do it — I can do it," he screams at the fight manager. And from that film on, he proved he could do anything. Equally, his mantra might also be identified as "I tried, goddammit, I tried," as he said to *Vanity Fair* in a 2002 interview.

The role of humanitarian is as important to Kirk Douglas as that of actor, and it cannot, and should not be, ignored. For his high school graduation, Douglas wrote in an essay, "Art can only be obtained through hunger — hunger for beauty or harmony or truth or justice." It is an ideal he has tried to live up to ever since. "I know the power of an American star in another country," he said in the 1960s, serving as a goodwill ambassador, for which he received the Presidential Medal of Freedom. He and his wife Anne have supported the Kirk Douglas High School facility for troubled children in Northridge, and helped fund 400 safe children's playgrounds since 1977. He has given his name to the Kirk Douglas Theatre in Culver City, which serves as a training ground for actors, directors and playwrights. A year ago, he lobbied the U.S. government to apologize for slavery. It is as if Kirk Douglas is always at the cutting edge, be it with his massive humanitarian efforts or simply blogging and chatting online with *MySpace*.

Screenwriter Dalton Trumbo was one of the Hollywood Ten, blacklisted during the McCarthy era. It was Kirk Douglas who rehabilitated him, insisting he receive screen credit on the actor's production of *Spartacus*. He recognized talent above politics by again hiring Dalton Trumbo for

Lonely Are the Brave. Breaking the blacklist is often described by the actor as his greatest achievement.

In *Lonely Are the Brave*, Douglas is a cowboy trying to live by his own code, but eventually beaten down by civilization. The performance reminds one very much of Kirk Douglas, the man, who has similarly been a maverick in terms of the roles that he has chosen to play. It should be no surprise that he chose to form his own production company, Bryna, named after his mother, or that he has not been shy about providing character notes to his directors. Douglas denies that he is a "Method Actor," and yet there is an intensity to his performances, suggestive of an inner quality, a determination to become the character. As long ago as 1957, a fan magazine writer commented that "If he wasn't sure, he acted sure. If he was sure, he was [in the actor's words] occasionally unbearable."

Lonely Are the Brave is often named by Kirk Douglas as his favorite film, but, arguably, the production which is most powerful in its message is *Paths of Glory*, directed by Stanley Kubrick, which, in terms of its anti-war stance is on a par with *All Quiet on the Western Front*. Here, as Colonel Dax, matched in dialogue delivery and argumentative style by Adolphe Menjou as General Broulard, Douglas ascends to a new level of brilliance.

One might be tempted to dismiss *Paths of Glory* as belonging to the past, of containing an outmoded message However, I can recall a few years ago in London hearing Mrs. Stanley Kubrick, who herself appears in the film, make the sad comment as to its pacifist message, "I wish it was an old fashioned film." One cannot help but be overwhelmingly moved by Kirk Douglas as the impassioned World War One French officer fighting for the lives of men who are to be sacrificed for the incompetence of their leaders. If only that same passion might be brought to the political arena today, if only there were an advocate with actor Kirk Douglas' skill in oratory and desire to confront the brutality and insanity of war. Don't let the dimple or the mischievous smile confuse you, that jutting jaw of his will brook no argument.

Paths of Glory was initially banned in France, but later, in 1985, Douglas received the Chevalier de la Legion d'Honneur for services to France in the Arts. It is not so much one country, France, but the entire world that benefits from Kirk Douglas productions such as Paths of Glory.

Like the Barrymores, the Douglas family has become something of a theatrical dynasty. At its head is Kirk Douglas, with the wit of a John Barrymore (of whom Douglas was in awe), the good taste and moral stature of Ethel (he turned down a role on screen with her in favor of the film that made him a star, *Champion*) and, yes, a little of the melodramatics of

Lionel (let us not forget *The List of Adrian Messenger*). The Douglas family ties extend from Russia, through Amsterdam, New York and Hollywood, California, to the shores of Wales. With a Welsh daughter-in-law, is it inappropriate to welcome Kirk Douglas as an honorary Britisher? The BAFTA Award for Contribution to Worldwide Film Entertainment could not be more apposite.

In his autobiography, *The Ragman's Son*, Kirk Douglas writes of the four shelves of the scripts which he has filmed. "I look at those scripts. How many millions of people around the world have seen those movies? How many did they enjoy? Did they really help someone forget their problems for a while? Did they get lost in what was happening on screen? Is it important? Has the world been altered? Is the world a better place to live in because of it?" There can be only one response. A resounding Yes.

[Kirk Douglas died in Los Angeles on February 5, 2020.]

Kent D. Eastin and Blackhawk Films

Films in Review, August/September 1981, pages 435, 441

Film collectors everywhere lost their best friend this April 14, when Kent D. Eastin, the founder and long-time president of Blackhawk Films died at the age of seventy-two.

Kent Eastin began his unique film career in July 1927, when he founded thea Eastin Camera Service in Illinois, and for the next few years began to build up a prominent 16mm film rental and sales organization. In 1935, Kent moved to Davenport, Iowa, and in 1939 he created Blackhawk Films there, establishing Davenport as a major city as far as any film collector is concerned. In the early 1950s, Blackhawk began making 8mm releases of railroad films; Eastin was a great train buff and deliberately planned the study in his house to overlook the tracks of the Rock Island Line.

For the next twenty years, Blackhawk Films grew in strength. It acquired exclusive distribution of Hal Roach's Our Gang and Laurel and Hardy series. It released the great features and the Biograph shorts of D.W. Griffith, being actively involved with the Museum of Modern Art in the 1975 restoration of the latter. Silent films really did live again and found new audiences thanks to Kent Eastin and Blackhawk Films. Long-forgotten comedy stars such as Billie Rhodes suddenly began to receive fan mail again. Thomas H. Ince's later features suddenly became available, and after so much speculation film historians found they were boring and lackluster. Everyone had the opportunity to study the development of Chaplin's pantomimic techniques in his early Keystone and Mutual comedies. Charley Chase was rescued from obscurity. The films of Douglas Fairbanks, Sr., Buster Keaton, Lon Chaney, and Rudolph Valentino were suddenly available to anyone with an 8mm or 16mm projector. All thanks to Kent Eastin and Blackhawk. And if you didn't have a projector, a reel, a can, a projector bulb, then Blackhawk could supply them also — all at reasonable prices.

But it was not just the variety and the sheer number of films that made Kent Eastin's Blackhawk Films so special. Primarily, it was the fact that one always knew the print quality would be excellent, that one was doing business with someone very unique in American business, a gentleman — and in Kent Eastin's case, a very gentle gentleman. As Blackhawk grew in stature and strength, it never ceased to be a family concern, a place where the president replied to one's letter personally. Quality and service were everything at Blackhawk.

There was another thing unique about Blackhawk, and that was those famous — some might say infamous — introductory titles. Sometimes they were one or two title cards long and sometimes as many as six or seven. In the early years, the authors were never identified, but later one discovered that those responsible included Kalton Lahue, Edward Wagenknecht and even Anthony Slide. I still cringe when I see one of those films with my introduction being screened, but sometimes I marvel that I managed to be so noncommittal and inconsequential about a film I detested or that, in the case of *The Juggernaut*, I managed to find a supposedly-satisfactory reason why Blackhawk was only releasing the last reel of a five-reel feature.

There was Blackhawk, and Blackhawk was Kent D. Eastin until 1975, when the company was acquired by Lee Enterprises. Today, the business principles that Kent Eastin instilled in the company are still maintained, but the project is geared more to the popular market and less to the film buff of a few years ago. However, what may happen to Blackhawk, it will remain a company inextricably linked to one man., the man who made film collecting a practical possibility for everyone in America, Kent D. Eastin.

[Lee Enterprises subsequently sold Blackhawk Films to the management, and in 1983, it was acquired by National Telefilm Associates (NTA). At the end of the decade, NTA sold the company to David Shepard, who had been associated with the company in the 1970s. At his death in 2017, Blackhawk Films was owned by French-based Lobster Films.]

Walter Forde
and *Land without Music*

Films in Review, May 1981, pages 301, 317

When I telephoned Walter Forde to tell him I was bringing over a print of his 1936 film, *Land without Music,* Walter's initial response was "that was a lousy picture all round." I was not unduly surprised by his reaction, for Walter Forde is one British director who has always been unsentimental and unduly modest about his many fine contributions to the cinema. In fact, Walter Forde's direction makes *Land without Music* move along at a snappy pace and prevents it from becoming just another turgid operetta. It compares more than favorably with similar types of films directed around the same period by Robert Z. Leonard at MGM.

Land without Music comes in the middle period of Walter Forde's film career, following *The Ghost Train* (1931), *Rome Express* (1933), *Chu-Chin-Chow* (1934), and *Bulldog Jack* (1935), among others. It was produced by the short-lived Capitol Films, which was lucky in obtaining Forde, who had just terminated his contract with Gaumont-British. (Gaumont-British's production head, Michael Balcon, has quite rightly described Walter as "probably one of the most underestimated directors in the British film industry".) Had not Capitol Films entered bankruptcy after the release of *Land without Music,* Walter Forde would have directed *The Pickwick Papers* for the company, with Edmund Gwenn as Mr. Pickwick.

The film of *Land without Music* is based on an original operetta by Oscar Straus, and set in the early 19th Century Duchy of Lucco, where all work is neglected in favor of music. When the Princess Regent (Diana Napier) bans music in order to force the people to work and pay off the National Debt, there is a popular uprising led by Lucco-born opera star Carlini (Richard Tauber) and a visiting American journalist (Jimmy Durante). The Princess Regent is forced to rescind the ban, and Durante's daughter (played by June Clyde) comes up with the answer to the country's economic problems: "Make music a national industry." Now if only Jimmy Carter had thought of that!

The role of the American journalist was to have been played by Eugene Pallette, but on the first day of shooting he walked off the picture — for reasons unknown — and as Durante happened to be appearing at the London Palladium at the time, he was persuaded to take over the role. It is a well-known fact that marvelous as Jimmy Durante was live on stage or on early, live television, his personality simply does not come across on film. He was a passable screen performer, but somehow the Durante verve is missing. In *Land without Music*, he, Tauber and Clyde interact well together, and Walter Forde confirms there was rapport on the set between all principals and is quick to stress that both Tauber and his wife, Diana Napier, were easy to work with.

The music, unfortunately, is not too memorable, except for one charming song, "Only a Simple Little Melody," which Tauber introduces at the secret concert he gives in an underground cave, and which becomes a love song between him and the Princess Regent. Like most opera stars, Richard Tauber could easily look pompous on film, but Walter Forde carefully avoids that by not allowing the camera to linger too long on the singer. When Tauber makes his first entrance, singing in his coach, Forde cuts to shots of the coachman yawning and the horse reacting to Tauber's singing. It is a cute idea, and here it works.

Land without Music was obviously a lavish production as the sets indicate. The exterior scenes have a look of Continental Europe to them, despite their all being shot on the back lot of the Denham Studios.

On the film's initial release, *Motion Picture Herald* (October 24, 1936) commented, "Those who appreciate finely rendered music will be enthusiastic about the picture, but in addition there is Schnozzola Durante, who makes the most of a hearty comedy part, and there is good romantic interest too."

Walter Forde is not the easiest of British directors to study in this country. Aside from *Land without Music*, only three of his other films are currently available for rental here: *Bulldog Jack*, *Flying Fortress* and *Sons of the Sea* (released in England as *Atlantic Ferry*). In addition, there is a splendid booklet on Walter Forde, compiled by Geoff Brown and published by the British Film Institute. Do not be put off by the fact that the B.F.I is the publisher. This is not another piece of academic, semiological twaddle prepared by second-rate film professors who cannot find a legitimate publisher, but rather it is a superb piece of film research, containing a very detailed filmography and an erudite and sympathetic introduction by Michael Balcon.

Lillian Gish: Star of Screen, Stage — and TV

Emmy Magazine, January/February 1984, pages 27-29

On March 1 [1984], Lillian Gish will receive the prestigious Life Achievement Award from the American Film Institute in recognition of a career of more than seventy years in the film industry. Through *Hearts of the World*, *Broken Blossoms*, *Way Down East*, *The Wind*, *Duel in the Sun*, *Portrait of Jennie*, *The Night of the Hunter*, *The Comedians*, and *A Wedding*, Lillian Gish has been an integral part of motion pictures. But in the history of show business, she is more than merely a movie star; she has also been an accomplished stage actress since before she entered films, and — what is generally forgotten today — she is a veteran television performer as well. Lillian Gish was there at the American Biograph Company when director D.W. Griffith created screen syntax; she was there when he made *The Birth of a Nation*. And she was also there when the age of American live television began.

Lillian herself has often remarked that the beginning of television was rather like the beginning of cinema — "You had just one chance to do it." But it was no longer 1912, when the actress had made her screen debut; it was now 1949. She was no longer a gawky, dreamy teenager, but rather a mature woman who brought an immediate dignity and quiet restraint to all of her television roles. She was elegant in a subdued fashion, and she spoke her lines with a soft but determined demeanor.

Lillian made her television debut on February 6, 1949, in NBC's Philco Playhouse production of *The Late Christopher Bean*. She played the harassed housemaid Abby, to whom the late painter of the title had left his fortune because she was the only person who had been kind to him. It was a role that Pauline Lord had first performed on stage in the original 1932 production of Sidney Howard's play of the same name. Lillian looked a little more attractive and considerably more ethereal than had Pauline Lord, and she was, as one critic had noted, "extremely appealing." The first television role was enhanced by the supportive playing of former silent star Bert Lytell and by the distinctive production of Fred Coe.

There was to be a two-year absence before Lillian returned to television, where her portrayals included appearances in live television presentations of plays that included *Ladies in Retirement* (1951), *The Joyous Season* (1951), *The Corner Drugstore* (1954), *The Quality of Mercy* (1954), and *The Sound and the Fury* (1955). Perhaps appropriately, her television career began in earnest with a Philco Playhouse program, *Birth of the Movies*, devoted to the life and work of D.W. Griffith, with whose career Lillian's was so interwoven and with whom her name is indelibly linked. Fred Coe produced, Delbert Mann directed, and H.R. Hays and Robert Alan Aurthur wrote the script based on Lillian's memoirs. Apart from the live drama with John Newland as Griffith, Jean Pearson as Lillian Gish (Grace Kelly had auditioned for the role) and Paul Mann as Griffith's cameraman, Billy Bitzer, the production also utilized clips from many of Griffith's films, including *The Birth of a Nation*, *Intolerance* and *Broken Blossoms*. Lillian Gish narrated.

The production, which aired on April 22, 1951, came in for a fair amount of criticism, largely because the network executives apparently seized on the program as an excuse for an attack on the film industry (which was actively fighting the incursion of television as a dominant factor in popular entertainment). *Variety*'s criticism was typically oxymoronic: "They built Griffith into a superman, at the same time caricaturing his successors in Hollywood as a group of money-grubbing businessmen who sacrificed any creative ideals to the all-important box office."

Lillian has written that one of the highlights of her years in television was meeting Grandma Moses, the American primitive painter, whom she portrayed in the March 28, 1952, Schlitz Playhouse of the Stars adaptation by David Shaw of Mrs. Moses' autobiography. Since Lillian, also, had come from a quieter, less hurried age and had also created works of art in her own particular medium, she was a natural to play Grandma Moses, and she brought a simple and sympathetic feeling to the characterization.

If Grandma Moses was a woman at peace with her family and her society, the fictitious Mrs. Carrie Watts, Lillian's next television characterization, was not. Watts was an elderly woman searching for her lost spirit through a trip back to her hometown, Bountiful. Televised on the Philco Playhouse on March 1, 1953, *The Trip to Bountiful*, written by Horton Foote, is probably Lillian's best-known television work. The production reunited Lillian and producer Fred Coe; the actress is an outspoken admirer of Coe's work, describing him as the "father of the [television] medium." That program also marked the beginning of an illustrious career for Lillian's co-star, Eva Marie Saint, who plays the young woman who befriends Mrs. Watt on the long bus ride. The show was also unusual in that it proved so successful on television that it was transferred to the stage, as a Theatre Guild presentation, with Gish and Saint recreating their original roles.

One of Lillian's pet projects has long been the creation of a governmental post of Secretary of Fine Arts; she is quick to point out that the United States is the only major country without a minister of culture. In the October 19, 1955, Kraft Television Theatre presentation of *I, Mrs. Bibb* by Paul Crabtree, Lillian had the opportunity to promote such a post. As Elizabeth M. Bibb, widow of a former senator, Lillian plays a woman who is caught between a sense of duty and a need to preserve her husband's memory as a great man when she discovers that he has apparently taken a bribe. Although not a major television production, *I, Mrs. Bibb* was expertly directed by Richard Dunlap[6] and captured the imagination of viewers. It is interesting to compare Lillian's performance with that of Marie Carroll as the Senator's secretary, Miss Lilly. While the latter practically tore the scenery apart with her melodramatics, Gish's performance is a model of dignity and simplicity of style. Here is a star from silent film, a medium widely considered to have been full of melodrama, giving a group of television performers an incomparable acting lesson.

Prior to appearing in *I, Mrs. Bibb*, Lillian had starred on screen in *The Night of the Hunter*, the only film to be directed by Charles Laughton. After her work in the feature, Laughton had written to Lillian that "I hope that my life, professionally, as well as personally, shall have a lot of Gish in it." Laughton's wish came true less than a year later when he hosted and narrated the February 11, 1955, Ford Star Jubilee presentation of *The Day Lincoln Was Shot* (produced by Paul Gregory, directed by Delbert Mann, and adapted by Terry and Denis Sanders and Jean Holloway from the book by Jim Bishop). The unusually long (ninety minute) production was notable for the performances of Lillian as Mary Todd Lincoln, Raymond Massey as the doomed president, and Jack Lemmon as John Wilkes Booth.

6. When writing this article, I spoke with Richard Dunlap, who told me that the union AFTRA had informed him that there was to be only limited time for rehearsal. When he informed Lillian, she responded that she had never allowed a union to tell her when to work. "Whenever you are willing to work I am." She was "very nervous," particularly about the long speeches, but would not use cue cards.

But if ever there was a perfect television program for Lillian Gish, it was *Morning's at Seven*, seen on NBC's Alcoa Hour on November 4, 1956. Skillfully adapted by Robert Wallsten from Paul Osborn's classic 1939 play, *Morning's at Seven* is a wonderful example of ensemble playing by a cast that includes Lillian Gish and her sister Dorothy, as well as June Lockhart, Evelyn Varden, Dorothy Stickney, and David Wayne. In a world of whimsical eccentricity, Lillian's character, Esther, is sensible and secure.

"God's in his Heaven; all's right with the world" are the last words in *Morning's at Seven*, and they were spoken by Lillian. But all was not well in the world of television. It was changing: live presentations were coming to an end, there was less of a need for versatile performers, and there was a corresponding demand for personalities to star in long-term series.

To be sure, Lillian Gish continued to be seen on television, notably in episodes of *The Defenders*, *Mr. Novak*, *Breaking Point*, and *Alfred Hitchcock Presents*. With her friend, Helen Hayes, she starred in the 1968 ABC presentation of *Arsenic and Old Lace*. In 1976, again for ABC, Lillian made her TV movie debut in *Twin Detectives*. She hosted the 1975 PBS series, *The Silent Years*, portrayed a high school teacher in a 1980 episode of *The Love Boat*, and played Kate Jackson's grandmother in a 1981 CBS Tuesday Night Movie, *Thin Ice*. And we saw her last December in a CBS movie adaptation of the play *Hobson's Choice*, co-starring Sharon Gless, Jack Warden and Richard Thomas.

As *I, Mrs. Bibb*, Lillian Gish remarked, "the legends in the history of our country are very important." And it is important that those legends live on. The AFI Life Achievement Award will add to the legend of Lillian Gish, film personality. What we also need are new television productions in the tradition of *The Trip to Bountiful* and *Morning's at Seven* to add to the legend of Lillian Gish, television star.

Filming Lillian Gish

American Cinematographer, June 1984, pages 42-48

In 1924, Joseph Hergesheimer wrote of Lillian Gish, "You have the quality which, in a Golden Age, would have an army against the walls of a city for seven years." That "quality," that mix of strength and ethereal beauty has fascinated photographers as much as it has directors and audiences for some seven decades now.

From 1912, when Lillian Gish first entered the film industry, the actress has been photographed by a considerable number of major cinematographers, including American Society of Cinematographers members, John Arnold, Joseph August, Stanley Cortez, George Folsey, Lee Garmes, Charles Lang, Jr., Roy Overbaugh, Franz Planer, Charles Rosher, and Clifford Stine, along with Billy Bitzer, Henri Decaé and Desmond Dickinson. Through the years, she has come to know as much, if not more, about how she should be photographed.

Twenty-seven-year-old Jon Kranhouse, who filmed Lillian Gish's most recent feature — officially recorded as her 101st film — recounts that when she was first introduced to him, the actress remarked, "Young man, I've been working under lights longer than you've been alive. It's very important that I have a high camera and a low light." She knew exactly what she wanted, and Kranhouse saw little reason for disputing her requirements. When, at one stage, he did, suggesting that a particular exterior scene be shot using natural light, Gish's first comment upon arriving at the set was, "Where are the lights?" She was so used to staring ahead straight into arc lights that she refused to accept Kranhouse's explanation regarding modern lenses and high speed films, simply repeating, "Where are the lights?" And, of course, eventually the lights were set to her specifications. Similarly, Richard Thomas, Gish's co-star in the 1983 television feature, *Hobson's Choice*, recalls his colleague's retort upon being informed that she was to be shot from a low camera angle: "If God had wished us to be filmed from that level, he would have put our eyes in our belly button."

When Lillian and Dorothy Gish appeared in their first film for D.W. Griffith and American Biograph in 1912 (a one-reel short titled *An Unseen Enemy*), the cinematographer was Billy Bitzer. Bitzer filmed Lillian through such screen classics as *The Birth of a Nation*, *Intolerance*, *Hearts of the World*, *Broken Blossoms*, and *Way Down East*. For all his importance as a pioneer, Bitzer was never very receptive to new ideas or sensitive to the needs of any particular scene or close-up. According to Gish, Andy Reid, who was Bitzer's electrician, set up the lights for each scene, and she insists, thanks to her experience back then, that "the electrician is just as important as the cinematographer. I spent more time with Andy Reid than I did with Billy Bitzer," adding, "They painted the faces on the screen in those days and I wish they would take the time to do that again."

Karl Struss pointed out that Bitzer has received at least one screen credit that is not legitimately his; although he receives co-credit with Struss as photographer on Griffith's 1928 production of *The Battle of the Sexes*, Bitzer was never present at the studio. Bitzer is also generally recognized as being solely responsible for the cinematography on *Way Down East*, including the climactic rescue of Lillian Gish from the ice flow, but as the following excerpt from an article by Lee Smith in the December 1, 1921 issue of *American Cinematographer* indicates, there were a battery of cameras filming the sequence.

"Our first action was to establish an outpost far above the falls to watch the ice for the break-up and here cameramen were stationed with instructions to keep their lenses trained on the river night and day. As there was nothing else to do one of these cameramen photographed the sunset every day and sent to Mr. Griffith the finest set of winter subsets in captivity. We were 35 days on this ice job and there were four to fourteen cameras always on the job, which accounts for the great variety of the ice scenes filmed and the perfection of the sequences. Not a possible angle of photography was overlooked and too much credit cannot be given the cameramen who worked under every difficulty imaginable. They conducted themselves like a lot of soldiers doing their duty calmly in the face of constant danger and the results as shown on the screen testify to their efficiency…Shooting the close-ups in the mill race was dangerous work, as the water was swift and treacherous. It was an engineering feat of no mean cleverness to make the ice act right at the right time, while the problems of the cameramen were endless. It was like shooting at flying targets with a rifle while standing on one foot on a pinnacle or on a slippery log over quicksand. The light was horrible, the weather cold and the winds raw, but the most annoying thing was the constant and terrifying grinding and washing of the ice, which kept one's nerves on edge every minute. Also the falls were roaring in our ears and the ice was disintegrating, but by herculean labor we shot the stuff and the whole world knows that it was good."

In reality, on *Way Down East*, Billy Bitzer shares credit with Hendrik Sartov — the first time that Bitzer did not receive solo credit on a Griffith production. Hendrik Sartov had been a portrait photographer in Hartsook's Los Angeles salon. He made some photographs of Lillian Gish in connection with *Hearts of the World*, and she was so impressed with Sartov's work that she persuaded Griffith to hire him, photographing occasional close-ups of the star beginning with *The Greatest Thing in Life* (1918). With Gish as his champion, Sartov quickly became Bitzer's equal in the Griffith organization. Although despised by many of his fellow cinematographers, including Bitzer who accused his rival of trying to steal his job (which he did), Sartov's influence on the Gish-Griffith features is very apparent.

With Sartov photographing Lillian, there is a decided improvement in the lighting and composition of the close-ups. They might occasionally be jarring and inappropriately placed in the action, but that is a fault that can be placed as much on the director as on the cinematographer. Above all, Sartov was able to film Lillian in such a way that the dark circles around her eyes — very noticeable in *The Birth of a Nation* and some of the Biograph shorts — were no longer apparent. Interestingly, Audrey Hepburn had a similar problem and she, like Gish, quickly came to rely on the cameraman Franz Planer (who photographed both actresses in *The Unforgiven*) to light her to best advantage.

Gish took Sartov with her to Metro-Goldwyn-Mayer as her personal cameraman — a unique requirement of her contract — and he worked on the actress' two 1926 films, *The Scarlet Letter* and *La Bohème*. However, after Gish left MGM, Sartov fell afoul of Louis B, Mayer. He was hired by William Randolph Hearst to photograph Marion Davies in *Quality Street* and *The Red Mill* (both 1927), but then for reasons unclear, he appears to have been blacklisted and never worked again in the industry. Last heard of in the early 1940s Sartov was working at a small photographic outlet in Pasadena.

Sartov and Gish were a happy combination. Less pleasant was the actress' dealing with George Hill, who photographed *Remodeling Her*

Husband (1920), the only feature to be directed by Lillian Gish, and starring sister Dorothy. Some years ago, Lillian recalled for me,

"Hill was just back from the war, and he had had shell shock and was hysterical. And I know I got my main set — the living room — so big and not high enough at the back, so that if he took the whole room in, shot over the top. He threw his hat in the air, and jumped and stamped on it, and had hysterics about that. I had to keep him calm. Oh, it was terrible."

Curiously, when Lillian went to Italy to film *Romola* and *The White Sister* between 1923 and 1925, she did not take Sartov with her, but instead was accompanied by Roy Overbaugh. *Romola* remains generally unrecognized as a pioneering work of cinematography, the first major feature to be filmed entirely — both exteriors and interiors — with panchromatic stock. Henry King, who directed both features, recalls,

"While I was making pictures in New York, I became associated with Gustave Deitz, who is now in Hollywood and who is an experimenter in panchromatic lines. At that time I was very interested in this type of negative and had used it in various scenes in my productions. Deitz was enthusiastic and told me that a photoplay filmed entirely with panchromatic would be a sensation. We began at that time a series of tests, using negatives in all sorts of different interior shots, and the excellent results obtained proved to us that the new negative could be used successfully under conditions where the common stock of negative had formerly been used exclusively. With Roy Overbaugh, the chief cinematographer, Deitz went with us to Italy, where we worked eleven months on *Romola*. We were surprised at the little light needed, for while it was generally suggested that panchromatic was slower than common stock, it proved a great deal faster."

Lillian Gish has appeared in sixteen sound features, few of which have achieved the lasting impact of her great silent classics. Two that are exceedingly pleasant offerings, but which are all too often ignored these days are *His Double Life* (1933) and *Follow Me, Boys!* (1966). The photography — by Arthur Edeson and Clifford Stine — is not of the type about which critics write, but it is ideally suited to the gentle nature of the stories. Gish is quiet, yet firm, in both, and just as her performance does not distract or disturb the viewer, so do the cinematographers capture the essence of her character without fuss or frivolity.

Asked to name Lillian Gish's three most important sound films, one would probably select *The Night of the Hunter*, *The Cobweb* and *A Wedding*. In *The Cobweb*, she is cast as an unpleasant supervisor in a mental institution — a far cry from the types of roles with which she is generally associated — fighting with the psychiatrist's wife as to the choice of drapes in the library; as one character remarks, "You can tell the doctors from the patients here by the fact that the doctors go home at night." It is an unusual role for Lillian in that she is neither sweet nor lovable, except at least in the eyes of her cinematographer George Folsey (who had photographed sister Dorothy in the 1923 production of *The Bright Shawl*). He recalls that Lillian was "so simple and easy to shoot; it was a pleasure and an honor to photograph a woman like that." Folsey also notes that Gish never forgot her former cameramen, and when she discovered Roy Overbaugh (by then retired) was a friend of Folsey's insisted he visit the set.

It is a curious coincidence that Charles Rosher should have been Mary Pickford's personal cameraman, and that his son should have filmed Pickford's closest friend and only important screen rival in Robert Altman's memorable 1978 film, *A Wedding*. In a film short on dignity and humor, Charles Rosher's camera brings a reality and an emotional calm to Lillian Gish's death scene (which occupies the opening ten minutes of the feature. Here Lillian is the family matriarch, Nettie, who dies in her bed before the wedding party gets underway. Rosher's camera moves the film from Gish to the party by the simple expedient of showing the cars arriving for the reception from the window of her bedroom, but in so doing takes away the life not only of the character but also of the film.

There can be no argument that Paul Gregory's 1955 production of *The Night of the Hunter* gave Lillian her greatest sound role, with Charles Laughton's handling his only directorial assignment. Stanley Cortez is quick — and correct — to hail Laughton as a genius, in his recreation of a melodramatic style reminiscent of D.W. Griffith at his best. (Cortez and Laughton spent days viewing all of Griffith's films.) Cortez, who worked as an assistant cameraman on Griffith's *Abraham Lincoln* (1930) and in a similar position on the 1930 Lillian Gish vehicle, *One Romantic Night*, has created a world of shadows and moonlight, in which the very unreality of many of the scenes become frighteningly real. As the God-fearing widow who saves the children from the wrath of the Satanic preacher Robert Mitchum, Lillian Gish is a dominating yet simplistic force for good.

"She has a lovely face to photograph," says Cortez. "I tried to create on screen an ethereal quality, even when she was wearing an apron in the kitchen. That quality came through in her voice and in her eyes. There are few persons we can photograph through their eyes, but Lillian Gish is one.

She is the most elegant, the most saintly, the most highly respected person on the set — not only as a person but as an actress. She has an air about her that commands respect. She represents tradition — the Griffith days."

The love affair between Lillian Gish and the motion picture is also, very much, a romance between the actress and her cameraman. Her manner not only commands respect, as Cortez has commented, but also professionalism. "She is very much alert," says Jon Kranhouse. He recalls for one scene on *Hambone and Hillie*, there was only an hour to film before the sun went down and due to a misunderstanding Lillian Gish had not received a page-and-a-half of dialogue until right before the scene. She spent five minutes learning the lines and got the scene perfect in the first take. On *The Night of the Hunter*, Stanley Cortez recalls she was so involved in what Charles Laughton was trying to do that she would come on the set and watch, just to be there, even when she was not working in a scene that day. "She was Miss Motion Picture History walking through or performing on the set," says Cortez. "She inspired everyone."

Giuseppina

Program Note for screening at Academy of
Motion Picture Arts and Sciences, "Oscar Docs: The First
Twenty Years 1941-1960," December 5, 2005

The oil industry has a remarkably fine record in the sponsorship of "quality" productions — including Robert Flaherty's *Louisiana Story*, financed by Standard Oil of New Jersey — and *Giuseppina* is one in a long line of short subjects from British Petroleum. The storyline is a simple one. Giuseppina is the daughter of a BP gas station owner in a small Italian community. She complains that "Nothing ever happens," and, rather like the doorman in *Grand Hotel*, her father points out that much does take place here. She watches as he deals with American, British and Argentinian tourists, as well as a newly-wed couple with a flat tire and a squeaky horse-drawn cart. The pacing is slow, the subtitles few and relatively unnecessary, sound often non-existent and music (at times dated) used only sparingly. The opening shots of a fairground might suggest a Felliniesque production, but *Giuseppina* is far closer in concept to the work of Jacques Tati. Unfortunately, Antonia Scalari in the title role is neither Tati nor Giulietta Massina, and her facial expressions are limited. She only seems to come alive dancing an ersatz tango with the Argentinian customer. Certainly it is the Argentinians who come out of the film relatively unscathed, unlike the Americans, who are brash and over-powering (just as they must appear to Europeans today), and the British who are, well, very insular and very English. The British *Monthly Film Bulletin* (September 1960) described the film as "thoroughly enjoyable," while the American *Film News* (May-June 1962) considered it "a lesson in and a treat for all adolescents." *Giuseppina* is good-humored and charming, and credit obviously belongs to one man, its producer, director and writer, James Hill (1919-1994), who began his career in the late 1930s with the GPO Film Unit, served in the RAF Film Unit during World

War Two, and is not to be confused with the American producer of the same name. In the 1940s, Hill was associated with the noted British film theorist and documentary filmmaker Paul Rotha, and in the 1950s was a leading director for the BP Film Unit. Hill was very much a journeyman documentarian. *Giuseppina* is hardly representative of his work; for example, concurrent with its release was Hill's *A Walk through the Forest*, dealing with the search for oil in Papua/New Guinea. James Hill turned to television and feature filmmaking while still active in documentary production. In 1966, he directed what is his best-known work, *Born Free*, the true-life story of lion conservation in Kenya, starring Virginia McKenna and husband Bill Travers as Joy and George Adamson — and, of course, Elsa the Lion. While Giuseppina may have some minor faults, it is still a delightful film, a pleasant and sentimental remembrance of an earlier era when gas stations actually provided service to their customers. As we watch Giuseppina's father offering the same level of service he provides to the little boy, "Signor Beppo," with his make-believe automobile, we can only wish that the oil industry of today recognize as does he that "Everyone is important."

[Running Time: 29 minutes. New York opening on August 20, 1960, paired with End of Innocence, *at the Paris Theatre. Los Angeles opening on May 19, 1961, paired with* Saturday Night and Sunday Morning, *at the Music Hall Theater. Winner of Best Documentary Short subject of 1960.]*

Griffith's Other Actors

Films in Review, October 1975, pages 475-481

It is not possible in this brief space to discuss the careers of all actors who worked with D.W. Griffith, so I am limiting this essay to those who have received little or no attention, particularly those not discussed elsewhere. This means excluding Robert Harron, Richard Barthelmess, Elmer Clifton, Ralph Graves, and Henry B. Walthall.[7]

It is far more difficult to define the typical Griffith actor than to pinpoint the characteristics of a Griffith actress (as I did in my 1973 book, *The Griffith Actresses*). The actors who worked for Griffith fall generally into two groups — handsome juveniles, typified by Walter Miller, Henry B. Walthall, Robert Harron, Elmer Clifton, Richard Barthelmess, Neil Hamilton, Ralph Graves, and Arthur Johnson; and character players such as Spottiswoode Aitken, Donald Crisp, George Siegmann, George Fawcett, Adolphe Lestina, Walter Long, Porter Strong, and Howard Gaye.

Griffith himself is not too helpful in explaining why he picked the actors he did. In a 1915 piece, he wrote, "good hair, good eyes, good teeth — these are essential for good photoplay actors." One would have hoped that Griffith looked for a little more, and of course he did. However, acting experience would not appear to have been of great importance to him. After choosing his players, he *taught* them to act. All his major male stars either had no acting experience, or came from a background of second-rate stock companies. In this way, Griffith felt assured that his players had no theatrical temperament — the director would supply that himself — and no arrogance.

"I demand the ability to work," wrote Griffith, "and to work pleasantly and uncomplainingly. It takes endless work to produce a big motion picture. Unless the stars are willing to be human and get right into the

---

7. Who can be found in my books, *The Idols of Silence* (1976) and *Silent Players* (2002).

work instead of hanging back and acting like superior beings, we cannot produce a good play."

One prominent Biograph leading man who is always overlooked is Walter Miller, who gives such fine performances in *Oil and Water*, *Death's Marathon* and *The Mothering Heart*, among others. The last might be considered Lillian Gish's picture — it is certainly her finest Biograph performance — but Walter Miller, playing opposite her, delivers a performance for which he need not be ashamed. Born in Atlanta, Georgia, in 1892, Miller joined the American Biograph Company in 1912, after some six years of experience in various stock companies. He claimed to have made his screen debut in *The Informer*, released on November 21, 1912, playing alongside Mary Pickford and Henry B. Walthall, but he can be glimpsed n "bit" parts in one or two Biograph productions shot prior to *The Informer*. Probably one reason Miller is forgotten today is that he did not go along with Griffith to Reliance-Majestic when the director left Biograph in 1913, but instead joined Universal.

After Universal, Miller took a downward path, switching companies rapidly, until by 1918 *Motion Picture Magazine* was asking what had become of "Biograph's one best bet as a leading man." However, Miller was not completely out of the film scene, continuing to work first with major companies, and later in not-so-major companies' offerings. Then in 1925, Pathé starred him opposite Allene Ray in a George B. Seitz serial, *Sunken Silver*, launching Miller on a new career as a leading man of serials. Through the rest of the silent era, he appeared in more than a dozen serials — *Snowed In*, *Melting Millions*, *King of the Kongo*, *The Man without a Face*, etc. — usually playing opposite Allene Ray. With the coming of sound, Walter Miller was also active, this time in Westerns rather than serials. In 1937 alone, he appeared in twenty-one "B" pictures. Miller collapsed and died at Republic Pictures on March 30, 1940. He never forgot his years at American Biograph; in the late 1910s, he published a series of photographs from Biograph productions in various trade papers. In 1918, his wife was quoted as saying, "Times have changed in an artistic sense, but somehow or other the good old days with the American Biograph, with Mr. Griffith to watch over us, were the best after all."

Another neglected actor, from an earlier Biograph period, is Arthur Johnson, who made his screen debut in the first film directed by Griffith, *The Adventures of Dollie*, released on July 14, 1908. Arthur Johnson has the honor of being the first player Griffith "discovered" for the screen. According to Johnson, Griffith's first comment to him was "You're too tall." Arthur Johnson was with American Biograph from 1908 through 1910, and became one of the first screen actors to have a special impact on the female cinema audience. His popularity led to Johnson's signing a contract with the Reliance Company, but soon, in the summer of 1911, he joined the Lubin Company, with whom he remained on and off as both an actor and director until his death in Philadelphia, on January 17, 1916, at the age of thirty-nine.

At Lubin, Johnson was starred with Lottie Briscoe, who said of him in a 1915 *Photoplay* interview, "As an actress, what I particularly like about Johnson's acting is his wonderful reserve power, his sincerity and his naturalness. To use technical slang, he never 'chews the scenery.' That is, he never overacts." But Johnson had a drinking problem, which was responsible for his frequent absences from the screen. Early in 1915, he was admitted to a hospital suffering from nervous prostration. Upon his return to films, with *Country Blood*, released on August 4, 1915, the *Dramatic Mirror* commented, "Doesn't it seem good to see Arthur Johnson on the screen once more?" In *Photoplay* (December 1926), Frederick James Smith asked Griffith to name the greatest actor he had directed. "He thought for a while. 'Arthur Johnson, I guess,' he said...'Johnson was matchless in everything — modern, romantic, comedy. He would have been a great film leader had he lived.'"

Death took two other Biograph actors at an early age. John R. Compson, who played opposite Florence Lawrence in the series of eleven Jones' family comedies released in late 1908 and early 1909, died of pneumonia on March 15, 1913. Compson, a jolly fat man, somewhat akin to John Bunny, created the "Bumptious" character with the Edison Company after leaving Biograph. Incidentally, so popular were the Jones' family comedies that both Essanay and Selig began releasing their own imitations.

Joseph Graybill — excellent as the sinister stranger in the 1912 *The Painted Lady* — had been with the American Biograph Company from 1910. He died in New York of acute meningitis on August 3, 1913, only days after signing a contract to star at Pathé. According to the *Moving Picture World* (August 2, 1913), Graybill was the author of one of the most famous of Biograph productions, *The Musketeers of Pig Alley*.

One only has to consider the majesty of Alfred Paget's portrayal of Belshazzar in *Intolerance*, and then compare this role with any of the many others he essayed earlier for Griffith at Biograph — particularly the gang leader in *The Musketeers of Pig Alley* — to realize what an extraordinarily versatile actor was this young Englishman. Paget joined American Biograph in 1910, initially playing Indian or Native American roles. Unlike many of his fellow Biographers, he did not follow Griffith to Reliance-Majestic but stayed with Biograph until the spring of 1915. After *Intolerance*, he remained with Griffith until America's entry into World War One, at which time he joined the Canadian Army. At the war's close, he returned briefly to film, Alfred Paget died in Winnipeg, Canada, on October 8, 1919, at the age of forty.

D.W. Griffith always had the happy knack of picking exactly the right character actor for a part. Once chosen, many such actors remained with him for several years. Who can forget George Siegmann's Silas Lynch in *The Birth of a Nation* or his portrayal of Von Strohm four years later in *Hearts of the World*? Spottiswoode Aitken's miserly uncle in *The Avenging Conscience* was every bit as fine in his work as kindly Dr. Cameron in *The Birth of a Nation*. Only the British cinema in the 1930s came near Griffith in the ability to create the perfect character actor.

Spottiswoode Aitken, who had several years on the stage under the direction of Augustin Daly before joining Griffith, compared the two men from an actor's viewpoint in a rather florid 1916 article in *Picture Play*: "And all that Daly did for the drama, art and actors, Griffith is doing in another and no less artistic field., where imagination reigns and brain words are formed to suit each individuality. In the darkness of the photoplay, the cryings and longings of the soul remain unseen, undisturbed, while soft music heals the wounded heart. The drama is not dead but lives, reincarnated, in the motion picture under the master mind of Griffith; and actors are fast gathering under his banner, for he carries the spirit of Daly — but without that rough exterior. He, too, has all the qualities that Daly had for picking talent and developing it, for bringing out the best in an actor and making him feel he has over him a master of art — and a friend." Born in Edinburgh in 1869, Aitken — sometimes spelt Aiken — had some twenty-seven years of stage experience behind him before joining Griffith at Biograph. He was featured in four Griffith features: *Home Sweet Home*, *The Avenging Conscience*, *The Birth of a Nation*, and *Intolerance*. In the last, as Brown Eye's father, he is as kindly and saintly as he was in *The Birth of a Nation*. Something of Aitken's status as an actor at this time may be gauged from the fact that he was featured on the cover of the October 14, 1914, issue of the *New York Dramatic Mirror*, a singular honor at that time for film actors (with the publication usually favoring performers from the stage). Aitken worked continuously in films until 1927, becoming frailer and frailer in appearance as the years passed. In *The Coast Patrol* (1925), he looks as if a breath of wind could blow him away. He died in Hollywood on February 25, 1933 at the age of sixty-five.

The classic silent screen villain is surely Walter Long. There has never been anything to equal the villainy and savagery of his portrayal of the renegade Negro, Gus, lusting after Mae Marsh in *The Birth of a Nation*. Commented *Variety* (March 12, 1915), "fiendish and with the lust of the beast in his eyes...Walter Long made Gus a hated, much despised type, his acting and makeup being complete." Born in Milford, New Hampshire, on March 5, 1888, Walter Long had many years on the legitimate stage and in vaudeville before joining Essanay in 1909. He appeared in only three Griffith features — *The Birth of a Nation*, *Intolerance* and *Scarlet Days* — but in all three he was up to no good. As the perfect screen villain, Long was very much in demand by producers through the late 1930s. One of his best non-Griffith performances is that of Captain Mitchell in *Moran of the Lady Letty* (1922), which incidentally is one of Valentino's best films. In her article, "Expert in Villainy," in *Picture Play* (January 1923), Celia Brynn described Walter Long: "His face is heavily lined, and there are deep wrinkles that run from his nose to his mouth. His lips are not nearly so thick as they appear on the screen, and his eyes are normally cheerful and honest, but when he scowls — as he did to illustrate a point in his conversation — the whole expression of his face changes. It becomes crafty, sensual, belligerent. You would not want to meet a physiognomy like that on a dark night without a gun in your hip pocket."

Walter Long was married to Luray or Laura Huntley, who had minor roles in some Griffith titles, and who died in the 1919 Spanish Influenza epidemic. Walter Long died in Los Angeles on July 4, 1952.

Close behind Walter Long as a master of villainy is George Siegmann, the man responsible for the destruction of Babylon in *Intolerance*. Siegmann appeared in five Griffith features — *The Avenging Conscience*, *The Birth of a Nation*, *Intolerance*, *Hearts of the World*, and *The Great Love* — and he was also an assistant director to Griffith, and casting director for both *The Birth of a Nation* and *Intolerance*. Born in New York in 1883, Siegmann began his career as an actor with Biograph in 1907, before Griffith appeared on the scene. He may have returned to Biograph at some later date, but he was certainly with Reliance in 1913, and according to the *Moving Picture World* (September 6, 1913), he had been there for three years, when Griffith took over the company. Siegmann's performance in *Hearts of the World* has suffered in terms of modern critical response because the name of the character he portrays is so similar to Von Stroheim, who also appears in the film in a very small role. Many — including Stroheim biographer, Thomas Quinn Curtiss, who has presumably never seen *Hearts of the World* — believe it was von Stroheim who played the lecherous villain who attacks Lillian Gish. George Siegmann's massive weight and build (225 pounds and six feet, two inches) helped to continue his demand by producers up until his death in Hollywood on June 22, 1928

Donald Crisp was another villainous brute, playing in *Broken Blossoms*, and to most Griffith devotees he is even more villainous for having attacked Griffith's integrity by claiming to have directed all the battle scenes in *The Birth of a Nation*. Certainly, Crisp contributed something to the film, as an article in the *Moving Picture World* (April 29, 1916) will testify, but he most assuredly did not direct any major scenes. There are stories in the *New York Dramatic Mirror* in 1915 poking fun at Donald Crisp for making exaggerated claims as to his skills as a costume designer and dancer, so possibly the younger Donald Crisp just had a vivid and fanciful imagination. At the time of Griffith's death, Donald Crisp paid tribute to the master in a dignified and moving speech. *[Even without his Griffith-related claims, Donald Crisp had quite an extraordinary career, appearing in more than 160 films, and directing more than seventy. He was born in London in July 1882, and died in Van Nuys, California, on May 25, 1974.]*

The character actor who appears in more Griffith features than any other player is George Fawcett, dubbed by *Photoplay* in 1920, as "The Grand Young Man of the Screen." Fawcett was with Griffith continually from *Intolerance* (in which he played the judge in the Babylonian sequence, a part considerably enlarged for the single-story release, *The Fall of Babylon*), through *The Greatest Question*. Fawcett had joined Vitagraph in the winter of 1919 to direct Corinne Griffith vehicles, but returned to Griffith as Dorothy Gish's director. His career as a director was short; in the 1920s, he returned to acting, and even worked again for Griffith in *Lady of the Pavements*. It says something for Fawcett's abilities as an actor that he appeared in over 100 feature films during the 1920s.

[George Fawcett acted in more than 150 films. He was born in Alexandria, Virginia, in August 1860, and died in Nantucket, Massachusetts, on June 6, 1939.]

The perennial black-face comedian in Griffith features was Porter Strong, who may be seen at his best — or his worst, whichever way you look at it — in *One Exciting Night*. After viewing this film, Al Jolson, the master of the blackface, commented, "I couldn't get enough of it, particularly the comedy of Mr. Porter Strong." Strong's film career, which was almost entirely in D.W. Griffith productions, began with *A Romance of Happy Valley* in 1919 and ended with *The White Rose* in 1923. Shortly after completing the latter, he died in New York on June 11, 1923, at the age of forty-four.

There were, of course, many other Griffith actors who never failed to please. At Biograph,, Wilfred Lucas, Charles Hill Mailes and Edna Foster (so good were her portrayals of little boys that I would like to dub her a honorary actor) come readily to mind. The English actor, Howard Gaye, was suitably moving and decorous as General Robert E. Lee in *The Birth of a Nation* and as Christ in *Intolerance*. There were also Ralph Lewis and Adolphe Lestina. As *Reel Life* (May 22, 1915) commented, "His portraiture of the much discussed character of Stoneman, the radical leader, in *The Birth of a Nation*, would be sufficient to rank [Ralph] Lewis at the very top of the dramatic profession. No more remarkable creation has vindicated the artistic value of motion pictures." Adolphe Lestina — a Griffith regular if ever there was one — could not have asked for a more satisfying role than that of the Confederate Officer who, lives in France rather than concede victory to the North in *The Girl Who Stayed at Home* (1919).

[Howard Gaye was born in Hitchin, England, in May 1878, and died in London on December 26, 1955. I had the good fortune to meet his widow and she entrusted me with his unpublished autobiography. Adolphe Lestina was born in New York in February 1861, and died in New Rochelle, on August 23, 1923.]

The directing tradition which Griffith established continues, but the Griffith acting tradition is gone forever. It could not have survived the coming of sound. Death took most of the actors before they might have received the same kind of attention paid to his great actresses, Lillian Gish, Blanche Sweet and Mary Pickford. The final word belongs to Marshall Neilan, who not only acted for Griffith but whose direction displayed all that was best in Griffith's technique. In a 1933 interview, he explained the director's methods for getting the best from his actors:

"He was the Belasco of the screen. He could take obscure people and instill confidence into them. His policy was to discover talent outside the ranks of the theater, and he could pick types, as Belasco did, with an unerring eye. At the same time he had a bag of tricks which never failed to work. For instance, he'd come into the studio in the morning, frowning and gloomy, speaking to no-one and immediately getting all the poor devils hoping to earn a few dollars that day into such a state of nerves they didn't know whether they were coming or going. Just when the whole outfit thought they were going to be fired, he'd start shooting, and he'd get from this tense situation a fine nervous scene, emotional and at the same time artistic."

Val Guest

Filmfax, June/July 1998, pages 100-106, 130

Sitting in the living room of the Palm Springs home of Val Guest and his wife, Yolande Donlan, looking out over a golf course which abuts their property, there is a possibility of seeing anyone or anything wander by — from ex-President Gerald Ford to a friendly rabbit. It is an elegant, but unexpected, setting in which to find a director, and screenwriter, who was an integral part of British cinema from the 1930s through the 1970s.

Born in London on December 11, 1911, Val Guest's career was matched in longevity and success only by that of Maurice Elvey, whose films generally lack the quality of those directed and/or written by Guest. There is no genre that Guest has not tackled, and it is perhaps unfortunate that, in the United States, he is generally known for his work in the science fiction and horror fields, for he is equally at ease with musicals and comedies. Indeed, it might well be argued that his major contribution to British cinema has been as author of some of the best comedies of the 1930s, starring the likes of Will Hay, the Crazy Gang and Arthur Askey.

There is a brilliant summation of the work of this quite extraordinary man in the Autumn 1958 issue of *Sight and Sound*:

> "Val Guest's talent lies in the skillful and immediate exploitation of the current fashion in popular entertainment. He can turn his hand to farce or horror with equal facility, and is one of the few people who have survived a career in the Thirties and followed it up with another, equally successful one in the Fifties. If few of his films survive as well as he has, they, at least, stand as a memorial to an extraordinary flair for catching the public's eye."

GUEST: My God! I think my father or mother must have written it. It's very nice of them to say it. I just try to keep going. I tried to do all sorts of pictures because, in the very early days, Noel Coward once said to me, "A little bit of advice, my boy: Never come out of the same trap twice."

SLIDE: How are you able to understand just what the public wants?

GUEST: I don't know what the public wants. My God, I would be a millionaire if I knew that. I have never, ever tried to do a film because I thought it was what the public wanted. That's fatal. I've always done a thing that really appealed to me and that I thought I'd like to go and see — that's the only level I've worked on. I had never done science fiction or horror. Never! And, one day, Yolande and I were going to Tangier for a holiday. Tony Hinds of Hammer said, "We've got a BBC play, *The Quatermass Xperiment*, which we're thinking of making into a picture." He said, "I'll be at the airport with the scripts." I think there were sixteen scripts — it ran for sixteen weeks on television. I took 'em all to Tangier, put them by the side of the bed, and never opened the packet. One day, Yo said to me, "What's all that? Are you going to read it?" I said, "It's not my cup of tea. I'm not into that sort of space thing." She said, "Since when have you been ethereal?" That's what she said to me! I read it and thought it would be a super-human job to get sixteen scripts into one film, but that's how I, very loathfully, got into that genre of film.

SLIDE: I don't really understand how in the 1930s, you came to be working for *The Hollywood Reporter*?

GUEST: I didn't work here. I was *The Hollywood Reporter*'s London editor. I had been doing a column in *Zit's New York Review*, which was a sort of lower grade *Daily Variety*, and Billy Wilkerson, who was the publisher of *The Hollywood Reporter*, asked if I would like to do a column for him. From doing a column, I said, "Why don't we start the thing up in London?" It was called *The London Reporter*, and was published inside *The Hollywood Reporter*.

SLIDE: Originally you were primarily an actor?

GUEST: I started out as an actor and writer, not a screenwriter. Somehow I got a contract with Warner Bros., as an actor.

SLIDE: There is a 1932 credit for you, *The Innocents of Chicago* [released in the U.S. as *Why Saps Go Home*], in which you played a gangster.

GUEST: Jesus, I hope nobody ever sees it. I was either a gangster, a dope fiend, or a pimp. Perfect casting. That was at B.I.P. Then, I got a contract with Warner Bros.-British. I don't think I was very good, and I thought I'd rather tell them before they told me. I was doing quite a bit of writing on the side, and they let me go on the understanding that, for the rest of my contract, they had first call on anything I wrote. They never took a thing!

SLIDE: In the 1930s, you were closely associated with director Marcel Varnel.

GUEST: That came about through *The Hollywood Reporter*. I wrote a review of a picture that he had made in Hollywood called *Chandu the Magician*. I thought it was awful and, with the brashness of youth, I wrote that, if I couldn't write a better film than this one with my hands tied behind my back, I'd get off the game. He got in touch with Billy Wilkerson and said, "If your reviewer is so goddam clever, let him write my next." I went and apologized to Marcel and said, "Of course I can't write your next film." He said, "I think you can." That's how I got into writing movies.

SLIDE: And that was *No Monkey Business* in 1935.

GUEST: Yes, with Gene Gerrard and June Clyde.

SLIDE: Let me ask you about the Will Hay films. When you are writing for a comedian like Hay, how do you set about making sure the material will fit?

GUEST: You have to know the character. He was a super-timer. He and Jack Benny were the same sort, and as a matter of fact, Benny, when asked about British comedians, said there were only two that he thought superb — one was Will Hay and the other was Alastair Sim. You got to know his timing and you got to know the sort of thing he could handle.

SLIDE: Would Will Hay work with you on the script?

GUEST: The first script he ever sat down with was one he made with Bill Beaudine, the American director — they brought him over to do *Windbag the Sailor*. Will Hay sat down and said he had a terrible time. He didn't know what to say, what to do. He thought it was a complete waste of time. You'd got to know your character. The secret of a comedy writer is to know whom he's writing for, because, in comedy, everybody's different.

SLIDE: You tend to have regular collaborators — Mariott Edgar, Robert Edmunds and J.O.C. Orton.

GUEST: George Mariott Edgar — he was always known as George. Very funny, because Moore Mariott [who worked in the Will Hay comedies] was also George. Jack Orton was not a collaborator at all. They used to give him a script and see if he could get any ideas. He got a credit now and then, but he never wrote scripts — he was an "ideas" man. There was another man like that, called Val Valentine, whom I never worked with. I was with George Edgar the whole time I was at Gainsborough.

SLIDE: How would you work together? Would you sit in the same room, talking out ideas?

GUEST: Yes. I'd probably get an idea how a scene went, and George would get an idea. So I'd say, "You do that one and I'll do this one." George wrote some great stuff. He was very good on old-time routines and things which we updated. He could dredge back into memory what everyone else had forgotten.

SLIDE: How did you first become collaborators?

GUEST: The first time I ever went to Gainsborough, I worked with Marcel Varnel. We had a joint contract. He couldn't direct what I didn't write, and I couldn't write what he didn't direct. We got that contract after our first picture, *All In* [1936], I think. Then [producer] Ted Black said, "We're thinking of signing up a music hall writer, Mariott Edgar," and that's how we met.

In the old Gainsborough days, there were four of us under contract: myself, George, Frank Launder, and Sidney Gilliat. Frank was the story editor. Now, Sidney and Frank did *The Lady Vanishes* [1938] for Hitchcock, but we were all a big family there, and we would kick this bit around, that bit around. Hitch used to wander in and out. He would ask, "Got a better line for this?" He had an office next door to mine, so it was easy to poke his head around. He had a rather sadistic, but enormous, sense of humor. I remember, once, I wandered onto the set; he beckoned me over, and said, "Are you a man of the world? I'm going to show you something." He took me behind the set, unzipped his fly, pulled his shirt up, and said, "Thirty shillings with two collars." That's the sort of badness that would suddenly come out of him.

SLIDE: What sort of money did you make back then?

GUEST: Peanuts — something like twenty-pounds a week

SLIDE: You wrote for [comedian] Arthur Askey.

GUEST: This is something I did because I was under contract. I never thought he was funny. He wasn't difficult at all but, oh, he was the meanest little bastard.

SLIDE: You wrote *Hi Gang* [1941] for Ben Lyon and Bebe Daniels.

GUEST: They became great friends. In fact, Yo and I used to go there every Sunday and have canasta parties. The Spanish Ambassador would be playing. Jeanette MacDonald would show up.

SLIDE: Was it through Arthur Askey that you became a director with *The Nose Has It* [1942]?

GUEST: No, I pulled Askey into it. *The Nose Has It* was a Ministry of Information short. The Ministry of Information asked me to write a thing about coughs and sneezes spread diseases — that old crap. And I got on my high horse and said, "Yes, I'll write it, but only if I can direct it." We didn't have Will Hay under contract — he'd gone — but we had Arthur Askey. So I wrote it for him. I had no other choice.

SLIDE: Once you had made that short, was it still a struggle to get Gainsborough to give you directing assignments?

GUEST: No. I was very lucky. I had very good press on that short. I took all the press clippings in, and said, "How about my doing a feature?" And Ted Black said, "OK. Write it and we'll see." It took two years because they wouldn't give me time off. I was under contract as a writer, and I still had to go on doing all the Gainsborough stuff.

SLIDE: Your first two feature films, as a director, *Miss London Ltd.* (1943) and *Bees in Paradise* (1944) were with Arthur Askey.

GUEST: Yes, because he was a very big box-office star. He was under contract to Gainsborough and so was I. I thought the only way to do it was to get more people around him who could do more things. Make it a musical.

SLIDE: Just after the end of the war, you wrote what was going to be the great British musical, *London Town* [released in the U.S. in 1953 as *My Heart Goes Crazy*], directed by Wesley Ruggles.

GUEST: Wes Ruggles.

SLIDE: What went wrong?

GUEST: Wes Ruggles. A sweet guy, a nice guy, but he hadn't got a clue. This guy had made *Cimarron* and all those fabulous old movies, but he's not a guy to do a musical. Also, I didn't write that. I wrote the Sid Field [comedy] stuff because I had worked with Sid at the Prince of Wales Theatre. I added things to his "photographer" and "golfing" sketches, and various odds and sods, going through the script. I certainly didn't write the picture. I pushed in a girlfriend whom I was trying to help along the way, named Kay Kendall. I wrote ad-libs for Sid; all his ad-libs had to be written and rehearsed!

SLIDE: Throughout the 1940s, you were writing and directing comedies. I guess the first break, although it's still a partial comedy, is *Murder at the Windmill* [1949].

GUEST: Yes, that was a turning point. What happened was, Daniel Angel, who was not a producer, came to me. He was married to Vivian Van Damm's daughter, and he came to me one day and said, "Old man Van Damm has always refused to have any picture made at the Windmill [a London theater specializing in burlesque, whose slogan was "We Never Closed"] but, I thought, if we gave him the right story, he would let us make a picture at the Windmill." And, I think, between ten o'clock that night and two o'clock the next morning, I'd written *Murder at the Windmill*. I just sat and did it. The old man said, "Yes, OK, go ahead." And Danny said, "Now what happens?" He said, "I'm not a producer. I don't know how to produce." That was his first picture. I also wrote the music and lyrics for it. [At this point, Yolande Donlan entered Val Guest's life. The daughter of character actor, Jimmy Donlan, Yolande, or Yo as Val Guest calls her, had been under contract to MGM as a dancer before understudying the Billie Dawn role in *Born Yesterday*. When Laurence Olivier decided to produce the play in Britain, he signed Yolande as its star, and she opened as Billie Dawn in Glasgow in October 1946. Yolande and Val Guest were married on September 11, 1954.]

GUEST: One of the small-part actors in her show was Michael Balfour and we were making *Just William's Luck* [1948]. It was on location. It was absolutely pissing down, and Michael, who was in my car, said to me, "You've got to come and see our show. There's a girl in it who's marvelous." He fixed me two seats, and that's how I first saw Yo. From then on, I started to talk her into doing films in England. I wrote *Miss Pilgrim's Progress* [1950] for her. I wrote a lot of pictures for her — *The Body Said No* [1950], *Mr. Drake's Duck* [1951] and *Penny Princess* [1952] — when she was not doing her plays. Then I wrote a play for her. We were very much entwined.

SLIDE: During this period, when you wrote a film but did not direct, would you have liked to be the director? I'm thinking of *Another Man's Poison* [1951], directed by Irving Rapper, and *Happy Go-Lovely* [1951], directed by Bruce Humberstone.

GUEST: Yes, I would have liked to direct Bette Davis. I probably would have lost ten years of my life. But Bette said she would do a film only if she had an Academy Award cameraman and a director she knew. So, I said, "Fine." I was pulled in on *Happy Go-Lovely*, Marcel Hellman wasn't quite certain sure how to go about a musical, and I was pulled in to tailor this for Vera Ellen and David Niven.

SLIDE: Tell me about Margaret Rutherford and *The Runaway Bus*.

GUEST: She was an enormous fan of [comedian] Frankie Howerd. That's how we got her for the picture. I wrote it with him in mind — it's a question of knowing somebody's style and writing a script for it. Frankie said to me, "I will make a film on one condition. You write a comedy-mystery so, if the comedy's no good, you've still got the mystery." And, he said, "I'm not going to star in it." My contract said it starred Margaret Rutherford and Frankie Howerd, but after the second day's rushes, Maggie Rutherford came to me and said, "I can't star above him." So, here you have two actors arguing not to be starred.

SLIDE: Was Margaret Rutherford a genuine eccentric?

GUEST: Absolutely. I said to our dress designer, "I want Maggie to wear her own clothes." We wanted her to look how she looked. Maggie was horrified. "I want new clothes." It was a terrible battle to get her to wear her own outfit, but finally she did.

SLIDE: And she insisted her husband, Stringer Davis, should be in the film?

GUEST: Yes, always, if you did a deal with Rutherford.

SLIDE: How did you write a part for him?

GUEST: That's easy enough. You write a couple of lines. I can't even remember what he played. He was a harmless, nice guy. I was never even aware of him on the set, he was such a nothing — a nice nothing.

SLIDE: You started your Hammer career with *Men of Sherwood Forest* [1954].

GUEST: I'll tell you a funny thing. My Robin Hood, Don Taylor, is now a respected film director in Hollywood, but he'll always be Robin Hood to me.

SLIDE: Your casting or their casting?

GUEST: It wasn't Hammer's casting. It was their American partner's casting. Forrest Tucker, Brian Donlevy…It was all casting from the other side.

SLIDE: With the two Quatermass films, you didn't watch the BBC series?

GUEST: Never did see them. And I'm very glad I didn't, because it might have swayed me one way or another. I must have been the only person in England who never saw them. When they asked me to do it, I said I'd only do it on one condition. I would like to shoot it like a newsreel — as though *Panorama* [a popular BBC news program] had told me to go out and cover the story. I would shoot it *cinéma verité* style, using hand-held cameras. And Tony Hinds agreed.

SLIDE: In writing a horror script, how do you know a scene will be horrific to an audience?

GUEST: You learn, in the trade of filmmaking, that to understate is far more dramatic than to overstate, or even dramatically state. That is the first thing. You learn the rudiments of impact, the impact of horror, the impact of light. Little tricks. For instance, if you have a terrible car smash and there's smoke coming out of the car and there are people in it, to put music on it kills it. But you have this terrifying scene and jazz music coming out of the car radio, to me, that is one hundred percent more exciting.

SLIDE: At what point do you decide how you want the music to work?

GUEST: Afterwards, you discuss the music. I had a terrible battle with the studio on a picture called *Yesterday's Enemy* [1959]. There was no score. I said, "I don't want a note of music in this. I want to play all the background with jungle noises." And the sound department did a fantastic job in getting monkeys, cheetahs, warthogs…We orchestrated that whole, very dramatic film simply with jungle noises. They thought I was mad when I said I did not want one note of music.

SLIDE: On *The Abominable Snowman* [1957], Nigel Kneale wrote the story and script. Your idea or Hammer's?

GUEST: He sold it on condition that he wrote the script. He's a good writer, but it was far too long for the screen. You could have got away with it, maybe, on television. So, I had to edit and redo bits, make it screenable. That's all.

SLIDE: In a situation like that, would you work on the script before or during shooting?

GUEST: Cut-and-dried before you were shooting. Absolutely. You get it pared down and corrected, and then you go on the floor. Don't extemporize.

SLIDE: Do you storyboard?

GUEST: Always. Never have I directed a film without my storyboards. I don't mean a picture board, but a board with every shot angled on it, little marks and tracks and scene numbers, so the entire unit knows where the camera is going to be.

SLIDE: Where did you shoot *The Abominable Snowman* [a.k.a. *The Abominable Snowman of the Himalayas*]?

GUEST: In the French Pyrenees: We were there for two weeks. The rest was the large stage at Pinewood.

SLIDE: Was it unusual for Hammer to allow location shooting, because of the cost?

GUEST: No. I mean, there were always locations around Bray. We went across to Hamburg for *Break in the Circle* [1955]. They didn't like it but they felt they had to. Incidentally, not one of the stars, not one of the actors, went to the Pyrenees. We had doubles. In later years, Forrest Tucker gave out a big story about how we filmed up in the Pyrenees, and he did this and that. It was typical Tuck.

SLIDE: *Camp on Blood Island* [1958]. Where was that shot?

GUEST: We never moved further than the sandpits just outside of Bray. The rest was built, a brilliant set, on the lot at Bray.

SLIDE: Did you ever get an American actor who resented being directed by a Britisher?

GUEST: No. Why would that be? Mostly, the American actors and actresses had a great respect for Britain and the British industry.

SLIDE: A lot of American actors complain of union tea breaks.

GUEST: That was terrible. The unions killed the British film industry. I remember when we were shooting a picture called *Jigsaw* [1962] down in Brighton, and we were getting through like wildfire. I was breaking early, about five o'clock, and my assistant director came to me and said, "We've got trouble guv, they're going on strike tomorrow." "Why?" Because they were not getting any overtime and they were used to overtime. That is their mentality. They struck. And we went two days without shooting.

SLIDE: And *Expresso Bongo* [1959]?

GUEST: We had known Wolf Mankowitz [the show's creator] for years, and we were invited to go and see him at the show. It was Yo who said to me, "Why don't we make a film of this?" So, we went back and mulled it over. We thought we really couldn't go to the South of France for the second act. Somehow, the pop scene was the story. We bought the screen rights, and worked on it. Brought the second act into London, so it all stayed in London. I found this young singer, Cliff Richard, singing in a bar in Soho. He had sung a number, "Living Doll," in some film before that, but this was his first acting film. I knew he was a bright kid. I thought he was going to last. He had a freshness about him that the other rock people didn't.

SLIDE: You wrote some of the music and lyrics for *Expresso Bongo*.

GUEST: That's right. I wrote it with Robert Farnum. I wrote the scores — and the lyrics — of all our musicals. You see, one of my jobs, in my youth was as a songwriter. I was under contract to Feldman's and Francis Day, the publishers. I was used to writing songs and numbers for people.

SLIDE: What about *The Day the Earth Caught Fire* [1961]?

GUEST: That's my favorite! It took me eight years before anyone would let me make it. Every time I finished a picture, people would ask me, "What are you going to do now?," and I'd say, "Look, I've got a story." And they would say, "Who wants to know about the bomb? Christ! Come on! Grow up!" The only way I got it made was, we, ourselves, put up *Bongo* as collateral, with British Film Finance. And I talked Mickey Balcon into coming in on it.

SLIDE: Leo McKern is an odd choice for a leading man.

GUEST: Leo is an old chum. I used to write Leo into practically every film, if I could. He was part of my stock company. Michael Goodliffe was another. Sid James. Gordon Jackson. A gang of wonderful, very good people. I used to write little parts in for them.

SLIDE: Did that include Reginald Beckwith, who was in many of your films in the 1950s?

GUEST: Not only was he our greatest chum, but he was also a partner in the film company we started, Conquest Productions, that later became Val Guest Productions. Yo, myself and Tony [Reginald] Beckwith.

SLIDE: Were you happy with *Casino Royale* [1967]?

GUEST [to his wife]: Yo, he just asked if I was happy with *Casino Royale*.

YO: You used to complain a bit. He's always happy when he's working.

GUEST: It was a madhouse production. Charlie [Charles] Feldman, who couldn't keep his mind made up for more than six hours. The sort of guy that, one day, you wanted to hug him, and the next, you wanted to throttle him. Charlie came to London, sent for me, and said, "Val, I want to do a send-up of all the Bond films. I would like to get a compendium of directors and a compendium of writers. We've got *Casino Royale*, but we can't use the book. The Bond pictures have [already] used everything in the book." Then he gave me a script that had been written by Terry Southern, a script that had been written by Ben Hecht. A treatment by Wolf Mankowitz. My contract was for eight weeks, and seven months later, I was still working, trying to salvage this. As it ended up, Charlie Feldman asked me to be coordinating director.

SLIDE: Did you work closely with Woody Allen?

GUEST: Woody came to London and, when we were getting the script ready for *Casino Royale*, Woody would come to our house. We'd sit down and knock out scenes together. Yo said, "We must invite him to a real English dinner — steak and kidney pudding." So Woody came to dinner. We had smoked salmon — that was OK. Then, we came to the main course, and Woody said, "What's this. I can't eat kidney." Jewish. Can't eat kidney

YO: Americans don't eat kidney. We had to make him an omelet after all this effort went into making him a typical English meal.

SLIDE: Would you have been happier if you had been sole director?

GUEST: No. I would have committed suicide. Ken Hughes had been on one segment. He had gone. There was Joe McGrath. [Peter] Sellers wanted him on. Sellers had him fired. Richard Talmadge, a great old-timer, did all our chase stuff. John Huston was going out of his mind and, finally, he got pissed off and went to Ireland to play poker. One day, Charlie Feldman said to me, "Somehow, we ought to join all these [segments] up." Of course! "Can you do it?" So, I did it only on condition that I write two of my chums through all of the joining up things because I knew, if I had two chums with whom to giggle, we'd get through. I wrote in David Niven and Ursula Andress as my links. I remember saying to Charlie, "You're out of your fucking mind. You cannot make a picture like this." It opened in ten theaters, in and around New York, and, at the end of the first week, my telephone in London went at three o'clock in the morning. Charlie Feldman calling. "Want to hear some figures?" I didn't. I wanted to go to sleep. He told me these figures from all these places, and said, "Now who's fucking mad?"

SLIDE: Why did your career end?

GUEST: I stopped directing. I think I had had enough. I went late into the 1970s. I did a couple for television, a few suspense things. I wanted to get on with my life. I was writing for other people. I'm still writing. I sold the remake rights to *The Day the Earth Caught Fire* to 20th Century-Fox, and I've done a rewrite, an update. And Warners is [going] to remake *Quatermass Xperiment* and call it *Xperiment*. Someone has taken an option to remake *Expresso Bongo* in London. So, I work.

SLIDE: Looking back, what are you most proud of?

GUEST: That I'm still standing, that I've survived.

SLIDE: I was thinking more in terms of specific films.

GUEST: I would think *The Day the Earth Caught Fire*. I'm glad to think that, on the subject of global warming, I was before my time. I must be perfectly honest. I've had a ball most of the time. I enjoyed it all. *The Day the Earth Caught Fire*, *Bongo*, *Yesterday's Enemy*, and *Jigsaw*, those four are the ones that I like best. But, I've had a wonderful time in this profession. I'm lucky that I've met so many people, that I've done so many things in so many different genres.

[Val Guest died in Palm Springs on May 10, 2006.]

William Haggar

Cinema Studies, June 1967, page 65

Many early fairground showmen made films for exhibition in their Bioscope shows, but few showmen had quite the success of William Haggar. Haggar traveled the fairgrounds of South Wales with his family, presenting theatrical shows. In the late 1890s he decided to change his tented theatre into a Bioscope Show, and at the same time decided to make his own films.

The first films were of topical items. His daughter, Mrs. L.M. Richards, believes that the first film her father made was of skaters on the lake at Aberdare Park. He later went on to make fictional films, the most famous of which are *The Life of Charles Peace*[8] (Mrs. Richards played Peace's assistant, dressed up as a boy), *Maria Marten*, *The Maid of Cefn Yddfa*, *Wanted a Wife* (a comedy), *The Poachers*, *Uncle Tom's Cabin*, and *East Lynne*. Haggar also made an entire comedy series of *Weary Willie and Tired Tim* stories. William Haggar's son, Walter, played Weary Willie.

In 1907, Haggar gave up travelling the fairgrounds, and built his first cinema in Aberdare. In 1910, he built cinemas in Llanelly and Mountain Ash; and in the same year he also bought the Theatre Royal, Llandudno, and turned it into a cinema. The Mountain Ash cinema is still in the hands of the Haggar family, and run by Mrs. Richards.

William Haggar made some experiments with sound on disc films in 1908, and these were advertised, "Can be heard two miles away." Unhappily, these early experimental films do not appear to have survived. As indeed do few of Haggar's films apart from *The Life of Charles Peace* and *The Maid of Cefn Yddfa*. It is for this reason probably that William Haggar is not very well-known. In fact, in the few places that the Haggar family are mentioned (such as the Low and Manvell *History of the British*

---

8. Charles Peace (1832-1879) was an infamous burglar and murderer, who has been the subject of several films, of which William Haggar's was the first.

Film), credit is always given to his son, Walter Haggar. But I can state quite emphatically that Walter Haggar only assisted in the making of his father's films.

William Haggar was a much-loved and respected man in the early film industry. His work for charity was well-known, and *Kinematograph Weekly* always characterized him as Father Christmas. He was responsible for the building of the Aberdare Hospital, and his Aberdare cinema was used regularly on Sundays for charity concerts. His daughter told me that during the depression in Wales, during the early 1930s, she would always hold competitions during the children's matinees, and give food or clothing as prizes.

With the death of William Haggar, at the age of seventy-three, on February 24, 1924, the film industry lost a great pioneer and the people of Wales lost a true benefactor.

Hull Cinemas: An Introduction

Cinema Studies, June 1963, pages 171-172

The number of cinemas in Hull has dwindled from over thirty during the 1930s to the present ten. The cinemas suffered greatly during World War II; on the nights of May 7 and 8, 1941, eight cinemas were completely destroyed by enemy actions. Amongst those cinemas was the Cecil (now rebuilt), which housed the offices of eleven Hull cinema companies. So not only were the actual cinemas destroyed, but also the complete records of those and several other cinemas. The only thing which did survive was the company's minutes book, which the managing director had taken home with him on the fatal night. This managing director, Brinley Evans, told me it took him practically six weeks to get over the shock of the loss of so many cinemas.

Many cinemas shut during the period 1958-1960, whether or not due to television, I would not like to hazard. However, it should be noted that Hull was very overpopulated with cinemas, and there had been one cinema seat for every nine inhabitants. Of the cinemas closed, not one has yet been demolished, but many standing empty have suffered from vandalism, and stand bleak and desolate, windows broken and doors boarded up. Some closed cinemas have been put to other uses, three are supermarkets, two bowling alleys, one a ballroom, and one a bingo and wrestling hall.

Hull has two very fine modern cinemas, the A.B.C. Regal and the Cecil. The A.B.C. is one of the largest cinemas in this country, and the only one able to provide both stage shows and Todd A.O. projection. The Cecil is probably the finest modern cinema in this country, and even John Davis, managing director of the Rank Organization, had to admit that his company had nothing to compare with the Cecil. The cinema is also the proud possessor of the largest CinemaScope screen in the country.

Very little has been written about Hull cinemas, other than an article in the *Hull Quarterly* for July 1935, and the biography of William Morton, the owner of several Hull cinemas, entitled *I Remember*, published privately in Hull. Of course the finest source of information is the minutes of the Watch Committee, which are easily accessible and a mine of information. The most surprising source of information is a magazine titled *Architecture Illustrated*, which contains photographs and plans of cinemas throughout the country, including two Hull cinemas — the A.B.C. Regal and the Dorchester. Cinema managers are a constant source of titbits on cinemas, as many of them, like R. Fall, who started as a projectionist in 1916, and is now manager of the Regent Cinema, have spent their whole lives in cinemas.

[Today, Hull has five cinemas, some of which are multi-screens.]

Hull Cinemas: William Morton

Cinema Studies, December 1963, pages 197-199

William Morton was born on January 24, 1838, at Royston in Hertfordshire. After a brief spell in the newspaper world, first as a printer and then as a journalist, he became the agent and manager for the illusionists, Maskelyne and Cooke. Later when the partnership was dissolved, he bought the Theatre Royal, Greenwich, and acted as the manger and licensee for that theatre. He came to Hull in 1894, and formed there a limited company with his son, W.F. Morton, as the managing director, to run three of the city's theatres, namely the Theatre Royal, the Alexandra and the Grand.

On Saturday, July 2, 1910, William Morton opened the first hall in Hull to be specifically designed as a cinema. It was named the Princes Hall, after a Baptist Chapel of that name, which had previously stood on the site, and was built at a cost of 10,000 pounds. The New Century Animated Picture Company of Leeds was the original owner of the site, but after representation from William Morton's company, Morton's Ltd., it agreed to let William Morton run the cinema, while they, as his partner, supplied the films.

The popularity and success of the Princes Hall made William Morton plan another cinema, not in the city centre, but in the suburbs of East Hull. This plan culminated in the opening on Saturday, November 16, 1912, of the Holderness Hall, Witham. The cinema was built in the style of a Roman Temple at a cost of 12,000 pounds. It contained three separate restaurants, each running independently of the cinema, and seating for 2,000 people, and the foyer was designed to allow over 1,200 people to queue whilst awaiting admission.

William Morton's third cinema was the Majestic, opened by the Lord Mayor of Hull on February 1, 1915. Its seating capacity was 1,100 and it occupied the site of the former Mechanics Institute (later the Bijou Theatre) on George Street. The first film was an American one, *The Charity Ball*, and the seat prices at the opening ranged from one shilling in the balcony to four pence in the stalls. The architect for the project, a Mr. Gaskell, built it in the style of a legitimate theatre with four private boxes at each side of the auditorium, the projection room being situated at the back of the cinema, contrary to the practice in most cinemas, and there was also an independent restaurant and reading room combined. It was in this cinema that William Morton had his offices from which he controlled his company up to his 97th year.

Morton's final venture into the cinema world was the conversion of the Grand Theatre into a cinema. It opened as a cinema on September 1, 1930, looking exactly as it had done as a legitimate theatre with the exception of a screen at the front of the stage; due to lack of space for a projection room, back projection was used. Its one claim to fame may be that it was the first provincial cinema to install hearing apparatus for the deaf.

The blow to the Morton Empire was struck on June 9, 1935, when W.F. Morton, William Morton's oldest son, died at Bridlington. The running of Morton's Ltd. had been entirely in his hands, and his death as well as being a great personal blow to William Morton, also put the fate of Morton's Ltd. in doubt. The end, in fact, came not long afterwards. On Saturday, June 29, 1935, the *Hull Daily Mail* announced, "Mr. William Morton, Grand Old Man of Hull entertainment, has severed his connection with the world of theatre and cinema, and the career of Morton's Ltd. and Morton's Pictures Ltd. is finished."

A meeting of the shareholders of the company was held on September 3 of that year in the Law Society's offices in Hull, when it was found that the company had a deficit of 45,525 pounds, seventeen shillings and one penny, and was to go into voluntary liquidation. How this had come about it is not easy to explain: the 1930s were boom years for the cinema and yet William Mortons's cinemas had run at a loss. The answer could perhaps be that cinemas better than Morton's had opened in the city, notably the Cecil in 1925 and the Regal in 1934, or perhaps the blame can be put on the drift of the city centre away from the George Street area, where most of William Morton's cinemas and theatres were situated. Or perhaps the answer was plainly that cinemas that were at the height of luxury in 1910, 1912 and 1915 were old-fashioned and shabby in 1935.

The Majestic and the Grand were sold to Hull Cinemas Ltd. The Majestic was closed for a short period for renovation, and reopened on August 5, 1935, as the Criterion. The Grand was entirely rebuilt, and was opened by the Lord Mayor of Hull on December 30, 1935 as the Dorchester. The Holderness Hall was sold to the defunct Gaumont-British Company who ran it as the Holderness Hall until 1950, when the name was changed to the Gaumont. In 1959, it was closed, to re-open again on March 3, 1960, as the Majestic Ballroom.

The Princes Hall was kept in the Morton Family, the lease being taken up by William Morton's youngest son, T.J. Morton, and on his death by his children, Robert and Marjorie Morton. In 1955, they sold it to two Hull businessmen, Norman Shenker and Maurice Kirman, who opened it on December 26, 1955, as the Curzon Cinema. In 1960, they sold it to another Hull businessman, who changed it into a supermarket.

William Morton died in his 100th year on July 8, 1938. Even then, he had been forgotten and only five people attended his funeral. A sad end for a man whom the *Hull Daily Mail* had called "The Grand Old Man of Hull Entertainment."

[I was assisted in the preparation of this article by Robert and Marjorie Morton, the Hull Daily Mail, *the Rank Organization, and the Kingston upon Hull Local History Library.]*

Bioscope Shows at Hull Fair

Cinema Studies, June 1965, pages 7-9

On April 1, 1299, Edward I granted to the inhabitants of Kingston upon Hull a charter giving them the right to hold "one fair in every year." Through the centuries, the character of the fair changed, until on its transfer in 1888 from the city centre to a large open space off Walton Street in West Hull, it merely provided pleasure and entertainment. The original charter stated that the fair was to be held on "the day of St. Augustine after Easter [May 26] and for twenty-nine days," but it is by tradition now held for one week, commencing on the nearest Saturday to October 11.

Hull had its first chance of seeing the new invention of cinematography at the Fair in 1896, when fairground showman Randall Williams presented his Electroscope "living pictures," direct from the Royal Agricultural Hall, London. The press was not unfavorably impressed. The *Hull and Lincolshire Times* (October 17, 1896) wrote, "Another interesting show is managed by Mr. Randall Williams, whose living pictures and tableaux vivants are well worth seeing." For the next two years, Randall Williams was to be a popular visitor to the fair. In 1898, he introduced the new, improved American Bioscope, of which he announced (in the *Hull Daily Mail,* October 10, 1898), "Fun without vulgarity. You can bring your children without the slightest fear." The veracity of this statement is somewhat in doubt, for in the "World's Fair" column of *The Era* (January 29, 1898), it was noticed that one of the highlights of Randall Williams' show is "a representation of a young lady taking a bath." Only a month after attending the fair, Randall Williams was dead, but the show continued to visit Hull under the management of his two sons, Richard and James Monte.

The Bioscope shows of the period invariably presented an outside entertainment of jugglers, clowns, dancers, etc., whose job was to attract customers. They would open at ten o'clock in the morning and continue through the day until eleven o'clock at night, giving a total of over thirty shows a day. The popularity of such shows may be judged by the fact that ladders had to be used to allow so many patrons at a time to approach the pay boxes. The ladders were held across the top of the steps to the show by two men, one holding each end; they would lift the ladder high enough to permit the required number of people to go under, and then lower it to avoid a rush on the doors. After the show, the pattrons left by side entrances to allow new customers to enter at the front.

By 1900, Bioscope shows had become a firm favorite at the Hull Fair and at fairs throughout the country. They were now beginning to show films of important world events; in 1898, a popular film at the Fair had been the Fitzsimmons and Jeffries prize fight for the championship of the world. Items of local interest were also to be seen; visitors to the Hull Fair were able to see the girls leaving the Danson Lane Factory of Reckitt and Sons. The local newspaper on October 11, 1900, reporting on its customary yearly inspection of the Fair wrote, "Living Pictures are all the rage this year. The cinematograph meets you at every turn."

Randall Williams owned the largest of the Bioscope Shows to attend Hull Fair, but there were many smaller ones which also attended from 1897 onwards. These early Bioscope Shows were presented as secondary entertainment to other shows, as in 1897, when both Bartlett's Menagerie and Testo's Masrionette Show presented films. After 1900, the attendance of Bioscope Shows in their own right was a regular feature, presented by such people as Captain Payne, Relph and Pedley, Savages, and President Kemp.

In 1903, the character of the Bioscope Shows began to change. They were beginning to look like small halls, with ornate fronts and giant organs to attract the attention of potential patrons. The Randall Williams' show had acquired an 89 key Gavioli organ, and Ralph and Pedley were not long following with a Marenghi Organ. The organ at this time was the most important feature of the booth; showmen were adding bigger and better organs, each trying to outbid his rivals. President Kemp had a Dreamland organ to attract his customers, while his chief rival, Captain Payne brought in 1909 a gigantic Limonaire.

A grave threat to all Bioscope showman came in 1909, when the Cinematograph Act came before parliament. This Act, in an attempt to secure safety at cinematograph exhibitions, would have forced the Bioscope shows to close their doors for good, if it had not been for the action of the Showmen's Guild. The Guild was responsible for the introduction into the Act of a special clause dealing with portable structures.

(For more information, see Thomas Murphy's *History of the Showmen's Guild*, The World's Fair, 1948.)

1913 was the last year Bioscope Shows attended Hull fair; there were only four that year — Asplands, Farrar and Tyler, Ben Hobson, and C. Ling. Randall Williams, who had attended every year since 1896, paid his last visit in 1912, for shortly after leaving the Hull Fair, the show burnt out at Thirsk Fair. The Bioscope Shows had lost their appeal to the citizens of Hull; the novelty had worn off. With over a dozen regular cinemas in the city, where was the excitement and glamour of sitting in a draughty, make-shift hall, watching a few minutes of faded film being projected onto a dilapidated screen? The invention which these showmen had fostered had outgrown them. It had grown out of its youthful vulgarity into art; the culturists had got hold of it.

Even today the Bioscope Shows have a certain appeal, although the men that ran them have been forgotten. Men like Edwin Lawrence, Felix Testo, Wadbrook, Donner and Crecraft, whose names were once household words in the fairgrounds of this country are forgotten, Yet they were the real pioneers of the cinema; they exhibited and, in many cases, made some of the earliest films. "Yes, Hull was the world's greatest fair, and we are not likely to see anything like it again, nor such wonderful sights, for the great shows have gone," said Arthur Sellman, who worked on Bioscope Shows at Hull Fair at the turn of the century.

Bioscope Shows, however, appear to be coming back into popularity. In August 1964, an old-time steam fair was held at White Waltham in Berkshire, and undoubtedly the outstanding attraction at the Fair was a Bioscope Show, presented in Tom Norman's Palladium, with an 89 Key Gavioli Organ on one side and the Savage Portable Light Engine No. 761, "Sarah," which had previously been with Anderson and Rowland's Bioscope Show on the other. In June 1965, another steam fair was held at Melton Mowbray in Leicestershire, which also contained a Bioscope Show, yet again presented in Tom Norman's Palladium. Over 400,000 people attended these fairs, and even *The Times* exhorted its readers to roll up for all the fun of the fair. Perhaps the days of the Bioscope Shows are not over yet?

Mama's Boys

Stallion, May 1987, pages 56, 58, 64

There was a time when songs about mothers were all the rage. Charles King sang "Your Mother and My Mother Too" in *Hollywood Revue of 1929*. George Jessel sang — it seemed interminably — "My Mother's Eyes" in *Lucky Boy*. "Mother of Mine, I Still Have You," sobbed Al Jolson in *The Jazz Singer*. Evelyn Herbert introduced the song "Mother" in the operetta *My Maryland*. Everyone loved his mother. The problem was some men loved their mothers a little too much. Mothers dominated their lives, and there was once a much accepted theory that domineering mothers created homosexual sons. And to prove such a theory, Hollywood offered the perfect stereotypes in two of its most pre-eminent character actors, Edward Everett Horton and Clifton Webb. Horton's screen persona, like Webb's, suggested a meticulous, obsessive, even prissy, personality — comic contrast to the conventional machismo of Hollywood's leading man types.

The phrase "Mama's Boy" had entered the language in the 1910s. It was used to refer to "wimps" and "sissies," who wouldn't fight, who hid behind their mothers' apron strings, and who never, never could win the girl. Indeed, the implication often was that once won, such men wouldn't know what to do with the girl. Harold Lloyd played such a character in 1922, but he called his film *Grandma's Boy*. Silent film star Charles Ray, who specialized in playing rural types, was often cast as a mother's boy.

The American silent screen also had its own real life mother's boy in actor J. Warren Kerrigan. Known as "The Gibson Man," in that he was as handsome as the Gibson Girl was beautiful, Jack Kerrigan was on screen from 1910 until 1924. He gained some sort of lasting fame late in his film career as the star of the 1923 classic Western, *The Covered Wagon*, and in his 1924 portrayal of the title role in *Captain Blood*, which was later to be played by Errol Flynn. Unfortunately, the 18th Century costume which Kerrigan wore did not exactly flatter him, and the producer of *Captain Blood*, Albert E. Smith, complained bitterly that his star looked much too effeminate.

J. Warren Kerrigan made a bad career move in May 1917 by announcing that he would not go off to war until it became essential. "I think that first they should take the great mass of men who aren't good for anything else, are good only for the lower grades of work," he told a reporter from the *Denver Times*. "Actors, musicians, great writers, artists of every kind — isn't it a pity when people are sacrificed who are capable of such things — of adding beauty to the world." He was promptly attacked by the fan magazine *Photoplay*, which editorialized against him as "one of the beautiful slackers."

The actor's entire life revolved around his mother. He entered films because he wanted to make a permanent home for his mother. He published his autobiography in 1914. It was dedicated to his mother, Sarah, and in it he published a credo, which began "I am a Christian," and ended:

"I am a law-abiding, peace-loving citizen, in no way unlike the general run of my fellow men, endowed by the grace of God with my share of ideals, hopes, possibly a trifle more that I deserve of happiness, and above all a great heartful of love for her to whom this book is affectionately dedicated, my MOTHER."

J. Warren Kerrigan died in 1947, at the age of sixty-seven. As might be expected, all the newspapers commented that he had never married.

If J. Warren Kerrigan took himself perhaps a little too seriously, the same cannot be said of Edward Everett Horton, who knew that his demeanor evoked comedy and actively worked to create a comic effect.

The archetypal screen fusspot, Edward Everett Horton never portrayed a suggestively homosexual character in any of the more than 120 films in which he appeared from 1922 through 1970. Thomas Mitchell might jokingly call him "Sister" in *Lost Horizon*, but that was because he displayed feminine traits, not because he showed any interest in other men. Horton was the quintessential sidekick, reliant as a friend or a valet, whose happiness came from worrying about and organizing the lives of his friends. He was a dominant character actor in films such as *The Front Page* (1931), *The Gay Divorcee* (1934), *Shall We Dance* (1937), *Arsenic and Old Lace* (1944), and *Pocketful of Miracles* (1961). In the first, he played Bensinger of the *Tribune*, an old maid of a reporter, the butt of his colleagues' jokes, continually concerned with the danger of disease. It was a masterly Horton performance.

The closest that Horton ever came to a gay scene on screen was in the decidedly risqué 1931 comedy, *Reaching for the Moon*, starring Douglas Fairbanks and Bebe Daniels. As Fairbanks' manservant, he gives his master a lesson in how to make love with Fairbanks playing the female role. The two are spotted by a workman whom Horton imperiously calls "My Man," and hastens to explain what's what in the situation. The workman responds, "I'm not your man and I know what's what."

Edward Everett Horton spent all his working life as an actor, a profession which he thoroughly enjoyed. "I have led a serene life. I gave up all mental activity at eighteen," he once told a reporter. His best known stage appearance was the title role in the Benn Levy farce, *Springtime for Henry*, which he played intermittently from 1932 onwards, and which has some surprisingly suggestive dialogue which it is certainly possible to misconstrue as gay-oriented.

Offscreen, Horton was devoted to his mother, Isabella, who died in August 1961, at the age of 101. In 1924, he purchased an estate in the San Fernando Valley region of Los Angeles, called "Belly Acres," where he and his mother might live together, with his brother occupying a house on the estate, and a third house rented to F. Scott Fitzgerald. When the City of Los Angeles built the Ventura Freeway through his property, rather than move, Horton arranged for the roadway to curve around his house. He was the first film star to have the street on which he lived, Edward Everett Horton Lane, named in his honor

The actor became known as "Hollywood Most Celebrated Bachelor." Asked in 1939, why he had never married, Horton explained, "I arouse nothing but respect, and not too much of that, in the opposite sex. It is one of the crosses I bear that I never seem to inspire cooperation on the part of designing females. I am a bachelor of some years standing — both public and private." There was a rumor around Hollywood that Horton would never play a part in which he was called upon to kiss a woman. Although he denied the accusation, and although he has played husbands in films such as *Holiday* (both the 1930 and 1938 versions) and *Design for Living* (1933), there does not appear to have been an occasion on screen when he kissed a woman on the lips.

Mrs. Horton and her son were inseparable, and the actor obviously enjoyed playing mother's boy well into old age. When he called his mother at the age of ninety-eight to tell her he was going to an after-theater party, she warned him, "That's fine, Edward, but remember don't eat too much and don't talk about yourself." Edward Everett Horton died nine years after his mother's passing, on September 29, 1970, at the age of eighty-four.

There was always something loveable about Edward Everett Horton's temper tantrums on screen, as he stamped his feet and looked suitably irritated, displaying all the mannerisms of a frustrated lover. The same cannot truly be said of Clifton Webb. His screen image was perhaps a little too close to his private one, that of a very bitchy and rather unpleasant character. Edward Everett Horton once admitted to the *New York Times* that he loved to prance about a little. Clifton Webb could never let himself go. As producer Darryl F. Zanuck remarked, "It isn't that Clifton won't unbend, it's just that he can't."

Clifton Webb came to films late in his career. He appeared in three nondescript silent films, but he did not make his sound film debut until *Laura* in 1944, more than thirty years after his stage debut on Broadway. On stage, he was an accomplished dancer, with his partners including Bonnie Glass, Mae Murray and Mary Hay. With Libby Holman, he introduced the song, "Moanin' Low," in the 1929 revue, *The Little Show*.

Because he was such a brilliant dancer, Clifton Webb was signed to a contract with MGM in 1935, with the studio's intending to groom him as a competitor to RKO contract star Fred Astaire. Joan Crawford was cast to play opposite Webb in what was to be his first film, *Elegance*, but nothing came of the project, supposedly because MGM studio head, Louis B. Mayer, was concerned at spending such a large sum of money to promote a new romantic man who was widely rumored to be homosexual.

Eventually Clifton Webb came to Hollywood because he was invited to do so by Rouben Mamoulian, who was as much noted for his work on stage as for the films which he had directed. However, Mamoulian quarreled with the studio, 20th Century-Fox, over the film *Laura*, and he was replaced by Otto Preminger. Clifton Webb is first seen in the film, as Waldo Lydecker, taking a bath. Blatantly, the character tries to titillate the straight cop played by Dana Andrews. The role established Webb as a major Hollywood star, and it was followed by memorable performances in *The Razor's Edge* (1946), *Mr. Belvedere Goes to College* (1949), *Cheaper by the Dozen* (1950), *Titanic* (1953), and *Three Coins in the Fountain* (1954), among others.

Accompanying Webb to Hollywood was his eccentric mother, Maybelle Parmalee Hollenbeck, from whom the actor was inseparable. She had been a typical stage mother, working hard, against her husband's wishes, to teach her son to be an actor. With him, she became a member of New York's more sophisticated society, and the pair, who behaved more like husband and wife than mother and son, continued their well-established routine of getting the best out of society on the move to Los Angeles.

"My dear man, I have always been a success," Webb told one reporter, adding that he wore pajamas tailored by Hawes and Curtis of London because "a man must look his best always, darling."

One of Webb's closest friends was Noel Coward. Indeed, Ruth Gordon had once discussed writing a play in which she was to portray Maybelle and Coward would appear as Webb. Coward writes frequently of the actor in his published diary. A typical entry is from Christmas Day, 1960, and reads, "He admitted to me under a pledge of deep secrecy the other morning that he was seventy-one. I expressed token amazement because the poor dear looks and behaves like ninety. There is much that is sweet about him but he is, and always has been, intolerably silly."

Silly was hardly the word to describe Webb's relationship with Maybelle. She was never away from his side, usually getting very drunk at parties given by her son. Webb might occasionally become irritated by her behavior, but his love for her was absolute. In 1948, deliberately choosing his words with care, he told gossip columnist Hedda Hopper, "Maybelle has been so much a part of my career, so thoroughly the *gay* companion of my work and travels."

Maybelle Webb died on October 18, 1950, at the age of ninety, and Webb was desolate. Noel Coward told him that at his age it was rather late to be orphaned, but Webb could not see the humor in the remark. He aged tremendously, made one last film, *Satan Never Sleeps* in 1962, and died at the age of seventy-two on October 13, 1966. "Age defeated him," commented Noel Coward, blithely upon being told of Webb's passing. The actor was buried next to his mother at Hollywood Park Cemetery's Abbey of the Psalms.

Interestingly, actor turned novelist Tom Tryon appears to have based the character of the homosexual actor in *Crowned Heads*, who is murdered by two young men that he has picked up, not on Ramon Novarro, but on Clifton Webb. The character in the novel, like Webb, is besotted with a woman whom the murderers believe to have been his wife, but who is, in reality, his mother.

Although two very different characters, both on screen and off, Edward Everett Horton and Clifton Webb represent Hollywood's idea of a Mama's Boy. Both survived and prospered in the film community because they were always amusing, offering good "clean" copy for the columnists, and steering well clear of any hint of sexual indiscretion. Hollywood could love a "Mama's Boy," just as long as he never openly loved another boy.

D.M. Marshman, Jr. and *Sunset Blvd.*

Leonard Maltin's Movie Crazy, January 22, 2017

On March 29, 1951, three men mounted the stage at the Pantages Theatre in Hollywood to accept the Academy Award for Best Story and Screenplay in acknowledgement of their work on *Sunset Blvd.* Two — Billy Wilder and Charles Brackett — were well known within the industry at the time and their reputations have not diminished with the passing years. The third man was probably pretty unfamiliar to most members of the audience that night and he remains very much the forgotten third man as far as the script for *Sunset Blvd.* is concerned. His name, as it appears on the film, was D.M. Marshman, Jr.

Donald McGill Marshman, Jr., or "Mac" as he was called by Wilder and Brackett, was born in Cleveland, Ohio, on December 21, 1922, the son of a trial lawyer, and graduated from Yale, where he received his B.A. in the Class of 1945. At college, Marshman had written a column for the *Yale News* and with T.O. Cole he had authored a three act comedy, *Poet's Corner* (unproduced but copyrighted in 1946). In 1946, Marshman joined the staff of *Life* magazine, initially identified as a staff writer and later, in the summer of 1947, as an assistant editor. Two of the most prominent articles that he wrote for *Life* are "A Bold Tennessean with a Katzenjammer Accent Is the Newest Top-Flight Director in Hollywood" (on Robert Siodmak), published in May 1946, and "The Second Rise of Joan Crawford," published in June 1947.

In June 1948, Marshman left *Life* to become movie critic for its sister publication, *Time*, replacing Hillis Mills. As was the custom at *Time* during that period neither man received credit for his work. Indeed, when Marshman left *Time*, he was succeeded by Robert Wernick, who also was unacknowledged.

Both Charles Brackett and Billy Wilder were familiar with Marshman's work as a critic, and, at the latter's suggestion, he was brought to Hollywood. The tall, booming-voiced Marshman effortlessly turned the duo into a trio. "Billy Wilder was the greatest talent; he had a good ear and would fuss and fuss with lines until they were right," recalled Marshman, "but Charlie was the finer man…I was very fond of him, you know, and he was extremely generous to me, both personally and professionally. [He was] the most agreeable of men. You'd want to have him at a party." The two men Marshman described as "professional friends, not social friends." Wilder would often tell Marshman that it should be "Goodrich and Hackett and Wilder and Brackett," referencing contemporary screenwriters Frances Goodrich and Albert Hackett.

The hiring of Marshman by the pair was not only as a screenwriter. As Marshman told me, the two men would play cribbage on a regular basis and on the way back from location for *The Emperor Waltz*, they were engaged in what had been their favorite pastime. The game involves one person playing, say, a deuce, the partner playing a deuce, the first one playing a deuce, and so on. Wilder played a deuce, and so did Brackett. Wilder played a second deuce and won the round. When the hands were revealed, Brackett had the fourth deuce, which he had not played. He refused to explain why to Wilder, and the two men never played cribbage again. When Marshman was hired, they discovered that he knew how to play cribbage, and so they could take it in turn to play with him.

Marshman was deemed "a smart fellow" by Brackett and Wilder after telling them that *The Emperor Waltz* was "a schmaltzy piece of fluff," with which the two men agreed wholeheartedly.

Unfortunately I did not make contact with Don Marshman until after I had completed the edit of the Charles Brackett diaries for publication by Columbia University Press. Marshman was familiar with the diaries, about which Brackett would talk often, but which he maintained were unpublishable. When we did connect, in the summer of 2014, he had much to relate about the making of *Sunset Blvd.*, most of it, to the best of my knowledge, previously unreported.

Marshman recounted that the original idea was "to do a movie where the hero was a secret Communist. He would be played by Gene Kelly." It took about two weeks to decide on the structure of the film as made, with the three men running through ideas or "Blue Skying," as they called it.

Generally, Marshman did not remember which lines in the script could be credited to which writer. It was very much a collaborative effort.

The one memorable line for which he does take credit is the scene in which Norma Desmond is buying a coat for her young protégé, and the salesman comments, "As long as the lady is paying for it, why not take the Vicuna?" As to the most famous lines in the film in which Norma Desmond insists, "It's the pictures that got small":

"Billy and I were working on that scene at his home. He never wrote anything. I would sit with a pencil and pad and we would talk how a scene would work. He had a very good ear for dialogue. I remember Gillis had to say, 'You used to be in pictures. You used to be big.' There was a very logical response, and I don't remember who said the actual words first. It was very obvious to say. It was not a matter of anyone looking at that as a choice line of dialogue."

The name "Norma Desmond" is generally thought to be taken from Norma Talmadge and William Desmond Taylor. Marshman agreed in regard to Norma Talmadge, but insisted that the "Desmond" is Florence Desmond. When I pointed out to him that Florence Desmond was a British actress who had not appeared in silent films, Marshman stated categorically that the three of them thought she had. Wilder and he always thought that the references to silent films would register with an audience that had grown up with silent films. "Blur the lines between reality and imagination."

It is doubtful that audiences wonder where Norma Desmond gets the gun with which she shoots Joe Gillis. But the three writers did and didn't know what to do about it, with hours of meetings spent on the subject. Charlie Brackett had the idea of a loyal housekeeper getting the gun but that would need her to be introduced to the audience. Ultimately, it was decided that at some point Norma Desmond had gone out and purchased the gun, and engaged audiences would not stop to think when that was and how she was able to do it.

Marshman told one fascinating anecdote in regard to the music by Franz Waxman, identified as "an old friend of Billy's." Utilizing the script, Waxman worked independently and the three writers did not hear the score until it was being recorded. All agreed, "It seemed to be fine." There is melodious music over the scene of William Holden and Nancy Olsen working on the script and walking around the studio at night. When Wilder praised the piece, Waxman explained that he had not written it, but rather he had taken the theme song from *Paramount on Parade*, which was also used for the Paramount newsreel, slowed the music down and made it very rich and very sentimental. Nobody recognized the original source.

After *Sunset Blvd.*, Brackett and Wilder split up. Marshman left Hollywood, married and traveled abroad. He returned in 1952 to work on the 20th Century-Fox production, *Taxi*, actually shot in New York. Released in 1953, *Taxi* stars Dan Dailey and Constance Smith, with Marshman sharing screenplay credit with Daniel Fuchs, and the story credited to Hans Jacoby and Fred Brady and in turn based on *Sans Laisser d'Adresse* by Alex Joffe and Jean Paul Le Chamois. "With six authors banging away furiously at their typewriters it is hard not to understand why the film is so full of sound, fury and bad dialogue," sourly commented *Cue* (January 24, 1953). The sole reason for *Taxi*'s having any modern interest is that it marked the film debut of John Cassavetes.

The second film, an RKO release, on which Marshman worked was also shot on location, this time in Mexico, and in Technicolor and 3-D. While the screenplay credit for *Second Chance* goes to Oscar Millard and Sydney Boehm, Marshman does receive acknowledgement for the story and adaptation of this melodrama involving the ex-girlfriend of a crime boss, played by Linda Darnell, who has linked up with a prizefighter played by Robert Mitchum. With a climax on a broken cable car in the Andes, *Second Chance* was praised by *Newsweek* (August 10, 1953) as "a very respectable example of thriller writing."

Charles Brackett was at 20th Century-Fox at this period, but he did not produce *Taxi*, too minor a film for someone of his reputation and, also, he was busily at work on the Marilyn Monroe vehicle, *Niagara*, released only a week after *Taxi* appeared. Marshman did, however, work with Brackett in the spring of 1953 on an unrealized project, *Jewel of India*.

In 1953, Marshman abandoned his Hollywood career and pursued a new one, in advertising, on the East Coast. As he recalled in a 2007 interview with his local newspaper,

"It became clear that these studios could not afford these tremendous payrolls. It became a catch-as-catch-can business. The big stars began making deals for themselves. And I figured it was a poor bet for me. To have a successful career, you had to be very, very talented, or very well connected, or you really wanted to do it more than anything else in the world. None of these things applied to me...I didn't think the movie business was going to be any kind of life for a gentleman. And I've never regretted it."

Initially, Marshman worked with the prestigious Young & Rubicam Agency. From 1974-1979, he conducted a fund-raising campaign for Yale University, worked as a professional speechwriter, and in 2010, he founded his own organization, Marshman Enterprises, in Milford, Pennsylvania.

Since 1955, he had lived in Darien, Connecticut, with his wife, Ann, the mother of his four children, and a reportedly tarnished and darkened Oscar.

Like his mentor, Charles Brackett, Marshman had been a staunch Republican, but as he explained to *Western Reserve Academy Magazine* (January 14, 2014), "Gave up my Republican registration and vote nine years ago after 60 years in the fold and feel better about it every day."

Don Marshman died in Darien, Connecticut, on September 17, 2015.

Mae Murray
and *A Mormon Maid*

Films in Review, February 1979, pages 108-109, 124

In view of her legendary status, it is surprising how few Mae Murray films are readily available for reassessment. One that has been accessible in 16mm is *A Mormon Maid*, dating not from the 1920s, an era with which she is most closely associated, but from the mid-1910s, when her career was just beginning. *A Mormon Maid* must be regarded as one of the better feature-length films from the 1910s to have survived.

A Mormon Maid was Mae Murray's sixth feature and the second to be directed by her future husband, Robert Z. Leonard. Mae Murray had come to Hollywood via the *Ziegfeld Follies*, and she seems to have made few concessions towards the realism which the film industry should have demanded from its stars. Her bee-stung lips, although not as pronounced as they were to become in the 1920s, are completely out of place in a film set it Utah in the 1840s.

As one might expect from the title, *A Mormon Maid* deals with the less savory aspects of early Mormonism, a religion which the film industry throughout the silent era had held to be suspect. In fact, *A Mormon Maid* makes little effort to isolate the religious beliefs which are the central part of the film from modern Mormonism. Perhaps the most virulent attack on the Church of Jesus Christ of Latter Day Saints is a British production from 1922, *Trapped by the Mormons*, produced by a notorious filmmaker of British trash by the name of H.B. Parkinson. The film stars Evelyn Brent, who perhaps wisely assured me she recalled nothing about the production when I screened *Trapped by the Mormons* for her shortly before her death in 1975. I do not recommend the film, but 16mm prints are available.

The Mae Murray vehicle tells the story of an honest, non-Mormon pioneer, played by Hobart Bosworth, who is forced into a "celestial marriage" (polygamy or plural marriage) by the Mormon Elders, a marriage which causes his wife (Edythe Chapman) to blow her brains out in one of the more impressive scenes from the film. In an earlier outburst of religious hatred, Miss Chapman had declared, "I'll take my chances with Indians — not Mormons." Meanwhile, Bosworth's daughter, Mae Murray, is being forced to become bride number four to Noah Beery, but saves herself by announcing that she is not a virgin, and cannot, therefore, under Mormon Law, be taken in wedlock. After much shooting and bloodshed, Mae. Bosworth and the young hero, Frank Borzage, giving one of the best performances I have seen from him, escape to the "Promised Land," which we assume is far removed from the Mormon "Promised Land" of Utah. The screenplay was by Charles Sarver, and based on a story, "The Deliverance," by Paul West.

Charles Rosher, who was later to become Mary Pickford's cameraman, was in charge of the photography, and a magnificent job he makes of it, from the beautiful opening shots of the covered wagons on the move to the final scene of Murray, Bosworth and Borzage standing in front of an open fire, with the light from the flames gently illuminating their faces. One superbly composed shot, reminiscent of *The Birth of a Nation*, has the Indians silhouetted agains the hilltop as they ride across the frame.

It is hard not to be reminded of *The Birth of a Nation* as one watches *A Mormon Maid*, particularly because the film features "The Avenging Angels — 400 South-bound fanatics," whose white robes and masks closely resemble those of the Ku Klux Klan, with the all-seeing eye of Mormon on their chests instead of the crosses of the Klan. The Avenging Angels of the film are obviously based on the Danites, but I am unable to locate any evidence as to the validity of their costumes or as to whether, as the film suggests, the Klan based its costumes on theirs. This theory certainly does not tally with Griffith's tale in *The Birth*, and, although all I know is what I see in the films, it sure is confusing when two films present one with differing statements.

It is the Avenging Angels who also provide some wonderful moments in *The Mormon Maid*. "The Flight for Freedom," as they chase after Murray, Bosworth and Borzage, demonstrates an impressive understanding of the best techniques of photography, editing and direction.

A Mormon Maid was a Jesse L. Lasky production, and yet, instead of being released by Paramount, it was distributed on a states-rights basis in the Spring of 1917 by Friedman-Hiller and Wilk. Why Lasky and Zukor should have turned it over to an independent distributor is unexplained. It can hardly have been the subject matter, which they must have been aware of prior to the film's production. It was certainly not the reviews, which were glowing. George Blaisdell in *The Moving Picture World* (March 3, 1917) wrote, "It is strong drama, with its full measure of suspense, with its accompaniment of the tragedies that ensue in a primitive region when men of strong will meet at the crossing of the paths." While Peter Milne in *Motion Picture News* (March 1, 1917) wrote, "Commercially worthy, its artistic merit is no less prominent."

Milne described Mae Murray's playing as Pickfordian, which is hardly accurate, although in the early scenes she does do a lot of jumping about a la Pickford. In those same early scenes where Mae Murray is the tomboy, the actress seems ill-at-ease, wandering about — or to be more precise leaping around — with a vacant stare on her face. She is better handling the more sophisticated, more dramatic later scenes, where the ever-present bee-stung lips are less disturbing.

A Mormon Maid is not, strictly speaking, a Mae Murray picture; there are too many other good actors in the production for that, not to mention a good director and photographer. For those who want to see Mae Murray, the star, there is *The Merry Widow* (1925). However, if you like Mae Murray and you like first-rate features from the 1910s, the five reels of *A Mormon Maid* are highly recommended.

The Prussian Image on the American Screen

Films in Review, December 1985, pages 608-618

It is perhaps somewhat ironic that modern Prussian history should have begun with the invasion of that country in the 13th Century by the Teutonic Knights. For as far as the American cinema has been concerned, the modern image of the Prussian began and ended with the Teutonic image, that of a steely, cold, unfeeling individual who raped not only women and children, but whole nations, and when he was not busy raping, he was consuming large quantities of sausage, sauerkraut and beer. It was an image which began on American cinema screens with the United States' entry into World War One, and faded almost completely in 1919, reappearing later only in films such as *All Quiet on the Western Front* and *Hell's Angels* and in the characterizations of Erich von Stroheim and Lucien Prival.

Prior to the First World War, the Prussian character was a comic one in films, a carryover from the American vaudeville stage. Ford Sterling was the best known "German comic" of the screen, a leading member of Mack Sennett's Keystone Kops. Weber and Fields, who introduced burlesque to the American stage, created the comic German characters of Mike and Meyer. These two comedians introduced parodies of German immigrants to the United States, with Fields as the tall and bullying Meyer and Weber as the plump, trustful and innocent Mike. Unlike the later Prussian image, there was nothing harsh about these German comedians, they were basically working-class German Jews, uneasy with a new language, English, and the basis of their appeal on stage was their misuse of English words, although, of course, Fields' brutality towards Weber — poking fingers in his eyes and hitting him over the head with a bladder — was closer to what became the standard image of the German or Prussian. Weber and Fields' characterizations made a somewhat uneasy transition to films in

1915, under the aegis of Mack Sennett, but they were never as popular on the screen as they had been on stage.

When America entered the First World War, these so-called German comics suddenly became Dutch comedians. The make-up and humor remained the same, but the ethnic background did not. It was a time of extraordinary concern with image and with names. Sauerkraut was renamed "liberty cabbage," while the humble hamburger became the "liberty burger." Film personalities were also affected by the First World War, with actors making subtle changes to their Germanic names. Actress Margarita Fischer Americanized her name by dropping the "c", while the malevolent character actor Gustav von Seyffertitz adopted the decidedly English name of G. Butler Clonebaugh for the duration.

Anti-German sentiment, and with it the negative Prussian image, took a while to manifest itself in American films after the outbreak of the war in Europe. Some features, such as D.W. Griffith's 1915 production of *Old Heidelberg*, directed by John Emerson, showed Prussians as peaceful, fun-loving people. The film presented a musical comedy view of Prussia, a land in which a prince (Wallace Reid) could fall in love with a serving girl (Dorothy Gish). Even the presence of Erich von Stroheim, as Prince Karl's valet Lutz, could not detract from the film's romantic message. However, not everyone was taken in, and the eminent critic Julian Johnson, writing in *Photoplay* (December 1915) commented, "It is only marred by peace propaganda weak as wet gunpowder, a very burlesquey monarch, and a pictorial implication that Teutonic people are, naturally, averse to the present war." *Old Heidelberg* had its origins in Wilhelm Meyer-Forster's *Alt Heidelberg, Schauspiel in funf Aufzugen*, which was the basis for the 1924 Sigmund Romberg musical, *The Student Prince*, and for the 1927 Ernst Lubitsch film, *The Student Prince in Old Heidelberg*, starring Ramon Novarro and Norma Shearer, which was one of the very few silent films of the 1920s to present a favorable view of the Prussian people. Interestingly, Ernst Lubitsch again depicted a favorable view of the Germans in the 1932 pacifist film, *The Man I Killed* (also known as *Broken Lullaby*), in which a young Frenchman who cannot erase the memory of one German soldier that he had killed during the War, visits the German's family, and falls in love with the dead man's sweetheart. *The Man I Killed* is one of the American cinema's most moving and sympathetic portrayals of the German people, thanks not only to Lubitsch's direction but also his players, Lionel Barrymore, Nancy Carroll, ZaSu Pitts, and Louise Carter.

Alla Nazimova, the great Russian-born actress, took her vaudeville playlet, *War Brides*, and turned it into a 1916 feature, which also showed

Germans as peace-loving people, only participating in the War because of the demands of their Kaiser.

Anti-German forces at work within the American film industry were at first subtle in their propaganda. Films promoting preparedness and American involvement in World War One began to appear in 1915, and in these films the villains were never identified or Prussians *per se*, but the fact that they wore German-style uniforms and helmets with steel spikes left filmgoers in little doubt as to the nationality of these men seen bayoneting babies and raping innocent women.

The most important of these anti-German propaganda productions were *The Battle Cry of Peace* (1915) and *The Fall of a Nation* (1916). The former was produced by English-born producer J. Stuart Blackton, who in point of fact did not become an American citizen until after the *Battle Cry of Peace* was completed, and there were rumors that the British Embassy in Washington, D.C. funneled funds to Blackton for the film's production. *The Fall of a Nation* was written and produced by Thomas Dixon, who, in response to charges that he deliberately selected Teutonic-looking extras to portray the warring villains of the film, explained, "Five hundred Germans applied to me for work in the battle scenes and I was glad to give it to them."

Mary Pickford produced her own anti-German film in 1916 with *The Little American*, in which she is seen being threatened with rape by Walter Long, who seemed to specialize in villainous racial stereotypes from the Negro renegade Gus in *The Birth of a Nation* to the Mexican tyrant, Santa Ana, in *Martyrs of the Alamo*. The German community in Chicago was particularly offended by *The Little American* and the film was banned for a while in that city. Although German-Americans did little to temper the cinema' image of the Prussian people, there were a number of films, financed by Germans, produced prior to America's entry into World War One, aimed at showing the British in an unfavorable light during the American Revolution, in particular "The Liberty Boys" series and *The Spirit of '76*.

The Prussian image became firmly entrenched in the American cinema as a negative one with the United States entry into the War — on April 6, 1917 — and it never really changed. Even long after World War One was over, the American film industry was still producing films such as *Three Faces East*, first filmed in 1926 and remade in 1930, in which a British spy (played by Jetta Goudal in 1926 and Constance Bennett in 1930) falls in love with and then cold-bloodedly murders a ruthless German spy (played first by Clive Brook and then by Erich von Stroheim).

Anti-Prussian, anti-German films from the period of World War One were all basically the same, heavy on propaganda and light on subtlety. In films such as *Arms and the Girl* (1917), *Field of Honor* (1918), *Firefly of France* (1918), *The Hun Within* (1918), *The Prussian Cur* (918), *Till I come Back to You* (1918), *The Yellow Dog* (1918), *The Claw of the Hun* (1918), and *The Hun within Our Gates* (1918), the Prussians were consistently villains without any redeeming features, many times brought to surrender or death by pure young women of American stock. Although a parody of such films, Charlie Chaplin's 1918 Bond-selling short, *The Bond* comes fairly close to the content of most of the industry's anti-German films with its depiction of the Kaiser menacing the white-robed, pure and virginal Statue of Liberty (played by Edna Purviance).

My Four Years in Germany, the first major motion picture to be produced by Warner Bros., is based on a series of articles by James W. Gerard, former U.S. ambassador to Germany, and purported to show incredible scenes of German brutality in Prussian prison camps, scenes which were in reality filmed by director William Nigh in a New Jersey studio.

"Last Sunday night at the Knickerbocker Theatre when the film received its premiere presentation there was hardly a minute when the house did not ring with applause that turned into cheers," reported Peter Milne in *Motion Picture News* (March 23, 1918). "All the wily diplomacy with which the heads of the German nation sought to deceive the United States through its representative, all the atrocities witnessed by Mr. Gerard, such as the mistreatment of the English prisoners, the deportation of helpless Belgian women, perpetrated without regard for any sense of international law — these and a large assortment of views of Allied troops on the march make capital seeing for the man who goes into the theatre ready to have his emotions stirred against the common enemy… There is no stone left unturned to arouse the audience to a sense that the German manner of conducting war is synonymous with barbarism. One witnesses the heart rending sight of helpless prisoners shot down before German firing squads because 'there will be less mouths to feed,' of English and Russian soldiers placed in the same pens together so that the former contact the diseases common among the latter and feeding of the prisoners as dogs."

The comic relief in *My Four Years in Germany* was provided by a burlesque of the German Emperor and the Crown Prince. But to many the Kaiser represented the ultimate in Prussian villainy, and he was the subject of a number of films, including *To Hell with the Kaiser* (1918), in which the Crown Prince rapes an innocent girl, and *The Kaiser's Finish* (1918), in which the illegitimate son of the Kaiser, living in the United States, goes to Germany, kills his father, and is killed in the process. One of the best-known anti-German films of World War One — and a film which, sadly, does not appear to have survived — is *The Kaiser, the Beast of Berlin* (1918), basically a series of incidents in the Kaiser's life, ending wishfully with his being turned over to the King of the Belgiums at the war's close and being placed in the care of a blacksmith who has suffered at the hands of the Germans. The Kaiser is shown in the film as a "human monster whose vanity and arrogance led him to undertake to dominate the entire world," and is portrayed, in a remarkable resemblance to the real Kaiser, by Rupert Julian. Julian (1885-1943) was a New Zealand-born actor and director, noted for his portrayals of the Kaiser — "he was more like the Kaiser than the Kaiser himself," recalled Jetta Goudal, who worked with him in *Three Faces East* — but Julian was also capable of other characterizations as different from the Kaiser as that of a peasant in *We Are French* (1917), suffering under the Prussian yoke. According to actress Ruth Clifford who worked frequently with Rupert Julian, "He took his characterizations very seriously and was a man of little humor."

The crudest characterization of the Kaiser and the German Royal Family appears in Mack Sennett's 1919 production of *Yankee Doodle in Berlin*, which also contains scenes of American planes, described as "Messengers of Democracy," indiscriminately dropping bombs on German cities, and finds humor in having an American soldier place hand grenades down inside the trousers of two German soldiers. *Yankee Doodle in Berlin* came too late to stir up anti-German feeling, and after *The Kaiser, the Beast of Berlin* there was little further need for films to arouse such hatred. Frederick James Smith in *Motion Picture Classic* (June 1918) commented, "We recommend *The Kaiser* if you have trouble working up an early morning hate," while the *New York Times* (March 10, 1918) reported that at the film's premiere the previous evening at New York's Broadway Theatre, "The audience applauded wildly when a young German captain, resenting an insult of the Kaiser, laid the monarch low with a right-hand uppercut to the jaw." (Needless to report, for such an insult to the Kaiser, the young captain was forced to commit suicide.)

Strangely enough, American audiences continued to have an interest in the Kaiser's activities long after the termination of World War One, and as late as 1930, moviegoers were being treated to films such as *The Kaiser in War and Peace*, which the *New York Times* (January 27, 1930) reported as "a seemingly endless and boring pictorial record of Wilhelm Hohenzollern's activities before and after his banishment to Doorn." *[A reference to the Dutch city to which the Kaiser was exiled and where he died.]*

Most film-goers and film performers involved in the American cinema's biased view of Germany during World War One had not had any direct involvement with an actual German atrocity. One actress who felt she had a personal message of German hatred to bring to American filmgoers was the French-born Rita Jolivet, a survivor of the sinking of the *Lusitania*, to whom theatrical entrepreneur Charles Frohman uttered his oft-quoted last words, "Why fear death? It is life's most beautiful adventure" before going down with the ship. Rita Jolivet was starred in the 1918 Metro drama, *Lest We Forget*, in which she portrayed a French opera singer who strangles the German diplomat who plotted the sinking of the *Lusitania*. Edward Weitzel in *The Moving Picture World* (February 16, 1918) found "much that is excellent" in the production, while Hazel Simpson Naylor in *Motion Picture Magazine* (May 1918) found it "all so terribly usual and filled with inconsistencies."

The most impressive film made concerning the sinking of the *Lusitania* and one that does, in a not too subtle fashion, color one's feelings about the German people is Winsor McCay's 1918 one-reel animated short, *The Sinking of the Lusitania*, consisting of 25,000 separate drawings. It ends with the image of a woman holding her baby above her head as she goes under the wave, followed by perhaps the greatest propaganda title ever conceived on film, "AND THEY TELL US NOT TO HATE THE HUN!" *The Sinking of the Lusitania* was not the only cartoon to present a negative Prussian image to the American people, but the other cartoons were more of the type of *Knocking the H--- out of Heinie* (1919).

However, it was not in animated shorts that Americans audience found humor in the Prussian image that they were seeing projected on their cinema screens, but rather in one of the classic short comedies of Charlie Chaplin, *Shoulder Arms*, released only one month prior to the signing of the Armistice which ended World War One on November 11, 1918. In his autobiography, Chaplin recalled that Cecil B. DeMille told him, "It's dangerous at this time to make fun of the war," but nonetheless the comedian decided to embark on the production of what finished up as a three-reel feature in which the Little Tramp begins as an awkward army recruit and finishes up capturing the Kaiser, the Crown Prince and Von Hindenburg. Of course at the film's close, it proves to have been nothing more than a dream, but it was a dream with which many a wishful American soldier could sympathize. Film historian Kevin Brownlow has written, "Chaplin's *Shoulder Arms* is the only film from the entire period to be remembered with unqualified admiration," which, perhaps, says a lot for Chaplin or, perhaps, says not very much for the films which the American cinema turned out during World War One in order to vilify the Prussian image.

In 1919, *Photoplay*, the most popular American fan magazine, described Erich von Stroheim as "the man who did much to make Germans popular objects upon which to commit mayhem during the late war." Never was a case so understated, for no-one approached Erich Von Stroheim in terms of portraying a totally negative German image on American cinema screens from World War One through World War Two. In the former, he was a Prussian and in the latter a Nazi, but the performance and the effect was much the same. He was also, of course, to present a very sympathetic Prussian image in one of the greatest films of all time, but that was not an American production but rather Jean Renoir's *La Grande Illusion*.

Erich von Stroheim (1885-1957) was born, of course, not in Prussia but in the Austrian capital of Vienna, and when audiences during World War One over-reacted towards him and his hateful Hun characterizations, von Sroheim would explain, "The Austrians are like the Germans about as much as much as the Irish are like the English." Through his portrayal of Prussians in films such as *For France* (1917), *The Hun Within* (1918) and *The Unbeliever* (1918), von Stroheim came some way to earning the title of "The Man You Love to Hate," but the anti-German film of his which really stands out as far as the actor's brutal and viscious performance as a Prussian Officer, Lieutenant von Eberhard, is concerned is *The Heart of Humanity*.

Directed by Allen Holubar and starring his wife, Dorothy Phillips, *The Heart of Humanity* was released by Universal after the War's end, but that did not prevent the producers from presenting Germans and Germany in a particularly unsavory light. Degenerate is perhaps the best word to describe the Erich von Stroheim character whether he be attempting to rape the heroine or throwing a baby, with cold-blooded abandon, out of a window. After seeing von Stroheim's work in *The Heart of Humanity*, the critic for the *New York Times* (December 22, 1918) commented, "Erich von Stroheim makes a German villain as convincingly villainous as any actor on the screen." Writing in *Photoplay* (March 1919), Julian Johnson described *The Heart of Humanity* as "the biggest, most elaborate and most mechanically clever of all the screen's war stories," but Johnson like all the other critics found the theme and construction too similar to D.W. Griffith's *Hearts of the World* and concluded the latter was by far the more superior production.

Many, including one of Erich von Stroheim's best-known biographers, have concluded that the Prussian Officer who attempts to rape Lillian Gish in *Hearts of the World* is played by Erich von Stroheim. This is simply not so. The confusion has arisen because the character name of the Officer is von Strohm (perhaps some private joke on director Griffith's part?), but he is played by George Siegmann, a long-time associate of D.W. Griffith who served as one of the assistant directors on *The Birth of a Nation*. *Hearts of the World* was produced at the suggestion of the British government. Erich von Stroheim served as technical consultant on the film, which was released in the spring of 1918. For the climax, D.W. Griffith resorts to his old, trusty and worthy device of the last-minute rescue. The heroine, Lillian Gish, is threatened with rape by the lustful, stereotypical Prussian Office, von Strohm, while French soldiers advance to the rescue. Von Strohm is not the only negative Prussian characterization in the film, for Germans are also seen ill-treating French villagers, and one German sergeant brutally beats the much-abused Miss Gish. Interestingly and characteristically, Griffith does not show Germans solely in a bad light; one group of German officers restrain von Strohm from an attempted rape of the girl. And, of course, *Hearts of the World* does depict more of the horrors than the glory of war.

World War One was the background for three further D.W. Griffith productions, *The Great Love* (1918), *The Greatest Thing in Life* (1918) and *The Girl Who Stayed at Home* (1919). The last is of particular interest for although it does not fail to show us Germans in an unfavorable light, it also gives us one of the few glimpses, in an American film produced during or immediately after the War, of a sympathetic German. As portrayed by David Butler, the character of Johann Kant is a totally compassionate one, and when the heroine, Carol Dempster, is threatened with rape by one of his countrymen, Johann Kant shoots him, crying out, "Fight men — not women." In a small part, in a little-known film, David Butler gives one of the most unusual portrayals of a Prussian on the American screen.

D.W. Griffith's involvement with Germany and the German people did not end with *The Girl Who Stayed at Home*. Two Griffith films of the 1920s do no harm to Prussia or its image. *Lady of the Pavements*, released by United Artists in 1929, tells of Karl von Arnim (William Boyd), an attaché of the Prussian legation in Paris, who is maneuvered by his jealous fiancée into falling in love with a prostitute. William Boyd does not look particularly Prussian, but then perhaps that is a good point in that it shows the American cinema had no longer a negative Prussian image to project.

In 1924, Griffith directed *Isn't Life Wonderful*, a film which many critics and historians consider his last great achievement. In it, the director takes a sobering and heartrending look at conditions in Germany following the 1918 Armistice. *Isn't Life Wonderful* showed Americans audiences the suffering of a poor German family and, daringly, asked America to sympathize with its one-time enemy. With his leading players, Carol Dempster and Neil Hamilton, the director explores the privations and the courage of the German people. *Isn't Life Wonderful* was shot in the small town of Kopenick on the outskirts of Berlin in the summer of 1924, and was based on a short story by a British Army Officer, Major Geoffrey Moss. The finished result is a film to which G.W. Pabst would have proudly affixed his name.

To return to the American cinema immediately after the end of World War One, there was still a strong, unfavorably Prussian image on view, and this was never more evident than in Thomas H. Ince's production of *Behind the Door* (1919), directed by Irvin Willat, and starring Hobart Bosworth, Wallace Beery and Jane Novak. One of the most sadistic films of all time, *Behind the Door* relates the tale of German-American taxidermist Oscar Krug (Bosworth), whose wife is captured by a German submarine crew, brutally raped and then dispatched to her death by way of the torpedo hatch. Krug eventually meets the captain of the submarine (Beery), takes him "behind the door," and proceeds to skin him alive. *Behind the Door* certainly revealed no change in the American film industry's attitude towards the German people.

The Four Horsemen of the Apocalypse, Rex Ingram's picturization of the popular novel by Vincente Blasco Ibanez, was more than an epic of families at war, for it presented the interesting and oft-repeated theme of cousin pitted against cousin. Descendents of Madariaga, a wealthy Argentinian cattleman, form two branches of the family, the Desnoyers in France and the von Hartrotts in Germany. The film is not so much a war spectacle as a study in racial traits, with the Germans shown in a decidedly bad light. The French are basically normal, dignified human beings, while the Germans are arrogant and autocratic.

The film received its world premiere in New York on February 10, 1921, and was hailed by critics as one of the greatest motion pictures of all time, being compared, favorably, with *The Birth of a Nation* and *Intolerance*. Its leading man, Rudolph Valentino was to become one of the legends of the silent screen, while Alice Terry, who was shortly to marry Rex Ingram, proved herself an actress of great dignity and beauty. The German roles were well handled by Alan Hale, Stuart Holmes, Jean Hersholt, and Wallace Beery. Interestingly, Alice Terry was to play a German — a spy — in Ingram's 1926 production of *Mare Nostrum*, again based on a novel by Vincente Blasco Ibanez. Alice Terry has rightfully claimed that her greatest screen portrayal was that of Freya Talberg in *Mare Nostrum*, a difficult role to which she brings sympathy and understanding, particularly in the final, moving execution scene.

In the 1920s, the German image in American films was roughly divided into two categories: Germans were spies in *The Love Light* (1921), *Friendly Enemies* (1925), *The Great Deception* (1926), *Secret Orders* (1926), *Convoy* (1927), and *Lost at the Front* (1927), while the problems, domestic and otherwise, affecting German-Americans were discussed in *His Foreign Wife* (1927), *The Way of All Flesh* (1927), *Sins of the Fathers* (1928), and *We Americans* (1928). German novelist Hermann Suderman provided the source material for four American films with German backgrounds: *Lily of the Dust* (1924), *Flesh and the Devil* (1926), *Wonder of Women* (1929), and *Sunrise — A Song of Two Humans* (1927), although the last does not specify the locale as Germany. Comedian Harry Langdon found himself entangled with German soldiers in *The Strong Man* (1926), and the German military was naturally on view in such classic American "war" films as *The Big Parade* (295), *What Price Glory* (1926) and *Wings* (1927). But none of these films are particularly relevant as far as the American cinema's image of Germans is concerned. *Barbed Wire*, a 1927 Paramount production based on a novel by the English writer, Hall Caine, was unusual in that it depicts a German soldier in a sympathetic fashion and the French villagers who refuse to shelter him after the Armistice as shameful and unforgiving. Pola Negri plays a sympathetic French peasant, while the German solider is portrayed by British actor Clive Brook.

John Ford, an American director whose Irish ancestry and animosity towards the English probably made him more sympathetic to the German people than most American producers, was responsible for *Four Sons*, released by Fox in 1928. Sincerely and movingly, *Four Sons* tells of a German mother with four sons who loses each of them in the War, with the exception of Joseph, who has emigrated to the United States where he opens a delicatessen and to where, after the War, he invites his mother to come and live. In an understanding review, Abel Green wrote in *Variety* (February 15, 1928):

> *The film is an achievement in artless realism. There isn't a moment when it does not live, and the whole production is utterly guiltless of theatrical device. Simple people, kind and happy, are suddenly engulfed in the conflict, and the tragedy comes upon the gentle villagers, among whom stalk the hateful military martinets. It is the arrogant military class that plays the villain. The people are the pitiful puppets.*

Howard Hughes' production of *Hell's Angels* (1930) marked a return to the old Prussian image of reserved and arrogant military types, flashing white teeth in steely smiles, and displaying a cold-blooded belief in God, Kaiser and country. When the captain of the zeppelin orders that any extra weight must be jettisoned to allow the ship greater speed and altitude, members of the crew silently and willingly jump to their deaths to lighten the ship's load. Lucien Prival appears as Baron von Kranz and, giving a marvelous performance with mannerisms borrowed from Erich von Stroheim, proceeds to bully the two brothers (Ben Lyon and James Hall) who are the heroes of the film. Prival gives exactly the same characterization in a 1930 Charley Chase comedy, *High C's*.

A totally different German image was to be seen in Universal's *All Quiet on the Western Front*, production on which began, under the direction of Lewis Milestone, at 11:00 a.m. on November 11, 1929 — exactly eleven years after the termination of hostilities in World War One. Here is a remarkable film on the horror and waste of war, based on a remarkable novel by Erich Maria Remarque. The film worked for American audiences because the characters were not American soldiers, but Germans experiencing and questioning the futility of war. The only suggestion of a stereotypical Prussian is in the character of the schoolmaster, who advocates the War and fills his students with warmongering propaganda. Otherwise the players in *All Quiet* — Lew Ayres, William Bakewell, John Wray, Louis Wolheim, and Slim Summerville — are human beings, not Germans particularly, not characters in a play, not unsympathetic Prussian stereotypes, but human beings. Indeed, few of the players are even Teutonic in appearance, adding to the universality of the production and its message.

Interestingly, in 1939, Universal released a version of *All Quiet* with added anti-Nazi narration. Following the famous scene in which the soldiers sit around and talk of the futility of war, the narrator intrudes to comment that such brave words today in Germany would find their speakers in a concentration camp, and the reissue version closes with a seven-minute montage of newsreel footage and the burning of the novel of *All Quiet on the Western Front*. The film had opened in Berlin in 1931 under the title of *Nothing New in the West*. Hitler's followers released white mice in the theatre during the initial presentation, and the film was soon banned. *All Quiet on the Western Front* was not seen again in Germany until 1952.

Universal released another film, in 1934, with a similar universal theme, but played out again with German characters. The production was *Little Man, What Now?*, directed by Frank Borzage and starring

Margaret Sullavan and Douglass Montgomery. It is the story of a poor couple who marry because the woman is expecting a child, and, like many of Frank Borzage's films, shows the two persevering and finding happiness in their love for each other and their love for their child. It is set in Germany, but it might just as well have taken place in the United States, so untypically German are the characters. However, reviewers were quick to point out that the story takes place in Germany prior to the rise to power of the Nazis.

German characters continued to appear in American films of the 1930s, but they are generally of minor interest and not always sympathetically handled. A typical German role is that of Gustav von Seyffertitz in Josef von Sternberg's *Shanghai Express* (1932), who fails to arouse any compassion from the viewer, even after he is branded by the villainous Chinese rebel leader, played by Warner Oland. And then, of course, as the 1930s drew to a close, the German image on the screen became a Nazi one.

All in all, Prussians and Germans have not been treated kindly on American cinema screens. The Prussian image of the Erich von Stroheim type with monocle, steely gaze and arrogant manner was established during World War One and the memory, if not the image, lingers on. As *Photoplay* once commented, "Things reached a point where ordinarily sane men, after witnessing Erich von Stroheim with his arrogant Prussian ways and his Germanic clothes, would go home and melt up the baby buggy, fashion it into a French knife and go downtown to join the Marines."

Prussians and Germans may be one and the same in reality, but on the American screen the two are far apart. Prussians, with the exception of *Lady of the Pavements*, have a totally malevolent connotation. Germans have fared better, but generally when the American film industry has provided a sympathetic depiction of the German people it has been on a very human, rather than national, level, and in films such as *All Quiet on the Western Front, The Man I Killed* and *Little Man What Now?*, there has been a universal message and the implication that the stories do not necessarily have to be set in Germany and peopled with Germans.

In a 1980 interview on American television, Chancellor Helmut Schmidt declared there was no such person as a typical German. As far as the history of the American cinema is concerned that is not the case.

[*This essay was originally published as part of the five-volume,* Preussen: Versuch einer Bilanch *(1981).]*

The Regulars

Films in Review, April 1978, pages 222-224

The social life of the Hollywood community in the 1920s is of some interest to both the sociologist and the film buff. Aside from its seamier aspects, such as the "Fatty" Arbuckle scandal, it has received little attention, and with the Hollywood of today such a squalid, vice-ridden area of Los Angeles, it is all too easy to imagine that is the way it has always been. Standing at the corner of Hollywood Boulevard and Highland Avenue now, there is no way one can conjure up images of a Hollywood Boulevard lined with pepper trees, and with tall grass gently swaying in the breeze created by the passing of the streetcars.

As the Hollywood Sign slowly collapses and decays, almost in unison with the town beneath it, it is important to record the social life which once took place in Hollywood's past, before that is but a memory, which, sadly, is what the Hollywood Sign may soon become.

One remembrance of Hollywood social life in the silent era was given to me by John Ford's widow, Mary: "We had one restaurant and that was the Oasis, and you could tell who was working because that was who the maître d' would bring the check to at dinner. The Oasis was on Hollywood Boulevard near the Taft Building. Then we had one nightclub called John's, and it was a place where you'd go downstairs on Hollywood Boulevard, but nobody went there. They had the Hollywood Hotel Thursday night dances — that was the thing! And if you wanted to go slumming, you went to Vernon. There was a nightclub there, and you could get liquor under the table. Leo McCarey was the bouncer out there before he became a film director."

A very different social gathering is recalled by two Hollywood stars of the 1920s, Virginia Brown Faire and Priscilla Bonner, who were prominent members of the Regulars. In the mid-1920s, Mary Pickford had formed "Our Girls" as an informal social club for prominent female stars.

It met weekly at Pickfair, and its members included May McAvoy, Bebe Daniels, Constance Talmadge, and Marion Davies. They were the "elder girls," as Priscilla Bonner comments. Several of the younger members of the film community considered "Our Girls" and its Pickfair setting a little too overbearing and conservative and determined to form their own club, which was to become known as The Regulars.

The exact date of the founding of The Regulars is not known; the club received little publicity during its existence and its members have no reason for remembering detailed information on its activities. Virginia Brown Faire recalls that she and a group of ingenues were playing in one of what were known as "Writers Cramps," an occasional variety show held to raise money for the Hollywood Writers Club. The actresses in the show decided to get together and form a club. It had no name at first, and a contest was organized to find one. In the meantime, the girls called themselves The Regulars, for want of a better name, and when a better name did come along, they had become known as The Regulars and decided to stick with that title. (Interestingly, the name they planned to call their club was the Thalians, which, of course, is the name of a well-known entertainment organization to this day.)

There were approximately seven founding members of The Regulars. Among the actresses who belonged at one time or another were Virginia Brown Faire, Priscilla and Margerie Bonner, Sally Eilers, Mary Philbin, Mary Astor, Marian Nixon, Jobyna Ralston, Esther Ralston, Sue Carol, Mary Brian, Pauline Curley, Dorothy Devore, Pauline Garon, and several lesser known personalities, including Menifee Johnson, an agent and casting director of whom Mary Astor writes with great affection in her autobiography, Grace Gordon, the niece of *Los Angeles Times* reporter Grace Kingsley, and Maryon Aye and Duane Thompson, two minor screen players.

Mary Philbin had to be picked up by another member of the group from her parent's bungalow on Fairfax Avenue — a home in which she still lives — and if she arrived home one minute late, she would be met on the doorstep by an irate father. Eventually her father would no longer allow her to attend meetings. Mary Astor's membership in the club was also short-lived, as her father insisted she be home by nine o'clock in the evening.

The Regulars met every Monday in rotation at a member's home. Dues were one dollar a week. "We didn't drink," recalls Virginia Brown Faire, "and we had cookies and tea. We were in a prissy era. The most exciting fun I ever had was at a party where we had ice-crean! We had certain rules and regulations, and oaths we took. One of them was no gossip. So rather than sit around and gossip, we would have a book review and general chatter, even go into geography and history, and generally try to improve ourselves."

Margerie Bonner was the intellectual of the group, and she would read poetry for the enlightenment of the others, and also handle the book reviews. A charming little film actress of the 1920s, Margerie was to marry the distinguished novelist Malcolm Lowry, author of *Under the Volcano*, in 1940, and since his death has edited several volumes of his letters and other writings.

Perhaps the last major event of the Regulars was a shower for Priscilla Bonner, given on August 15, 1928, prior to Miss Bonner's wedding the following month. Present at the party hosted by The Regulars' member Alice Mills were the Misses Eiler, Nixon, Jobyna Ralston, Cordelia Kamm, Margerie Bonner, Dorothy Manners, and Mrs. William Friedman.

The Regulars remained in existence past the coming of sound, but too many of its members left the industry and its demise was inevitable. "I think we went our different ways," says Virginia Brown Faire. "Some got working too hard, and others married, and their husbands didn't want them to be gone on Monday nights."

The history of The Regulars serves as a reminder of a happier period in Hollywood history. In no other decade of the film industry could a club such as The Regulars have existed. No stars of a later era would have taken delight in such simple pleasures. That Hollywood Sign will never again look down on the innocence and fun of The Regulars.

Wendy Richard

Films in Review, October 1992, pages 303-306

Public television viewers have the unique opportunity of seeing Wendy Richard in two distinct periods of her career, fifteen years apart, and in two very different roles, as Shirley Brahms in *Are You Being Served?* and as Pauline Fowler in *Eastenders.*

Based on her work in those two long-running shows, one might well imagine that Wendy Richard is one of the busiest actresses under contract to the BBC, and in many respects this is true, with other series including *Not on Your Nellie, Please Sir!* and *Dad's Army.* Last year she taped a six-part sequel to *Are You Being Served?*, titled *Grace and Favour,* and this May began taping a second series of episodes. The original series of *Grace and Favour,* which brings back not only Wendy Richard, but also Mollie Sugden, John Inman, Frank Thornton, and Nicholas Smith, began airing on some PBS stations earlier this year.

I have long been attracted by the work of Wendy Richard, watching her devlop from a blonde bimbo to a character actress, while never losing her working class accent or the streak of common sense with which all her characters are imbued. It was, therefore, with a great deal of pleasure that I accepted an invitation to spent some time with Wendy at her local London pub, and to chat about a career which began in 1960 and still has, I suspect, new heights to reach.

Born in the North of England, Wendy Richard trained at the Italia Conti School before obtaining one of her first television roles in an episode of *Dixon of Dock Green,* starring Jack Warner and based on the character he played in the 1949 film, *The Blue Lamp.* Her first big break came in 1962, when she was featured on a pop record called "Come Outside" with Mike Sarne. Sarne went on to direct Mae West in *Myra Breckinridge* (1970), thought he was more important than she was and quickly disappeared from view. Wendy Richard, who received all of fifteen pounds for her work on this number one hit record, went on to appear in her first television series for the BBC, *Harpers West One*, which like *Are You Being Served?* is set in a department store.

Her first film appearance was in *No Blade of Grass* (1970), directed by Cornel Wilde and starring Nigel Davenport, a drama of the danger of industrial pollution based on John Christopher's novel *Death of Grass*. It was the last film made at MGM Borehamwood Studios. "I can say I successfully closed down Borehamwood Studios," states Wendy — and Wilde's work on the film did not impress the actress: "It came from a brilliant book, but Cornel Wilde, God rest his soul, I don't think he did it justice when it came to the screenplay. He seemed to go over the top and get some egg on his face."

Richard's first important film role came the following year with *Gumshoe* (1971), which starred Albert Finney and Billie Whitelaw, and was the first feature from Stephen Frears. "It was a brilliant little cameo part, which I was fortunate enough to get," recalls Wendy, "and from that one scene I got so much work." *Gumshoe* was followed by two films based on popular British television series: *On the Buses* (1971), which the *Monthly Film Bulletin* described as "a new low in British production," and *Bless This House* (1972). The last was directed by Gerald Thomas, who directed Wendy in two of the "Carry On" films, *Carry On Matron* (1971) and *Carry On Girls* (1973). Wendy was Miss Willing in the first and Ida Downs in the second, and although typical of the "bosomy" females of the series, there was no suggestion that she might become a regular.

Both British and American audiences really got to know Wendy Richard with the series *Are You Being Served?*, seen on the BBC from 1974 through 1984, and still playing on PBS stations across the United States. Utilizing what is best described as "seaside postcard humor," writers David Croft and Jeremy Lloyd created a series which raises the art of *double entendre* to a new level, and one which introduced a new catchphrase to the English language, "Are you free?"

Set in the ladies' and gentlemen's ready-to-wear department of Grace Brothers Department Store, the series featured Wendy Richard as Miss Brahms, Mollie Sugden as Mrs. Slocombe, John Inman as Mr. Humphries, Frank Thornton as Captain Peacock, Trevor Bannister as Mr. Lucas, Arthur Brough as Ernest Grainger, Nicholas Smith as Cuthbert Rumbold, and Harold Bennett as "Young" Mr. Grace. Mrs. Slocombe's continued concern for her "pussy" is probably the most outrageous aspect of the program, followed closely by Mr. Humphries' mincing walk and camp humor, which has not always gone over well with members of the gay community.

References to the Queen's Own Regiment and sailors always brings a smile to Mr. Humphries' face, as readily as the sight of Miss Brahms' miniskirted legs brings drool to the lips of Mr. Lucas and Captain Peacock. Ladies' undies and gentlemen's trousers always come down as quickly as in any sex drama, except here they are displayed only on counter tops and manikins. And only Mr. Humphries would remember to warm the end of his tape measure before checking an inside leg measurement.

Are You Being Served? is in the great tradition of British Music Hall, and one is reminded of this constantly by the appearances of the last of a dying breed of Music Hall performers throughout the series in its later years. Arthur English was a regular as the store's delivery man, and who should pop up in one episode, as a store customer, but Reg Dixon, who once appeared on variety bills complaining he felt "proper poorly" and singing the sentimental ballad "Confidentially."

Through the years, Wendy Richard has worked with a number of major comedians, who learned their craft in Music Halls, including Harry Secombe and Frankie Howerd (who died earlier this year).

"Harry Secombe was an absolute sweetheart, a lovely man, a gentleman, one of the old school. I was terrified of Frankie Howerd the first time I met him. Then I realized he doesn't suffer fools gladly, that he's a very professional man. If you're working with him, you've got to be on the ball as well. And I've found out as I get older I get less tolerant of some people who cannot conduct themselves in a professional manner, and so I knew exactly what he meant. I know that you have to learn your lines and you have to be punctual, all that sort of thing, which unfortunately some of the youngsters in *Eastenders* haven't quite learned.

Being professional, however, did not stop the cast of *Are You Being Served?* from amusing themselves at dress rehearsals, as Wendy recalls,

"We had a Christmas episode once, and this particular Christmas we had a model Santa Claus who stood there with his coat opened and said, 'Ho, ho, ho, little boy, do I have a surprise for you.' And we had a new designer on the show, and I said to her, well you know…She got two large Christmas balls and a Christmas cracker and hung them there, and the camera crew and everybody was hysterical. And Mollie Sugden said, 'What are they laughing at?' So I said, 'I don't know.' And she said, 'There wasn't anything wrong when I looked.' She must have gone up during the break and looked under the coat. She was naïve about some of the jokes — I was too about some of them. I'm a terrible giggler. Have you seen the German week episode, where I'm absolutely hysterical. I'm wetting myself."

Wendy Richard does take offense at the notion that her character is merely a blonde bimbo: "Really Miss Brahms isn't a bimbo; she's the most sensible of the whole lot. They come up with these silly, potty ideas, and a lot of times she can put them down with one-liners, because she knows they're all potty."

There is no question that Wendy is extremely fond of Miss Brahms — even her dog is named Shirley Brahms Mark 2. The part led her back to the screen for a 1977 film version of the series, directed by Bob Kellett and written by Croft and Lloyd. All the cast members were present, supposedly on Spain's Costa Plonka. "That was a bit of a disappointment actually," says Wendy. "You see I didn't think the film was very good. It was on a very cheap budget. And as far as we got was Gatwick Airport, to a Dan Air training plane. Considering the success of the program, they could have put a bit more money into it." The series was also brought to the legitimate stage. "John Inman was a great help to me, because I didn't know how to do stage make-up" — and Wendy has continued to appear in the theater, making the obligatory appearance in *No Sex Please, We're British*, and also playing principal boy Dandini and the fairy godmother in four pantomime productions of *Cinderella*. "I like playing principal boys," she notes, "I do, if I may boast, have a good pair of legs. I can strut about the stage, wave my arms, and do the thigh slapping."

In 1986, Wendy Richard became a regular on the popular BBC drama series *Eastenders*, which is seen on Tuesdays and Thursdays in the United Kingdom, and airs on a number of PBS stations, usually as two episodes back to back.

It might be easy to dismiss *Eastenders* as just another soap opera, but, in reality, it is one of the most impressive series on television, blending *cinema verité* style photography with a gritty and realistic storyline involving the various inhabitants of Albert Square in London's East End. The one reason why the show is not more popular in the United States may well be its realism. The accents are the accents of Britain's working class, and the use of natural sound as background in virtually all of the scenes requires the viewer to pay attention, something which most of the television audience is not used to doing.

Eastenders is videotaped at the BBC's studio at Elstree, utilizing both sound stages and a complete "mock-up" of Albert Square. The outdoor set is far more than mere frontages. The "buildings" allow for the actors to go upstairs, and the open doors of any of the frontages reveal fully dressed interiors. The set includes a complement of automobiles, taxis, trucks, and buses, and the use of hand-held cameras allows for the actors to move around the set, around vehicles, through a central park area, and past street stalls without a cut in the action.

Producing two thirty-minute programs a week is hard work for the cast.

"We normally work a five-and-a-half day work week. When we first started, we used to do studio days from 9:00 in the morning to 10:00 at night. Fortunately, we stopped that, and now we normally work from 8:00 to 6:30, unless, of course, there's a night shoot, which can go on till 2:00 or 3:00 in the morning. We have very little rehearsal time, so you really have to be on the ball, and we work on anything from six to eight different scripts a week, and they all dovetail one into another. We also do extra episodes so we can have two weeks off at Christmas. It is actually like being on a treadmill — once you're on it, that's it and you can't get off."

Usually attired in a frumpy woolen cardigan and her hair a mess, Wendy Richard plays Pauline, wife of one of life's losers, Arthur Fowler. American audiences have only just learned what British audiences knew for a year or more, that Pauline's son, Mark, has tested positive for the HIV virus. Wendy sees Pauline as a strong woman: "I think because she married Arthur and settled down, she didn't have much of a life. Her life has only been with Arthur. You see Arthur is basically a weak character, and Pauline is the strong one. That's what it boils down to."

While she is proud to be a part of one of the most popular series on British television, and one that is currently seen on fifteen PBS stations, she does object at times to the storyline's going beyond the realms of fantasy. When I mentioned to her that because of the length of time between the program's being produced in Britain and aired in the United States, the BBC had told PBS stations that five years of the series would not be seen over here, Wendy's response was "Well, you missed a lot of rubbish in some respects."

In reality, Wendy Richard has much of the down-to-earth, common sense approach to life of Pauline Fowler. However, unlike her television persona, she still has an attractive figure, with long blonde hair, looking rather like Diana Dors might have looked at that same age had she taken care of herself. There is little question that Wendy Richard a.k.a Shirley Brahms could still turn on Mr. Lucas or Captain Peacock today.

Unfortunately Mr. Lucas, in the person of Trevor Bannister, has not returned for *Are You Being Served*'s sequel. Arthur Brough (Mr. Grainger) and Harold Bennett ("Young" Mr. Grace) are also unable to return, having passed on to that great department store in the sky. Certainly, television audiences will be back for the sequel, *Grace and Favour*, and throughout the land the announcement of the show's presentation on local PBS stations will be met with the cry, "I'm Free."

[Wendy Richard was born in Middlesborough, on July 20, 1943, and died in London on February 26, 2009. As well as meeting in London for lunch on a number of occasions, she also visited me twice in Los Angeles. She was an expensive lunch/pub guest, as the only alcoholic beverage she drank was champagne.]

Vivienne Segal

Film Fan Monthly, October 1972, pages 19-26

One of my favorite sound films has always been *Viennese Nights*, and quite naturally, the film has given me great affection for its leading lady, Vivienne Segal. When I came out to Los Angeles, therefore, I lost no time in tracking down Miss Segal, whom I found living in a pleasantly-sized, single-story house in an upper middle-class neighborhood, bordering on the city of Beverly Hills.

Still a very attractive woman, Vivienne Segal lives alone with her two dogs; she moved to California when she separated from her husband, former CBS executive Hubbell Robinson, whom she married in 1950. (Her first marriage, from 1923-1926, to actor Robert Ames ended in divorce.) Autographed photographs on the grand piano from, among others, Richard Rodgers and Noel Coward, testify to the greatness of her career as a Broadway musical comedy star, but it was her all-too-brief film career that interested me.

Vivienne Segal was born in Philadelphia on April 19, 1897, the daughter of a well-known child specialist, Dr. Bernard Segal. Her mother had always wanted to be an actress, but the mother's parents had been opposed to such a career. It was that opposition that persuaded Mrs. Segal to allow her daughter to go on the stage, in order to compensate for own theatrical frustrations. Vivienne studied music under Mrs. Phillips-Jenkins, and appeared in a number of amateur productions with the Philadelphia Operatic Society. One Spring day in 1915, Mrs. Segal took her daughter to sing for Sigmund Romberg and J.J. Shubert at the latter's office in New York. Thirty days later a cable arrived, asking Vivienne to appear at the Broadway Theatre, Long Branch, New Jersey, where Romberg's *The Blue Paradise* was in rehearsal. After listening to the rehearsal, Vivienne was asked if she could play the dual role of Mizzi and Gaby at the show's New York opening in five days' time.

On August 5, 1915, Vivienne Segal made her professional debut at New York's Casino Theatre. Her singing of "Auf Wiedersehen" in *The Blue Paradise* stopped the show and she became — as they say in show business — an overnight star. Year after year, musical comedy lead followed musical comedy lead for Vivienne Segal. As Seymour Peck once commented in the *New York Times*, Vivienne Segal was "a noble, good and slightly tiresome musical heroine."

The movies first entered Vivienne Segal's life in 1927 when she appeared in a Vitaphone short for Warner Bros., taking its title from the song, "Will You Remember?" from Romberg's *Maytime*. She and co-star, John Charles Thomas, were billed as "America's foremost baritone and Broadway's most notable operetta star." A second Vitaphone short, *Fifi*, directed by Roy Mack, was released some six years later (in 1933), and was based on Victor Herbert's *Mademoiselle Modiste*. Supporting Miss Segal were Charles Judels, Albert (Van) Dekker, Philip Ryder, and William Ingersoll. "God, did we look awful," remembers Vivienne in reference to Will You Remember? "Our faces were absolutely pasty; we looked like clowns."

Warner Bros., in the first flush of the film musical craze, signed Vivienne Segal to a contract for five feature films, at a salary of $2,000.00 a week. In reality, only four were produced, and for only one year, 1930, was Vivienne Segal a film star. By the time Vivienne was ready to begin work on her fifth feature, musicals were box office poison, and the contract was cancelled with, one suspects, no regrets on either side. All four features were filmed in Technicolor (three of them by Dev Jennings); "I was just a guinea pig for Technicolor," was Miss Segal's rueful comment.

The first film to go into production was *Song of the West*, directed by Ray Enright, and its release caused only a faint ripple in the film industry. Adapted by Harvey Thew from the operetta *Rainbow* by Lawrence Stallings, Oscar Hammerstein II and Vincent Youmans, Warner Bros. found it necessary to ask Grant Clarke and Harry Askt to write additional songs for the film. Miss Segal could never understand why the studio found it worthwhile to purchase stage musicals and operettas for her, and then completely rewrite them, discard most of the original songs and then commission people of lesser stature than the original composers to write new compositions. She once asked this question of one of the company's leading executives, and was told that as a contract player she was required to do as she was told and not query the actions of Warner Bros.

Set in 1849 and 1850, *Song of the West* concerns a colonel's daughter (Vivienne Segal) and a cavalry scout (John Boles) who journey together from the East to San Francisco where they open a gambling den. The scout is framed by his associates and, rather than face dishonor, agrees to return to the army, where he and Vivienne Segal's character really belong, and where they find true happiness. Supporting players included Joe E. Brown, Marie Wells, Sam Hardy, and Eddie Gribbon.

The film opened at the Warner Theatre, New York, on February 27, 1930, to universally bad notices. *Variety* commented that "as unreeled this film is just a nice-looking program feature. No more — no less." "Owing to a mediocre script and uninspired direction, what might have been a magnificent outdoor operetta, all Technicolor, is pretty feeble," wrote *Photoplay*. The *New York Times* thought that Vivienne Segal "at times seems to be a victim of the temperamental microphone." *Song of the West* was certainly an inauspicious start to Vivienne Segal's feature film career, and her next was little better.

Golden Dawn, which followed, is still remembered by Vivienne. "God almighty!" was her reaction to my admission of having recently seen the production. Ray Enright was again the director of what must surely have been the most extraordinary musical ever produced on stage up until then. (It had a brief run on Broadway in 1927.) Written by Otto Harbach, Oscar Hammerstein II, Emmerich Kalman, and Herbert Stothart, *Golden Dawn* is set in German East Africa during the First World War. Halfway through the film, a reverse in the fortunes of the German troops means the locale becomes British East Africa. Vivienne plays a native girl whom everyone excepting the cast of the film know to be really a white girl, kidnapped and brought up by the natives. Because of her white skin, the natives decide that she must be a Goddess, thus allowing for such delightful dialogue as Vivienne's reply of "I go to be Goddess," to the hero's announcement, "I go to the new camp."

A lack of rain persuades the natives to sacrifice their new goddess in order to appease the Gods, despite a warning from the British governor: "Wise men of Africa, England is your friend. The British government will not tolerate the sacrifice of a white woman." However, like all emergent Black nations, this one cared little for the wrath of the British government, and went ahead with its plans to sacrifice Miss Segal. Luckily, a rainstorm freed her for the arms of her waiting lover, Walter Woolf, who by this time had discovered that she wasn't a native girl at all, and so might be loved without fear of offending a 1930 white cinema audience or the Black Pride Movement.

Among the songs are "I Crack My Whip" or "The Whip Song," splendidly sung by Noah Beery. Jr. in blackface; "In a Jungle Bungalow

(Where the tiger lilies grow)"; and my favorite, "My Bwana," which gives Vivienne the opportunity to sing such tender lines as "Who is never in the wrong? — My Bwana. Who gives laws both good and strong? — My Bwana."

"You felt like an ass, but what could you do? It was my livelihood" is Miss Segal's excuse and plea for forgiveness. (In all fairness to Messrs. Harbach, Hammerstein, Kalman, and Stothart, I should perhaps point out that the responsibility for "In a Jungle Bungalow" rests with those perpetrators of additional songs, Grant Clarke and Harry Akst.)

Sharing acting honors with Vivienne Segal in *Golden Dawn* are Alice Gentle and Marion Byron, and providing comedy relief (!) are Lupino Lane and Lee Moran. The reviewers again were not kind. *Photoplay* warned its readers, "If you're tired of players who break into song and dance without provocation, this won't help a bit...It's pretty dull." *Variety* agreed: "The all-colored and seemingly expensively produced sounded singer [sic] appears overloaded with songs — There are five within the first 15 minutes...Story is trite or tripe." Only the *New York Times* found a kind word to write, "Vivienne Segal as Dawn sings well and looks well."

Miss Segal's third feature film was *Bride of the Regiment*, released in the U.K. as *Lady of the Rose*. Yet again, Warner Bros. took an old operetta, *The Lady in Ermine* by Rudolph Schanzer and Ernst Welisch, asked Ray Harris to "adapt" it for the screen, and asked Al Bryan, Eddie Ward and Al Dubin to write additional songs. And finally, as the film starred one of Broadway's leading musical comedy stars, the company decided that the leading lady should have only one number,

Set in the days of the Austro-Hungarian Empire, Vivienne is seen as a newly-married Italian Countess, attempting to protect her husband (Allan Prior) by pleasing the invading Austrian Hussars, led by Colonel Vulton (Walter Pidgeon), while at the same time trying not to become too intimate with them. There were some fine comedy players (Louise Fazenda, Ford Sterling and Lupino Lane) in support, but the film and the songs, such as "When Hearts Were Young," "Broken-Hearted Lover" and "Dream Away" are long forgotten.

Bride of the Regiment meant a new director for Vivienne Segal, John Francis Dillon, and this change meant slightly better reviews, at least from *Variety*, which thought the film "entertaining all the way with good comedy sprinkled throughout in liberal doses, picture deserves returns above the average." Of the leading lady, *Variety* wrote, "Miss Segal plays particularly well. Besides a looker and on the screen striking a close resemblance to Mary Pickford, the star from the legit records and photographs with excellence." *Photoplay* was not so kind, writing, "This is another of First National's gorgeously dressed, sumptuously mounted and very slow-paced operettas taken from the theater. It positively glitters, and some of its Technicolor is grand, but it is a ponderous piece of business."

Vivienne Segal's fourth and final film for Warner Bros., *Viennese Nights* opened at New York's Warner Theatre on November 26, 1930, to excellent notices. The first operetta written directly for the screen — by Oscar Hammerstein II and Sigmund Romberg — *Viennese Nights* was undoubtedly, and Miss Segal agrees with me on this, her finest film. It was also a disastrous flop as far as America was concerned; the public had grown tired of musicals, even musicals as good as *Viennese Nights*.

Viewing the film today and reading the contemporary reviews, it does not seem possible that the public could so easily have dismissed the production. *International Photographer* wrote, "Nothing the Warners have done in twenty years or more of catering to picturegoers will give them a better claim to the consideration of their patrons than *Viennese Nights*... *Viennese Nights* has in its generous length not only the entertainment quality that attaches to excellent music and singing but all the illusion and deeply moving heart interest that would be found in an unusually good screen drama." *Variety* wrote, "Vivienne Segal has at last her opportunity in this picture." Similarly, the *New York Times* wrote, "Vivienne Segal has at last her opportunity in this picture, for not only is her voice nicely recorded, but she looks far more attractive than she has in any other cinema productions." And *Photoplay*, which had never previously found anything to praise in a Vivienne Segal film, commented, "The best operetta of recent months — a thing of beauty, with lilting music by Sigmund Romberg (oh, what waltzes!) and excellent singing and acting by a large cast. Vivienne Segal and Alexander Gray outdo themselves in the romantic leads…If you are weary of just plain talk, you'll enjoy this to the full."

Set in "Vienna of the glamorous days and romantic nights," *Viennese Nights* is the story of Elsa (Vivienne Segal) and her love for the poor musician, Otto (Alexander Gray), and how she is tricked by her father (Jean Hersholt) into marrying the wealthy but unfaithful Count Franz (Walter Pidgeon). The years pass and Elsa goes with her granddaughter Barbara (Alice Day) to hear a symphony by a young American with whom Barbara has eloped. The music irritates Elsa until suddenly she hears one of the symphony's themes. It is "I Bring a Love Song," the tune that Otto had composed for her so many years before. Yes, the composer is Otto's grandson. Elsa asks to be driven to the garden where Otto had declared his love for her so many years before. She slumps over, and the ghost of the young Elsa rises from her body to step into the arms of the young Otto, proving that "true beauty, true love is indestructible, and knows no age, no death, no end."

Sounds familiar? Well, of course, it's the theme of Noel Coward's *Bitter Sweet, Smilin' Through*, and, as the *New York Times*, pointed out Jessie Fothergill's novel, *The First Violin*. No matter, *Viennese Nights* in the expert hands of director Alan Crosland and cinematographer James Van Trees is a magnificent film, and does not suffer from comparison with any other work. The key scene in which Otto declares his love for Elsa contains some of the screen's most perfect dialogue. Earlier in the day, Otto had played his composition on the violin for the Academy of Music. Now, in the evening, he is talking of it to Elsa. "There's something more, Elsa. Words to fit the music I played this afternoon. I want the music to be played and loved all over the world, but the words are for you, for you, and no-one but you will ever hear them." He begins to sing "I Bring a Love Song." The dialogue then continues.

> OTTO: "Someday a great symphony orchestra will play that tune."
>
> ELSA: "I can close my eyes and imagine it. The violins, the cellos. I'll be seated in a box somewhere so proud of you."
>
> OTTO: "The world will applaud, but it will always be our song, just your's and mine."

[I am quoting the dialogue from memory.]

Aside from "I Bring a Love Song," the production also features "You Will Remember Vienna" (first sung by Walter Pidgeon and Bert Roach) and "When You Have No Man to Love" (sung by Vivienne Segal and Louise Fazenda).

Although unsuccessful in America, *Viennese Nights* was highly popular in the U.K., running for over a year in London's West End. The Leicester Square Theatre opened on December 19, 1930 with *Viennese Nights*. (Also on the same bill was Movietone News, *Little Covered Wagon* [A Talking Chimp Comedy], and, on stage, The Victoria Girls and Balliol and Merton "in an entirely new and sensational dancing presentation.") The review of the film in the trade paper, *The Bioscope*, typifies the reaction of the British critics:

"The musical and pictorial features of the film will appeal to every cultivated audience, while the sentimentality of the story will be more generally popular... Vivienne Segal plays the part of Elsa through the three periods of youth, maturity and old age and achieves considerable success in a very difficult task, her personal charm being apparent in every stage."

[I saw what was perhaps the only surviving nitrate print of Viennese Nights *in London in the late 1960s. It was in black-and-white, perhaps suggesting the film was released in the U.K. not in Technicolor but in black-and-white only, perhaps in an effort to save costs. It was not until many years later that Robert Gitt and the UCLA Film and Television Archive preserved and restored* Viennese Nights *in two-color Technicolor.]*

The lack of public response in the United States to *Viennese Nights*, coupled with the generally poor reception of the three earlier Warner Bros. features, meant an end to Vivienne Segal's contract. Little stage work was forthcoming at that time, and so, in order to support herself and her mother, Vivienne commenced a radio series, which brought in a steady income of $200.00 a week.

Miss Segal was not, however, entirely unhappy about leaving Warner Bros. The type of picture she had been required to accept dissatisfied her. She bemoaned, "Once an ingénue, always an ingénue, I used to say. How long do you think I can be eighteen?" She longed to play the type of role in the 1930s that Alice Brady made her own. That longing was not to be satisfied by the last film performance that Vivienne was to give.

She was signed by Metro-Goldwyn-Mayer to co-star in the screen version of the Jerome Kern and Otto Harbach Broadway hit, *The Cat and the Fiddle*. Jeanette MacDonald and Ramon Novarro were her fellow co-stars, working under the direction of William K. Howard. MGM executives were unhappy with the musical's serious tone, and hired Bella and Samuel Spewack to make various alterations. One such dramatic alteration, according to Vivienne, was the major reduction of her role. "It was fouled up so you wouldn't believe — orders of Miss MacDonald. That was the picture that ruined my career. They absolutely ruined me. No-one would cast me after that." Vivienne recalls that on the first day of shooting, Jeanette MacDonald walked on the set and greeted her co-star with "Hello, Viv. Have you seen your part? It stinks!"

Shot (by Harold Rosson) in 1933, *The Cat and the Fiddle* opened at New York's Capitol Theatre on February 18, 1934. *Variety* noted "Vivienne Segal draws the unsympathetic vamp role, and didn't get much sympathy from the photographer either. Miss Segal is really a much better looker than she is shown to be here."

Vivienne had two numbers, "Ha Cha Cha" and "A New Love Is Old," and Arthur Freed told her that her singing was the finest ever heard at the studio. Technicolor was used for the final production number in the film, but, as *Variety* pointed out, "the change to color in the last few feet doesn't help much since the picture is over by then, and nothing can make much difference."

The remainder of the 1930s saw Vivienne occupied with relatively unimportant stage work until 1940 when she was signed to play Mrs. Vera Simpson in *Pal Joey*, a new musical by Richard Rodgers and Lorenz Hart, based on a series of short stories by John O'Hara, which first appeared in *The New Yorker*. With legendary George Abbott directing, and with Gene Kelly as Joey Evans and June Havoc as Gladys Bumps, *Pal Joey* opened at New York's Ethel Barrymore Theatre on December 25, 1940, and ran for 374 performances. Vivienne Segal, singing three numbers, "What Is a Man" (originally titled "Love Is My Friend"), "In My Little Den of Iniquity," and, of course, "Bewitched, Bothered and Bewildered," won widespread public and critical praise. It is a tribute to Vivienne's ageless and changeless personality and singing voice that she was asked to play the same role in the 1952 revival, which opened at the Broadhurst Theatre on January 3, 1952, and ran for 542 performances. This time, Harold Lang played Joey and Helen Gallagher was Gladys.

I asked Vivienne if she regretted not being asked to portray the role that she had made her own in George Sidney's 1957 screen version of *Pal Joey*, She responded,

"God no, especially after I saw the film. The play was really excellent. That's one thing I was very proud of. There's nothing in it to be ashamed of. When I did the revival eleven years later, there was not one word had to be changed; John O'Hara had written such a marvelous story."

Rita Hayworth plays Mrs. Simpson in the film version, which, incidentally, bears little resemblance to the original stage musical.

In 1956, Vivienne was signed to appear in Joe Pasternak's remake of *The Women*, called *The Opposite Sex*, which David Miller directed at Metro-Goldwyn-Mayer. But after one day on the picture, she walked out. Miss Segal has been glimpsed occasionally on television in such series as *The Alfred Hitchcock Show* and *Perry Mason*.

A heart ailment makes it unlikely that Vivienne Segal will ever again be seen on screen or stage. However, in the unlikely event that Columbia Pictures decide to remake *Pal Joey*, I can assure the studio that

Vivienne Segal still looks and acts young enough to play Mrs. Simpson, and so immortalize on film one of the Broadway musical stage's greatest performances.

[Vivienne Segal died in Beverly Hills on December 29, 1992.]

Jim Sheridan

Program Note for 2004 Britannia Awards,
hosted by BAFTA/LA

Viewing a Jim Sheridan film can be a disturbing experience for an English audience. His is not the Ireland of the poetry of Yeats; his films are not inhabited by Oscar Wilde's epigrammatical characters. If anything, Jim Sheridan's productions are perhaps closest to the nightmare world of Sheridan Le Fanu, with just a hint of Jonathan Swift. Jim Sheridan's Ireland and his Irish men and women can often appear to be the images of our own self-induced bad dreams, the country and the people that England and the English have wronged for centuries, and which, as *In the Name of the Father*, the English are still unjustly persecuting. The so-called Guildford Four may have been allegedly tortured into confessing their responsibility for an IRA bombing, but there is nothing alleged about their conviction of fifteen years in prison.

Not that anyone can claim Jim Sheridan hates the English. He sees himself as a successor to George Bernard Shaw and Oscar Wilde, forcing us to look at ourselves and exposing our worst foibles. If, as he maintains, there are two kinds of cinema — films that lift one out of oneself and the other that drives you into yourself — then Jim Sheridan's productions have forced us to turn introspective, to accept and to move on and away from the Anglo-Irish tragedies of the past. There is still the story of the 1970s IRA hunger strike at Belfast's Maze Prison to be told[9], but, basically, Jim Sheridan has helped us to deal with what are often self-inflicted societal wounds relative to the IRA and the troubles in Northern Ireland.

John Ford may have created the romanticized cinematic vision of Ireland, but Jim Sheridan is responsible for the modern Ireland of the motion picture, a real world inhabited by real people, ranging from Daniel

---

9. It has since been the subject of director Steve McQueen's 2008 film *The Hunger*.

Day Lewis' poetic Christy Brown in *My Left Foot*, to the Richard Harris character in *The Field*, emotionally attached to the plot of land that he has tended for twenty years and is about to lose to a wealthy Irish-American. It is a land in which a former IRA member must try to rebuild his life in *The Boxer*, and where the fight for Civil Rights in Northern Ireland came to a climax in Derry in 1972 in *Bloody Sunday*, produced by Sheridan and directed by Paul Greengrass. With his script for *Into the West*, directed by Mike Newell, Sheridan introduced us to those poverty-ridden souls, the Tinkers (or gypsies) of Ireland, whose traditional culture, poor and forlorn as it might be, is being destroyed not by the English but by the Irish welfare state. The pain that is so much a part of the Irish psyche is here, and only through the telling can the pain be eased.

Yet in all this raw reality, there is a strong streak of Irish lyricism. No more so than in Jim Sheridan's most recent film, *In America*, based in part on his family's own immigrant experience in the United States, and co-scripted with his two daughters, Kirsten and Naomi. *In America* is a modern fairy tale, completed with potent references to drugs and AIDS, but this love letter to New York is also heavy with Celtic mysticism. Is it divine intervention that pays the hospital bill? After all, as the first great Irish filmmaker, Rex Ingram, pointed out, if any race is God's chosen people, it is the Irish. And one line, "Daddy, can we keep the pigeons," brilliantly sums up Sheridan's fascination with and love for the wonderment of life.

Jim Sheridan was born [1949] and grew up in Dublin — his brother. Peter, has written a book on their early years titled *44 — A Dublin Memoir* — and it was here that he ran an experimental theatre, the Projects Art Centre. To pay the rent, Sheridan organized Friday night concerts, where one of the bands was a group of college kids called U2, whose anthem is heard on the track of *Bloody Sunday*; *My Left Foot*'s producer Noel Pearson cast Sheridan in a stage version of *Borstal Boy*, the screen adaptation of which Sheridan, in turn, produced in 2000.

As an actor, Sheridan has also been seen on screen in John Boorman's *The General*, and one is very much aware of that special relationship that he has with the acting fraternity, ranging from Oscar-winning Brenda Fricker in *My Left Foot* to the much under-rated Paddy Considine, Samantha Morton, and the incredible presence of Djimon Hounsou in *In America*. The actor most associated with the director is Daniel Day Lewis (the star of three of Sheridan's films), and the pair are as compatible in their way as Robert De Niro is to Martin Scorsese. It's an odd combination, the upper class English Lewis, and an Irish director, whose roots can either be described as upper working class or lower middle class. And yet the actor notes they both have similar psychological roots and that Sheridan is writing if not directly about him, then about his own emotional make-up.

Sheridan left Ireland in 1981 for Canada, and a year later came across the border to New York. There, he drove a cab and worked as artistic director at the Irish Arts Centre, which introduced Americans to the work of playwright Brian Friel. Sheridan and his family lived in the Hell's Kitchen district of New York, and his production company is so named.

In the past thirteen years, Jim Sheridan has directed only five feature films, which he has also written in whole or part. As he notes, writing comes first and directing second. He is not a prolific director, but he is a conscientious and formidable talent, who never strays from his own personal perspective on life. Warm and friendly, Jim Sheridan is quintessentially Irish, and yet his films are international in appeal and universal in their conscience. "I don't see films as nationalistic," he once commented. "I am making films about my heart."

With a Jim Sheridan around, the English had better look out. As Frank McCourt defined "Irish Alzheimer's," "They forget everything except the grudge." And with Jim Sheridan around, his fellow international filmmakers had best not rest on their laurels. When *The Field* became Ireland's number one box office hit, Sheridan proved not only to the British, but also to his fellow countrymen that Irish can be best.

Writing of Jim Sheridan back in 1990 that venerable editor of *Daily Variety*, Thomas M. Prior, described him as a man of integrity and talent: "Would that there were more Jim Sheridans in the world." Slainte to that.

[Since this essay was written, Jim Sheridan has not really produced or directed anything of major significance, seemingly concentrating on documentary work.]

Sherlock Holmes and the Éclair Company

Bexhill-on-Sea Observer, May 18, 1968

Believe it or not, some fifty-five years ago Bexhill-on-Sea rivaled Hollywood as a center of film production. In the summer of 1913, the Éclair Film Company of France came to Bexhill with the object of making a series of films of the adventures of Sherlock Holmes. They made nine films in all, based on the short stories of Sir Arthur Conan Doyle which were so popular a feature of the *Strand* magazine.

The Éclair Company set up its headquarters at the Manor House. Scenes for the Sherlock Holmes films were shot here and at the old Kursaal [demolished 1936].

Holmes was played by Mr. [Georges] Tréville, and some local residents can recall seeing him as Sherlock Holmes pacing up and down the lawns in front of the Manor House. The Éclair Company decided that the character of Dr. Watson was uninteresting and boring and entirely superfluous to the plot, and therefore did not include him in the series.

Sir Arthur Conan Doyle took a personal interest in the making of these films, and was on hand to supervise the production. It was said that the total cost of the films was in the region of 30,000 pounds — a fantastic sum in those days.

The nine films were released in September 1913, and were favorably received by both public and press. One film magazine of the period wrote, "The scenery, which is very beautiful, is shown to the greatest advantage by the most perfect photography, and the uniform excellence of the cast adds greatly to the interest of the subjects."

Sadly, none of these Sherlock Holmes films is known to exist today, and if the old Manor House is demolished *[as it was in 1968]*, there will be no reminder of their ever having been made.

There have been many later films of the adventures of that most famous of private detectives. But can they have really have been as exciting as those local pioneering productions from the early days of the cinema?

[Written more than fifty years ago, this typifies my determination as a young man to write about film history and find a publication outlet, even if only in a local newspaper.]

John Stuart

Films in Review, March 1980, pages 166-167

John Stuart died last year, on October 18. He had appeared in more than 150 British films, from *Her Son* in 1920 through *Superman* in 1978, and yet he was basically unknown in this country. For one thing, he never actually played in an American film, although the first talkie in which he appeared and which was probably Britain's first sound feature, *Kitty*, directed by Victor Saville, was filmed in part at Paramount's Astoria Studios on Long Island. John Stuart was also an actor who never particularly stood out in British films, perhaps because he was too much the typically gentle, soft-spoken Englishman, who could fit so perfectly into the background of the film and never obtrude his own personality.

I got to know John in the late 1960s and became very fond of him. He was a nice guy to have a drink with at Sunday lunchtime at the local pub. He was never an actor in the sense that he acted offstage, but at the same time he was always delighted to be asked for an autograph, and could produce an autographed photograph at the slightest provocation. He had written a very, very slim autobiography, which like John was pallid and lacking in sensationalism, and in order to get it a wider circulation, I arranged for *The Silent Picture* to publish it in 1971 under the title, which John chose, of *Caught in the Act*. It says something of the man that John Stuart patiently numbered and signed every one of the thousand copies that we printed.[10]

Americans will know John Stuart if not by name at least by face in *Madonna of the Seven Moons* (1944), *Quatermass* (1956), *Sink the Bismarck!* (1959), and *Village of the Damned* (1959). As a child growing up in England in the 1940s and 1950s, I got to know John Stuart as the star of an early

---

10. This is not strictly true, as he only signed and numbered the copies that were actually sold, probably less than 100.

science fiction serial on television, *Lost Planet*. American film buffs will know John Stuart through the two Alfred Hitchcock features in which he starred, and because of *Atlantic*. New Yorkers who attend William K. Everson's screenings will know him from *Abdul the Damned* (1935).

The Pleasure Garden is important as Hitchcock's first feature, but it is not a particularly brilliant piece of filmmaking, and John Stuart is not particularly outstanding. He does have a spot more dramatic opportunity with *Number 17* (1932), a fairly short, fast-paced production which is fun and, if one ignores the use of too many obvious miniatures, a good production. It would have been a nice gesture, and something that John Stuart desperately hoped for, if Hitchcock had offered the actor a small, cameo role in *Frenzy*, shot on location in the U.K. in 1972.

Atlantic was shot at the British International Pictures studios at Elstree in 1929 by E.A. Dupont. The director made both British and German language versions, with the German version being that country's first all-sound film, starring Willie Forst, Lucie Mannheim and Fritz Kortner. Unfortunately, that version does not appear to be available, but the English-language one is, starring John Stuart, along with Madeleine Carroll, Franklin Dyall, Elaline Terriss, John Longden, and Donald Calthrop. It would be easy to dismiss *Atlantic* as one of the worst sound films ever made; the dialogue is handled so slowly, with each actor taking an eternity to make a one line speech, while the *Titanic* is slowly sinking. However, it is an early talkie, and many early talkies suffer from this problem. It would be easy to blame the actors, and John Stuart has pointed out to me that Dupont gave his actors absolutely no direction. He was interested in the technicalities of the production. He did not understand English. And, perhaps the biggest problem of all, E.A. Dupont would sit underneath the camera during the shooting paying the greatest amount of attention to the bottle of liquor in his lap.

Other John Stuart films that have surfaced in the United States include *Mine Own Executioner*, *Men of Sherwood Forest*, *Courageous Mr. Penn* (British title *Penn of Pennsylvania*), *Mrs. Fitzherbert*, *Reach for the Sky*, and the 1959 version of *The Mummy*. Unfortunately, all these films are from what may be best described as John Stuart's later career, when he was only a supporting player, and it is unfortunate that prints of such John Stuart starring vehicles as *Kitty*, *The Wandering Jew*, *Love's Old Sweet Song*, *This Week of Grace*, *Hindle Wakes*, and *Abdul the Damned* are not available in this country.

In the last few years of his life, John Stuart had problems getting parts. He was loath to admit that he could no longer remember his lines.

Richard Attenborough found a small part for him in *Young Winston* (1973), a part which assured him a good screen credit but did not require any dialogue. It was also good that John was able to end his career with a role in *Superman*. Yet again, as the 10th Elder of Krypton, he was only glimpsed briefly at the beginning of the film and perhaps had two words to speak, but his name was up there, only a little below the names of the principals, in the credits.

There is no question that John Stuart will be missed by all buffs of British films. I know that with his passing a very special part of my life in England has ended.

Thursday's Children

Program Note for screening at Academy of
Motion Picture Arts and Sciences, "Oscar Docs: The First
Twenty Years 1941-1960." November 14, 2005

Taking its title from an 1838 nursery rhyme by A.E. Bray that tells us "Thursday's child has far to go," *Thursday's Children* is Lindsay Anderson's fifth documentary, and the first in which he moves away from the industrial or informational genre. Here is a humanistic study of individuals — deaf children and their education at the Royal School for the Deaf in the English seaside resort of Margate. Anderson's co-director and writer, and originator of the project, is Guy Brenton of the BBC. Together with cinematographer Walter Lassally at the start of his brilliant career, the three men constituted the entire film crew. Ironically, in view of the subject matter, there was no live sound recording; in fact the primitive quality of the filmmaking strengthens the film's emotional power. Shot in June 1953, *Thursday's Children* provided Anderson with his first opportunity to work in 35mm, and, inadvertently, it led to his being permitted to join the British film union and thus continue and expand his career. The charm and easy grace of the children in *Thursday's Children* obviously leads to a comparison with Anderson's *If...* (1968), set in a British public school. While the teenage boys in the latter may "speak" just as poignantly, if more violently, to the audience, the children here, laughing and clowning for the camera, are no anarchists, but are shown as eager to learn and join a society that is to them silent. The sensitivity of the film and the audience reaction to it (which overcomes the heavy emphasis on a rather unfortunately titled children's story) is at odds with Anderson's perception as a cold and distant filmmaker. If anything, *Thursday's Children* has closer ties to the director's last and heavily sentimental effort, *The Whales of August*. The influence is obviously that of the great British documentarian Humphrey Jennings, and Richard Burton's narration is, at times, reminiscent of the former's 1945 production of *A Diary for Timothy*. (Just as in recent years, a documentary was produced featuring the child in *A Diary for Timothy* and the world since he came into it, so one wishes there might be an update on the "stars" of *Thursday's Children*, on Robert and Rosemary, and on John "who does not know what a word is.") Humphrey Jennings relied on the poetry of images, and similarly Anderson finds elegiac qualities in his children and the obvious dedication of the two teachers, Miss Taylor and Miss Massey, pictured in the film. Only in retrospect does one realize the underlying cruelty of a system that separates children from their parents, treats them as little more than orphans, and relies on a teacher to "translate" a letter from home. Look at the faces of the children who, unlike Dennis, have not received a letter. As a result of winning the Oscar, *Thursday's Children* received a limited theatrical release in the U.K., playing the Granada Theatre circuit, accompanying Republic's Susan Hayward vehicle, *Untamed*. In *Films and Filming* (December 1954), Peter Brinson described it as "simple and unpretentious in style," while Anderson's friend and biographer Gavin Lambert wrote in *Sight and Sound* (Summer 1955) of its "unusual purity of emotional response." *Thursday's Children* is deserving of acknowledgment as Lindsay Anderson's best documentary production, alongside *Every Day except Christmas* (1957), and as his only recognition by the Academy of Motion Picture Arts and Sciences.

[20 Minutes. New York opening on December 17, 1954, paired with Jour de Fete *at the Normandie Theatre. Winner of Best Documentary Short Subject of 1954.*]

Elisabeth Welch

Films in Review, October 1987, pages 480-483

As any New Yorker who has seen *Jerome Kern Goes to Hollywood* [11] can testify, its star, Elisabeth Welch, remains one of the great Black singers of the 20th Century, a chanteuse with an easy and relaxed style. So deceptively simple is that style, so professional her presentation, that one is inclined to forget how great an entertainer she is. Her enunciation is so crisp and clear, so very English, that one finds it hard to believe she is a native New Yorker. She is so carefully and elegantly attired, her hairstyle boyishly youthful, that one forgets one is in the presence of a singer approaching her 65th year in show business. So much a part of the stage and of sophisticated nightclub life does she appear, that few recall Elisabeth Welch's career also embraces motion pictures.

Elisabeth Welch was born in New York on February 27, 1904. She intended to become a social worker, and recalls, "I belonged to the Episcopalian Church and we had what is called a settlement, where I taught children raffia work and embroidery during the school holidays." She had always sung and was a member of the Sunday School Choir.

On October 29, 1923, the [Flournoy] Miller and [Aubrey] Lyles musical, *Runnin' Wild,* opened at New York's Colonial Theatre, and in the cast was Elisabeth Welch, in the role of Ruth Little. As she remembers, the show contained one historical moment: "I was always called a loud alto and they picked my voice to sing 'Charleston.' I couldn't dance — still can't. It's a terrible song and the verse is terrible. I came on and sang it, and then the girls came on and danced away." Elisabeth Welch recreated that moment in the 1980 show *Black Broadway,* which also featured Adelaide Hall, who had been in the original production of *Runnin' Wild.*

---

11. Opened at the Ritz Theatre on January 23, 1986.

Strangely, *Runnin' Wild* means little to Elisabeth Welch and she always claims that her first legitimate stage appearance was in the revue, *Blackbirds of 1928*. From there, she went into nightclubs, with appearances at two major Parisian nightspots, Le Boeuf sur le Toit and Chez Florence (replacing Mabel Mercer). Returning to New York, Elisabeth Welch was persuaded by Peggy Hopkins Joyce to perform Cole Porter's "Love for Sale" as part of her nightclub act. (At that time, it was permissible to perform show songs prior to the opening of the show, and so Elisabeth Welch was the first to sing "Love for Sale" before it was officially heard, sung by Kathryn Crawford in *The New Yorkers*.)

As Elisabeth Welch says, the song was "beautiful poetry for me, because it was like one of the street cries of London. It is a street cry. Kathryn Crawford was pink and white and blonde and totally unsuited for such a number."

After her introduction of "Love for Sale," Elisabeth Welch recalls,

"About ten days later, three gentlemen came into the club and the manager said, 'Elisabeth, will you sing "Love for Sale" for those gentlemen over there? Later, I found they were Ray Goetz, who was the producer of *The New Yorkers*, Monty Woolley, who was directing it, and Irving Berlin, who was a great friend of Cole Porter's. They heard me sing it, and then there was a little tete-a-tete, and finally, two or three days later, my manager called me up and said, 'They want you to go into *The New Yorkers*.' It's very amusing, because one of the three said, 'But she's colored,' and it was Berlin who said, 'You're in charge of the show, and if you want the girl then you make it right for her.' Three days later, the manager said, 'They're still in conference as to how they can get you in that spot.' The most amusing thing was it was a street scene at night, and instead of Park Avenue and a canopy which said some swank name of a club, all they did was change the canopy to the Cotton Club and made Park Avenue into Lenox Avenue, which they could have done in ten minutes."

Cole Porter and Elisabeth Welch did not meet until 1932 in Paris, where the composer had the singer come to his apartment and perform "Love for Sale:" "He played the piano, which was terrible, because he was not what you call an accompanist." Next year, the composer wrote the song "Solomon" for Elisabeth Welch to introduce in the Gertrude Lawrence vehicle *Nymph Errant*. By this time, Elisabeth Welch had settled in London, where she introduced "Stormy Weather" in the revue, *Dark Doings* at the Leicester Square Theatre.

Since 1933, Elisabeth Welch has made London her home, although she retains her American citizenship. "My mother was Scottish," she notes, "and I say what is the point of my taking out British citizenship? I'm half British anyhow. I regard myself as American, but I'm English in thought and interest." Elisabeth Welch is also very English in accent these days. She has the regality of Queen Elizabeth, the Queen Mother, mixed with the simple philosophy of Ethel Waters. Missing is the vulgarity of Josephine Baker or the ethnic aggression of Lena Horne.

In England, Elisabeth Welch has appeared in vaudeville, and been seen in shows such as *Let's Raise the Curtain* (1936), *No Time for Comedy* (1941), *Happy and Glorious* (1944), *Tuppence Coloured* (1947), *Penny Plain* (1951), *The Crooked Mile* (1959), *Cindy Ella or I Got a Shoe* (1962), and *Pippin* (1963). Ivor Novello wrote two songs for her in *Glamorous Night* (1935), and she has great admiration for the composer: "Ivor Novello was a great romantic. I don't think he would be accepted particularly now, because of what some people would call his schmaltz. But I don't say schmaltz. I call it romance. He was in love with love." Novello took Elisabeth to her first opera: "I head Grace Moore of all people doing Mimi, and she was dreadful."

Elisabeth Welch's early stage career was unusual in that her performances were limited to one or two songs in cameo roles, but those songs and those roles were ones to which the public responded and which audiences remembered. Her film career was very similar in that she generally appeared in British films as a nightclub singer, performed one song, and that was that. Her film career began with a 1934 melodrama titled *Death at Broadcasting House*, in which Elisabeth appeared as herself singing "Lazy Lady." Her only comment is, "I always say they should have left all the other words out and just called it *Death!*"

Death at Broadcasting House was followed by Elisabeth Welch's two most important films, *Song of Freedom* (1936) and *Big Fella* (1937), in both of which she is leading lady to Paul Robeson. She replaced Robeson's first lady lady in his British films, Nina Mae McKinney: "She didn't like me at all," remembers Elisabeth. "She hated me. C.B. Cochran [the great British theatrical impresario] was the one who told me about her. He called me to his office when I finally got to London and I think he wanted to 'case' me, because he thought he was getting another demon like Nina Mae McKinney. She turned out to be a swine. As a lot of people do, she thought that being a star, you must be temperamental, you must be nasty. Cochran said he gave her money to bury her father at least four times and her mother twice."

In *Song of Freedom*, Elisabeth Welch was perhaps as *Variety* (September 9, 1936) commented, "a little too refined for a dock laborer's mate."

However, the film is one of Robeson's best, with three delightful songs, "Sleepy River," "Lonely Road" and "Stepping Stone," plus the title song. *Variety* (July 7, 1937) wrote that "Elisabeth Welch gives a sweet, womanly portrayal" in *Big Fella*, a lesser Robeson opus. Both films were directed by J. Elder Willis, a minor figure in British film history of whom Elisabeth Welch remembers nothing. "I'm afraid I didn't have the knowledge to be interested in him, nor was I interested. I just thought he was a known director. He was a charming man, and that's all I know. You see one knew of Cavalcanti, one knew he was a great director, one knew his worth. I didn't know anything about Willis, but I didn't query."

Despite Paul Robeson's later denunciation of both films, Elisabeth Welch states, "There were no lines he objected to in *Song of Freedom*. In later years he was very nasty about that film *Sanders of the River*. He said they had tricked him into that. I don't know how or why. That's his comment, but I have no evidence of it.

"He was a lovely man. We discussed politics naturally. But I'm not politically minded, although I follow. And I have my own theories. He said you've got to be a citizen of the world because of this [she points to the color of her skin]. I said, 'I've got so many bloods in me, I'm part of the world. I don't stand up for one or the other, only for what's right, for decency.' He wanted to convert me, but he was very gentle about it. I'll take anyone's arguments if they have a sense of humor with it. And, of course, he laughed so easily. We became great friends. I loved him and he always came to see me when I was playing."

There were no more "meaty" parts for Elisabeth Welch until *Fiddlers Three* in 1944, a vehicle for comedian Tommy Trinder, directed by Harry Watt, in which Trinder and Sonny Hale are transported back to ancient Rome after a thunderstorm breaks out while they are taking shelter under the altar stone of Stonehenge. The plot has similarities to *A Connecticut Yankee*, but is delightfully risqué thanks to performances by Francis L. Sullivan as Nero and Frances Day as Poppeia. Elisabeth Welch appears as slave girl Thora.

Fiddlers Three was an exception, and Elisabeth Welch's film career in the 1940s was otherwise limited to appearing as a nightclub singer in Brian Desmond Hurst's *Alibi* (1942) and the Cavalcanti-directed *Dead of Night* (1945). "There was a stupid song I sang in *Dead of Night*," she recalled. "I was supposed to be Bricktop, and it was supposed to be Bricktop's nightclub. You saw about three musicians. It was tatty."

I asked Elisabeth for some general comments on what was involved in those one-song appearances:

"They had the scene set. I would come out. I had gown fittings in town. The car would take me out, sometimes it would be in the morning, sometimes in the afternoon. I wandered around and met people. Of course in those days, Alexander Korda used to go through *Spotlight* [the British casting directory] and get the names of all the actors and actresses for crowd work. In a one-song film I never selected my own song. I don't think we lip-synched . You know I can't remember, but I think we did it live. I really do. I remember re-takes with Paul [Robeson] and I'm sure it was live."

The last decade or so [the 1970s and 1980s], Elisabeth Welch has been busy with her stage career, including a 1979 tribute to her at London's Royal Festival Hall. She was seen briefly and uncredited in *Revenge of the Pink Panther*; and in Derek Jarman's version of *The Tempest* (1979), she appears as a Goddess singing "Stormy Weather" during the wedding feast. Jarman heard her singing at the Royal Opera House, Covent Garden, in a benefit for the Friends of the Opera, and decided he must have her for his film. When told what she had to do, Elisabeth replied, "You're joking," but now she says, "It was a lot of fun. He's a good director and anyone with any sense wants that."

Through a world war and race riots, Elisabeth Welch has stuck with England, one of a small group of emigré Negro entertainers that has included Paul Robeson and Adelaide Hall (with whom she entertained the troops during World War Two). Skin color has never played a part in her life. "I've never thought of it," she maintains. "I was brought up in a mixed neighborhood, 63rd Street and Amsterdam Avenue, that was primarily Irish, secondly Italian, thirdly Negro, and then the mixes of all the European countries. I went to a mixed school, Julia Richman High. I never thought of race. I'm lucky. It never hit me."

[Elisabeth Welch died at the actors' retirement home, Denville Hall in Northwood, London, on July 15, 2003.]

Lawrence Welk

Emmy Magazine, September/October 1982, pages 40, 70

April 11, 1982, was a sad day in the history of television. The critics and intelligentsia showed few signs of mourning, but for millions of devoted American television viewers it was a particularly emotional day — on that date, the last original *Lawrence Welk Show* was aired. It was time to say farewell to accordionist Myron Floren, pianist Bob Ralston, dancers Bobby Burgess, Jack Imel and Arthur Duncan, and singers Tom Netherton, Joe Feeney, Anacani, Ava Barber, the Aldridge Twins, the Otwell Twins, and Guy and Ralna Hovis. Above all, it was farewell to Norma Zimmer, Welk's "Champagne Lady" since August 1961, a beautiful, ageless testimony to the benefits of Geritol and the *Lawrence Welk Show*.

The supporting cast might go on to other things, but there could be no new *Lawrence Welk Show* without the boss. He might have been little more than a figurehead in the show's last years, doing nothing more than reading introductions from cue cards, but he was the one who held the various components of the show together, the man with whom the audience had grown up. Back in the late 1940s, it was Lawrence Welk's band to whose music young people had danced at Santa Monica's Aragon Ballroom and elsewhere. Those same teenagers had grown old with Welk, and to them he was the center of stability in a world of changing musical tastes. Welk had always asserted that "an entertainer's obligation is to his audience," and his audience has always respected him for that.

Lawrence Welk seems to have always been a part of American television. He was first seen on a local Los Angeles show in 1951; in 1955, he moved over to ABC network television as a summer replacement, ended up staying, and quickly became one of the network's most popular stars. His program easily beat out such competition as Herb Shriner, Jimmy Durante, Robert Montgomery, and Sid Caeser; in 1965, the show received a higher rating than a competing program guest-starring the Beatles. Welk's was one of the first ABC programs to be broadcast in color.

At a taping I attended last year of a *Lawrence Welk Show*, it was obvious that not only was Mr. Welk, as he is referred to by the longtime members of his company, having fun, but so were his orchestra and his performers. During much of the show, the boss was wandering through the audience [which that night included composer Meredith Willson] and chatting with them, while his staff was making frantic efforts to get him back in front of the camera for his next introduction. There was no sign of the oft-mentioned Welk nervousness. One was conscious only of a tireless and energetic performer anxious that everyone had a good time.

The show did, unfortunately, have its share of troubles over the years. In 1959, Welk fired his original champagne lady, Alice Lon, because she displayed (at least as far as Welk was concerned) too much of her shapely legs on air. That firing and the resultant bad publicity it caused for Welk is representative of the problems he encountered when other members of his musical family left the show (notably the Lennon Sisters in 1968 and Cissy King in 1978), often under unexplained circumstances. Critics claimed that Welk was at fault in letting such personalities go, but audiences seemed to remain faithful to Welk alone, not to individual members of his musical family — no member of the company has ever been quite as popular as they were when working under his guidance.

When ABC cancelled the *Lawrence Welk Show* in September 1971, it was not necessarily because his audience had decreased, but because it was considered "too old" by network standards. Watching the *Lawrence Welk Show* on television, one is aware that his sponsors' products are for a certain age group — those who wore false teeth, took medicinal aids such as Geritol, or used skin creams such as Oil of Olay; the show did not sell youth-oriented products, the backbone of television advertising. Though Welk did have an audience that could woo sponsors, the networks did not have the savvy, or perhaps the time, to pursue that audience.

The reason for Welk's success is simple: his motto has always been to play the type of music his audience can understand. He takes little, if any, notice of what his critics have to say. Welk's show never won an Emmy or any other major television award, but he claims not to have been concerned about such matters. "I have tried to dedicate myself to pleasing the public that comes to see me," Welk asserts. "That has been my cup of tea. The main thing you have to do is show the folks a good time."

The headquarters of Lawrence Welk's musical empire is located in a sparklingly modern, all-white office building overlooking the Pacific

Ocean in Santa Monica. In the park across the street from Welk's office, elderly residents of Santa Monica are lawn bowling. Half a block away, more senior citizens wander in and out of a high-rise apartment building that is owned by Welk and called, appropriately enough, Champagne Towers. The area is a perfect setting for Welk.

When he greets visitors, Welk's enthusiasm is equal to that he displayed during the taping of his shows. In his large office (singularly devoid of any sign of paperwork), he plays recordings of Dixieland jazz for me. It is his favorite style of music, but one which he is unwilling to force on a television audience that he feels will not share his interest. (Welk also insists that I listen to some popular German-style dance music and has his publicist, Bernice McGeehan, join him in a dance around the office so that I may see "how Germans dance.") Both Welk and his offices seem quiet and subdued until music begins to play; indeed, Welk will hold a record in his hands throughout our conversation.

Born on March 11, 1903, in Strasburg, North Dakota; Lawrence Welk was the son of German immigrants from Alsace Lorraine. His father taught him to play the accordion, and although he was unable to read music, Welk used the medium as an escape from farm labor. By 1927, he had his own six-piece band, Lawrence Welk's Hotsy Totsy Boys.

By the late 1930s, Lawrence Welk was leading a larger orchestra and playing in major Chicago hotels and theaters. In 1939, while performing at the Chicago Theatre, he added the bubble machine that was to become so closely associated with his television shows. It was around that same time that he began referring to his style of playing as "champagne music." Welk became a fixture at the Aragon Ballroom in 1950 and played there through 1961, when he moved over to the Hollywood Palladium, where for many years he taped his shows. The Lawrence Welk Orchestra gave its last live performance with its leader at the Concord (California) Pavilion on June 13, 1982.

Welk once said that "Music changes but I don't." Yet in reality, Welk's musical style as seen on his television show did change drastically through the years.

George Cates has been associated with Lawrence Welk for thirty-two years, since March 1951; at that time, Cates was head of Coral Records, for whom Welk and his orchestra recorded many best-selling albums. Cates, who later became the show's musical director, recalls the economics and the reasoning behind the changes in Welk's style: "When Lawrence came out to California he had what was literally known as a small band. When the television show started progressing, he came to me and said there was so much money coming in he'd like to add strings, so we added three violins. Then we added a trombone section. Instead of taking the earnings that were coming in and just wasting them, he built up an organization. We added more vocalists, and became more of a show than a dance band. Then we started to get comments that we should have more band music, [that] we couldn't play champagne music because it all sounds alike."

Although Welk himself feels that giving the public music to dance to has been crucial to his success, in recent years he has allowed George Cates to emphasize concert numbers more and recreate the big band sound associated with the Dorseys and with Glenn Miller — a sound that is unsuited to the style of dancing that Welk and much of his audience understand.

The demise of the *Lawrence Welk Show* on network television has brought a bonus not only for Welk fans but also for all interested in the history of television. Through MCA, the Welk Organization is syndicating *Memories with Lawrence Welk*, sixty-minute programs culled from the many hundreds of Welk shows of the past which were taped in color. All have new introductions and commentaries by Welk himself, recorded at the Lawrence Welk Village, a vacation complex in Escondido. This new series gives younger fans an opportunity to become acquainted with some of the earlier members of the Welk musical family, notably "da lovely Lemmon Sisters" (regulars on the show from 1955 through 1968), ragtime pianist Jo Ann Castle, country singer Lynn Anderson, violinist Aladdin, and band vocalist Larry Dean. (Because the new series seems limited to those shows that were televised in color, we will be denied a look at the original Champagne Lady, Alice Lon.)[12]

Lawrence Welk was, and is, the most popular musician in American television history. "All my life I have enjoyed what I was doing," says Welk, "but still I knew this would have to stop someplace if I didn't want to play when I was an old man. I've always felt a little sad when the dance was over."

Lawrence Welk started his television musical tempo back in 1951, and some thirty years later it is still unmatched. May we continue to enjoy the music and these memories of Lawrence Welk for many years to come.

[Lawrence Welk died in Santa Monica, California, on May 17, 1992.]

12. Since this article was originally published, black-and-white episodes have been aired, including those with Alice Lon.

Betty White: Life after Sixty

Emmy Magazine, September/October, 1985, pages 69-70

Betty white is very defensive of television. "I'm a television child; I grew up in television, and I just like the medium," she says, "I can throw the same rocks that you can throw at it, but it's a field that I know and that I'm comfortable in. I might throw rocks at people's taste, but now, more and more every day, it's your problem if you're watching lousy television."

She has been a part of television since 1949, after moving over from radio to join KLAC-Los Angeles (now KCOP) as an assistant to disc jockey Al Jarvis. Yes, there were once disc jockeys on television, and in time, Betty White became one herself, replacing Al Jarvis. According to television commentator Jack Lait, Jr., "She was pretty terrible. She had an irritating habit of blinking her eyes at the camera, a sure sign of nervousness and self-consciousness." Betty persevered, however, with help from station manager Don Fedderson, she learned through experience and hard work. By 1954, Lait was hailing White as "a girl with ease and assurance, with poise and personality, a girl who knew what she was doing and knew how to do it."

Life with Elizabeth was the show that brought White to national attention. First seen live in 1952, the show ultimately consisted of sixty-five episodes filmed for syndication from 1953-1955. Produced by Don Fedderson and written by George Tibbles, the series was unique in its day for presenting in each show three unrelated episodes in the life of Elizabeth, her husband Alvin (played by Del Moore), and their St. Bernard (played by Betty's own dog, Stormy). Usually set in the couple's living room, *Life with Elizabeth* had a natural spontaneity to it, and the viewer was given the feeling that he was very much a part of the show as each episode ending with announcer Jack Narz asking, "Elizabeth, aren't you ashamed of yourself" and White vehemently shaking her head.

Jack Narz's brother, Tom Kennedy, was the announcer for White's next series, *Date with the Angels* (ABC, 1957-1958), in which she portrayed newlywed Vicki Angel, a character of gentle humor, reminiscent of an intelligent Gracie Allen. In addition to her situation comedies, Betty White was a regular on *The Jack Paar Show* (as *The Tonight Show* was called from 1957-1962). For twenty years she hosted the Tournament of Roses Parade, and there were regular appearances on endless game shows, from *Make the Connection* in 1955 through the syndicated *Liar's Club* and *Match Game P.M.*

There is probably no-one in Los Angeles television that Betty White does not know. As she re-watches an episode of *Life with Elizabeth*, she spots friends from the past, identifies minor character actors, even gives credit to the harpist on the show, Helen Hutchinson. At the same time, she does not long for a return to live television. She thinks tape is better than film, particularly as far as comedy is concerned. "Those were the good old days," she says, "but these are even better."

To most television viewers, Betty White is Sue Ann Nivens, a character she played on *The Mary Tyler Moore Show* from 1973-1977, and for which she won two Emmys. As the cookery expert star of fictitious station WJM's *Happy Homemaker Show*, Sue Ann Nivens dispensed malice with a silver tongue while on the trail of suitable men to share her bed. "I think Sue Ann lived to offend," says White, "That was her second hobby — I know what her first was."

That role on *The Mary Tyler Moore Show* came dangerously close to typecasting White. CBS followed the show with the short-lived (1977-1978) series *The Betty White Show* — also the title of a 1958 ABC variety show — which left the viewer with the erroneous impression that White was capable of portraying only losers with a malicious sense of humor. For Sue Ann Nivens was, to a certain extent a loser, a woman with a past but not much of a future, and Joyce Whitman, the character on the later show, also faced an uncertain future as an actress in decline, who was eager for success as the star of a television series.

However, there is another and in some respects more important link between the two characters. They were both women on the wrong side of middle age. *The Mary Tyler Moore Show* recognized the age factor in Sue Ann Nivens' life and deserves credit for presenting in the character a woman who was still capable of living life to its fullest, building a successful career for herself and enjoying an active sex life.

The Betty White Show failed to consider adequately that side of its leading lady's character. It was trying too hard to parody television. Betty White's new television series, scheduled to air this fall on NBC, returns to the positive premise of the Sue Ann Nivens character — without the malice. *The Golden Girls* is a study of four independent women — played by Betty White, Bea Arthur, Rue McClanahan, and Estelle Getty — who are spending their "golden years" in Miami. According to White, the show "sets out to prove, once and for all, that one does not self-destruct at sixty and that a viable later life is not only possible but fairly certain."

White was given her choice of portraying either Blanche or Rose. She chose the latter, with Rue McClanahan taking the part of Blanche, a widowed Southern Lady with a strong interest in men. "I play a complete opposite of Sue Ann — rather naïve," says White. "I'm a grief counsellor. I'm completely literal, I take every word for its full meaning. I am not dinky, just a little out to lunch, but ladylike about it. Blanche would have come out really like Sue Ann if I played it, but not if Rue plays it. Rue says she's playing Betty, and I'm playing her, all the parts she's always done and all the parts I've always done."

The Golden Girls is one of the first television series to recognize that television audiences are getting older. Those folks who went out every Saturday night in the 1950s are now staying at home. They expect network shows with a higher degree of quality, and one hopes that *The Golden Girls* will answer that need.

The series is also important for Betty White as she comes to the midway stage of her fourth decade in television and enters her early sixties. She may have won a 1983 Emmy for her work as hostess of the daytime game show *Just Men!* but she is far more than just a television personality who can talk. As she herself comments, she is not a comedienne, but an actress with a sense of comedy.

White is proud of television, and she has given her best to it, rejecting all offers of films — she made only one some thirty-five years ago — and Broadway shows. At the same time, television has been good to her and she knows it. She has become such a major personality that she can use television as a forum in which to speak of those things that concern her deeply, particularly animals. She is president of the Morris Animal Fund, a member of the board of directors of the Los Angeles Zoo, and she produced the syndicated show, *The Pet Set*, in the early 1970s.

As I watch Betty White rolling around on the kitchen floor playing with my 100-pound Labrador retriever, I am reminded yet again that the perfectly composed and attired Sue Ann Nivens is a far cry from Betty White. There is life after sixty.

*[*The Golden Girls, *created by Susan Harris, ran on NBC from 1985 through 1992. Betty White has been nominated for many Emmys, and won in 1976* (The Mary Tyler Moore Show), *1986* (The Golden Girls), *1996* (The John Larroquette Show), *and 2010* (Saturday Night Live). *She also received a Lifetime Achievement Award in 2015.]*

Norman Lloyd

I have known Norman Lloyd since late 1977. My partner, Robert Gitt and I had the good fortune to become friendly with Jean Renoir and his adorable wife, Dido, and most Sunday afternoons, we would drive up to the Renoir home on Leona Drive in Beverly Hills and screen films for Jean. Norman and his wife, Peggy, would generally stop by on their way home from the Sunday afternoon members' screenings at the Academy of Motion Picture Arts and Sciences, and the afternoon visit to the Renoirs would end with a glass of wine, often a slice of ice cream cake (provided by a neighbor who was always identified as the Countess), and amusing dialogue from Norman.

[Norman Lloyd should need no introduction. He is a legendary actor, director and producer, involved in film, theatre, radio, and television, who has worked with such equally legendary directors as Orson Welles, Alfred Hitchcock, Jean Renoir, and Charlie Chaplin. Born in New York in November 1914, he first came to prominence in the theatre, working with Orson Welles' Mercury Theatre as Cinna the Poet in the 1937 production of Shakespeare's *Julius Caesar*. He gained far wider fame with his villainous performance in Hitchcock's *Saboteur* in 1941. More recently, he was featured in Judd Apatow's film, *Trainwreck*, in 2015. Along the way, Norman has been seen in films such as *The Southerner*, *Spellbound*, *Limelight*, and *Dead Poet's Society*, as well as such television series as *Alfred Hitchcock Presents* (as actor and director) and *St. Elsewhere*.]

It has never been my intention to write about Norman, because, quite frankly, I feel too close to him and to Peggy. However, through the years, I have kept notes on our meetings, and I thought this might be an ideal opportunity to share his comments on various film personalities he has known and also on other subjects. Whatever else one might say about Norman, he always had a way with words:

Boudu Saved from Drowning — "It was not based on a play but on Renoir's dog, Jerry, a mongrel which looked like a terrier. Each day in Paris, Jean would see the dog come home as he worked in his study. One day at four o'clock, it did not return, and a worried Jean found it at the pound, where the people told him the dog was picked up sitting on the trolley tracks. He took the dog home, but the dog failed to return a second day, and was found at the pound, having been picked up on the trolley tracks. The same thing happened a third day. Jean could not understand the dog's behavior until he learned that next door to the pound was the slaughterhouse where the workers, feeling sorry for the dogs in the pound — many of whom had only a short time to live — were feeding them choice pieces of meat, liver, kidney etc. Jerry had never eaten so well in his life, and so each day he returned to the trolley tracks to be picked up, taken to the pound, and fed."

Nigel Bruce — "I sought his advice when I first wanted to be an actor. Never could understand what he was saying because of his accent."

Charlie Chaplin — "A unique combination of an astute businessman and a mad creative genius, the problem being you had to know which one you were dealing with at any particular time…You must remember Charlie was *sui generis*, if I may quote the Latin [in a class by himself], Charlie is beholden to nobody,"

"Michael Chaplin came up to his father, dragging an expensive sweater on the ground, and Chaplin verbally lashed into him about its worth and the poverty he had lived through as a child. It destroyed the boy."

George Coulouris — "Extremely outgoing, lacking in shyness, and always eager to go on stage."

Gary Cooper — "The most beautiful thing I've seen on a horse."

Samantha Eggar — "An unrecognized talent."[13]

Hans Eisler — "He would constantly drink sherry and eat salami. Once he collapsed, and, asked if he was OK, responded, "I feel as if forty frogs are copulating on my tongue."

Frances Farmer — "She was a beautiful lady. We all lived together, the Group Theatre, that summer on Long Island. We played baseball. She was a tomboy. Sandy Meisner and I played the male leads in *Quiet City*, and she played the female lead, but because of the makeup of the play we had no scenes together."

W.C. Fields — "He would rant at Paramount about the fucking Jews who ran the studio. Told it was not only anti-Semitic, but also wrong in

---

13. At our house, Norman once asked Samantha if she had ever appeared on Broadway. She responded, "No, but I have starred at the Old Vic.

that Y. Frank Freeman was Catholic, Fields responded, 'Catholics, they're the worst type of Jews.'"

Greta Garbo — "She had the most perfect face for movies."

Samuel Goldwyn — "At a birthday party for Sam Goldwyn, Jr., there was silence as he blew out the candles on his cake and made a wish, and Sam Goldwyn, Sr. was heard to remark, 'He should wish for a good story.'"

Great films — "They don't make great films anymore. That's why I'm not working."

Lawrence Harvey — "Everyone of a certain generation had two minutes of sex with Lawrence Harvey."

Henry Hathaway– "Crazy — half-mad — but a real nice guy."[14]

Bernard Herrmann — "He was directing a score for a John Houseman production. Suddenly he stopped the music, turned to Houseman, and said, 'Jack, I warned you — there is a fascist element in the woodwind section.'"

John Houseman — "He stayed with us, and slept only in his pajama top. In the morning he goes down the driveway to pick up the newspaper, bending over only in his pajama top. You could drive a truck through the crack."

Van Johnson — "I cannot imagine wanting to see Van Johnson in anything."

Jury Duty — "The age scared them a little bit. It scares me too."

Jack Larson Announcing His Return to Acting — "It is the greatest setback for the acing profession since the death of Larry Olivier." [The next day, Jack Larson told me, "Norman is madly jealous because he doesn't have any work."]

Charles Laughton — (In *Galileo* he took off his shirt on stage to wash) "He had the most beautiful of breasts, more beautiful than any woman."

"Elsa Lanchester was not good for Charles Laughton. She frightened him politically by warning him of the danger of working with Brecht in *Galileo*."

"Charles Laughton always believed that actors should act with their balls — clank, clank, clank across the stage. Hence Shelley Winters' performance in *The Night of the Hunter*."

Robert Lewis (founder of the Actors Studio) — "Had a face like a skinned testicle."

Ida Lupino — "My only involvement with a woman director was when I hired Ida Lupino to direct Claire Trevor in one of the Alfred Hitchcock television programs. I asked Trevor how she was getting on with Lupino,

---

14. Hathaway directed Norman in the Tyrone Power Western, *Rawhide* (1951).

and she replied, 'This is the first time I've had a director who spent more time with the hairdresser than I do.'"

Method Acting — "When an actor cannot remember his lines, he becomes a method actor."

Naturalism — "An actress forgets her lines and thus is naturalism born."

Marshall Neilan — "The last time I saw Marshall Neilan, he was walking up Cahuenga Boulevard, carrying his laundry."

Harold Pinter — "After reading a script by Harold Pinter, Alfred Hitchcock said, 'I don't do this sort of thing.'"

Jean Renoir — "He ran all his films for us one year, talking of how determined he was that his films be far removed from his father's work. But he realized, after seeing them, that they were all influenced by his father's art."

Ralph Richardson — "While in town, he meets Joan Fontaine and Olivia de Havilland, and describes each as 'a terrible actress.' Then he asks, 'Is it hereditary?'"

Sex — "Sex is polo for the poor."

The Southerner — "There was a little dog supposed to chase a cow, but every time it saw the cow it ran away. Eventually, Jean [Renoir] picked it up, yelled 'Act, you idiot,' and threw it at the cow. It still ran away!"

Stage Presence — "Chaplin said that the two men with the greatest stage presence were Al Jolson in the U.S. and Herbert Beerbohm Tree in England."

Gloria Swanson — "Gloria Swanson visited Noel Coward after having rejuvenating goat gland injections. Coward was asked by a friend how she looked, and replied, 'a very old twelve.'"

The Third Man — "That's the way to make a picture — each scene plays itself out and carries weight. Back then, there were mature actors in films. Now, there are just juveniles."

Orson Welles — "The fact is that Orson and I had a very, I would say, tense relationship. That was because both our egos were impossible. I would eye Orson and he would get it. A very sensitive guy. And he knew I wasn't buying him 100%. But he did some great things. You know the best thing I ever saw Orson do as an actor was when he did the fat man, Falstaff, at the end. He was left alone on stage and sort of crying out for help. Everything was falling apart for him. And he did that scene with such emotion and fervor that I'd never seen him do in anything before… But don't get me wrong. He was the greatest theatre director we ever had. But he was a pain in the ass. As I suppose all great men are."

And, in conclusion, a quote from Peggy Lloyd: "It's fun to be old and gaga. You don't have to worry about all this shit, like remembering people's names."

[Robert Gitt and I visited Norman for the last time on the morning of Thursday, May 6, 2021. He had aged a lot since our previous visit, looked weak and was unwilling or unable to speak. He fell asleep soon after our arrival. He died a few days later on Tuesday, May 11th, 2020.]

Anthony Slide Bibliography

Michael Balcon — Producer, pamphlet (British Film Institute/John Player Lecture Series, 1969)

Lillian Gish — Actress, pamphlet (British Film Institute/John Player Lecture Series, 1969)

Early American Cinema (Tantivy Press/A.S. Barnes, 1970)

The Griffith Actresses (A.S. Barnes, 1973)

The Films of D.W. Griffith, with Edward Wagenknecht (Crown, 1975)

The Idols of Silence (A.S. Barnes, 1976)

The Big V: A History of the Vitagraph Company (Scarecrow Press, 1976/ revised edition, 1987)

Early Women Directors (A.S. Barnes, 1977/Reprinted in 1984 by Da Capo with new introduction/German language edition published 1982)

Aspects of American Film History prior to 1920 (Scarecrow Press, 1978)

Films on Film History (Scarecrow Press, 1979)

The Kindergarten of the Movies: A History of the Fine Arts Company (Scarecrow Press, 1980)

Fifty Great American Silent Films: 1912-1920, with Edward Wagenknecht (Dover, 1980)

The Vaudevillians (Arlington House, 1981)

Great Radio Personalities in Historic Photographs (Dover, 1982/revised edition, Vestal Press, 1988)

Selected Film Criticism: 1896-1911, editor (Scarecrow Press, 1982)

Selected Film Criticism: 1912-1920, editor (Scarecrow Press, 1982)

Selected Film Criticism: 1921-1930, editor (Scarecrow Press, 1982)

Selected Film Criticism: 1931-1940, editor (Scarecrow Press, 1982)

Selected Film Criticism: 1941-1950, editor (Scarecrow Press, 1982)

A Collector's Guide to Movie Memorabilia (Wallace-Homestead, 1983)

Selected Film Criticism: Foreign Films, 1930-1950, editor (Scarecrow Press, 1984)

Selected Film Criticism: 1951-1960, editor (Scarecrow Press, 1985)

Fifty Classic British Films: 1932-1980 (Dover, 1985)

International Film, Radio and Television Journals, editor (Greenwood Press, 1985)

The Best of Rob Wagner's Script, editor (Scarecrow Press, 1985)

Selected Theatre Criticism: 1900-1919, editor (Scarecrow Press, 1985)

Selected Theatre Criticism: 1921-1930, editor (Scarecrow Press, 1985)

A Collector's Guide to TV Memorabilia (Wallace-Homestead, 1985)

Filmfront: A Reprint Edition, editor (Scarecrow Press, 1986)

Selected Theatre Criticism: 1931-1950, editor (Scarecrow Press, 1986)

The Movie Posters of Batiste Madalena, co-editor (Harry Abrams, 1986)

The American Film Industry: A Historical Dictionary (Greenwood Press, 1986)

Great Pretenders: A History of Female and Male Impersonation in the Performing Arts (Wallace-Homestead, 1986)

The Memoirs of Alice Guy Blaché, editor (Scarecrow Press, 1986/revised and reprinted, Scarecrow Press, 1996)

Celebrity Articles from The Screen Guild Magazine, editor as Anna Kate Sterling (Scarecrow Press, 1987)

Cinematographers on the Art and Craft of Cinematography, editor as Anna Kate Sterling (Scarecrow Press, 1987)

The Best of Shadowland, editor as Anna Kate Sterling (Scarecrow Press, 1987)

Fifty Classic French Films: 1912-1982 (Dover, 1987)

Selected Radio and Television Criticism, editor (Scarecrow Press, 1987)

Selected Vaudeville Criticism, editor (Scarecrow Press, 1987)

100 Rare Books from the Margaret Herrick Library, pamphlet (Academy of Motion Picture Arts and Sciences, 1987)

The Cinema and Ireland (McFarland, 1988)

Sourcebook for the Performing Arts: A Directory of Collections, Resources, Scholars, and Critics in Theatre, Film and Television, co-editor (Greenwood Press, 1988)

The Picture Dancing on a Screen: Poetry of the Cinema, editor (Vestal Press, 1988)

The International Film Industry: A Historical Dictionary (Greenwood Press, 1989)

Highlights and Shadows: The Memoirs of a Hollywood Cameraman, Charles G. Clarke, editor (Scarecrow Press, 1989)

Silent Portraits (Vestal Press, 1990)

The Television Industry: A Historical Dictionary (Greenwood Press, 1991)

Nitrate Won't Wait: A History of Film Preservation in the United States (McFarland, 1992/paperback edition, 2000)

They Also Wrote for the Fan Magazines: Film Articles by Literary Giants from ee cummings to Eleanor Roosevelt (McFarland, 1992)

The Slide Area: Film Book Reviews, 1989-1991 (Scarecrow Press, 1992)

Before Video: A History of the Non-Theatrical Film (Greenwood Press, 1992)

Robert Goldstein and "The Spirit of '76" (Scarecrow Press, 1993)

Gay and Lesbian Themes and Characters in Mystery Novels (McFarland, 1993)

Encyclopedia of Vaudeville (Greenwood Press, 1994/revised edition, University Press of Mississippi, 2011)

The Hollywood Novel (McFarland, 1995)

Some Joe You Don't Know: An American Biographical Guide to British Television Personalities (Greenwood Press, 1996)

Lois Weber: The Director Who Lost Her Way in History (Greenwood Press, 1996)

The Silent Feminists: America's First Women Directors (Scarecrow Press, 1996/revised version of *Early Women Directors*)

Directing: Learn from the Masters by Tay Garnett, editor (Scarecrow Press, 1996)

DeToth on DeToth: Put the Drama in Front of the Camera (Faber and Faber, 1997)

Before, In and After Hollywood: The Autobiography of Joseph Henabery, editor (Scarecrow Press, 1997)

Ravished Armenia and the Story of Aurora Mardiganian (Scarecrow Press, 1997)

The New Historical Dictionary of the American Film Industry (Scarecrow Press, 1998/paperback edition, 2001)

On Acting and Actors: Essays by Alexander Knox, editor (Scarecrow Press, 1998)

Eccentrics of Comedy (Scarecrow Press, 1998)

Banned in the USA: British Films in the United States and Their Censorship, 1933-1960 (I.B. Tauris/St. Martin's Press, 1998)

Actors on Red Alert: Career Interviews with Five Actors and Actresses Affected by the Blacklist (Scarecrow Press, 1999)

Silent Players: A Biographical and Autobiographical Study of 100 Silent Film Actors and Actresses (Universiy Press of Kentucky, 2002)

Lost Gay Novels: A Reference Guide to Fifty Works from the First Half of the Twentieth Century (Haworth Press, 2003)

The Encyclopedia of British Film, associate editor (Methuen, 2003/later, revised reprints by Methuen and Manchester University Press)

American Racist: The Life and Films of Thomas Dixon (University Press of Kentucky, 2004)

Silent Topics: Essays on Undocumented Areas of Silent Film (Scarecrow Press, 2005)

New York City Vaudeville (Arcadia Publishing, 2006)

Now Playing: Hand-Painted Poster Art from the 1910s through the 1960s (Academy Imprints/Angel City Press, 2007)

Incorrect Entertainment, or Trash from the Past: A History of Political Incorrectness and Bad Taste in Twentieth Century American Popular Culture (BearManor Media, 2007)

Frank Lloyd: Master of Screen Melodrama (BearManor Media, 2009)

A Man Named Smith: The Novels and Screen Legacy of Thorne Smith (BearManor Media, 2010)

Inside the Hollywood Fan Magazine: A History of Star Makers, Fabricators, and Gossip Mongers (University Press of Mississippi, 2010)

D.W. Griffith: Interviews, editor (University Press of Mississippi, 2012)

Hollywood Unknowns: A History of Extras, Bit Players, and Stand-Ins (University Press of Mississippi, 2012)

Ravished Armenia and the Story of Aurora Mardiganian (University Press of Mississippi, 2013/Turkish Language Edition, 2017)

"It's the Pictures That Got Small": Charles Brackett on Billy Wilder and Hollywood's Golden Age (Columbia University Press, 2015)

She Could Be Chaplin: The Comedic Brilliance of Alice Howell (University Press of Mississippi, 2016)

Magnificent Obsession: The Outrageous History of Film Buffs, Collectors, Scholars, and Fanatics (University Press of Mississippi, 2018)

Wake Up at the Back There!: It's Jimmy Edwards (BearManor Media, 2018)

I Thank You: The Arthur Askey Story (BearManor Media, 2020)

Scarecrow Press "Filmmakers" Series, Edited by Anthony Slide

1. *James Whale* by James Curtis (1982)

2. *Cinema Stylists* by John Belton (1983)

3. *Harry Langdon* by William Schelly (1982)

4. *William A. Wellman* by Frank Thompson (1983)

5. *Stanley Donen* by Andrew Casper (1983)

6. *Brian De Palma* by Michael Bliss (1983)

7. *J. Stuart Blackton* by Marion Blackton Trimble (1985)

8. *Martin Scorsese and Michael Cimino* by Michael Bliss (1985)

9. *Franklin J. Schaffner* by Erwin Kim (1985)

10. *D.W. Griffith and the Biograph Company* by Cooper C. Graham, Steven Higgins, Elaine Mancini, and João Luiz Vieira (1985)

11. *Some Day We'll Laugh: An Autobiography* by Esther Ralston (1985)

12. *The Memoirs of Alice Guy Blaché*, translated by Roberta and Simone Blaché (1986); 2nd edition (1996)

13. *Leni Riefenstahl and "Olympia"* by Cooper C. Graham (1986)

14. *Robert Florey* by Brian Staves (1987)

15. *Henry King's America* by Walter Coppedge (1986)

16. *Aldous Huxley and Film* by Virginia M. Clark (1987)

17. *Five American Cinematographers* by Scott Eyman (1987)

18. *Cinematographers on the Art and Craft of Cinematography*, edited by Anna Kate Sterling (1987)

19. *Stars of the Silents* by Edward Wagenknecht (1987)

20. *Twentieth Century-Fox* by Aubrey Solomon (1988)

21. *Highlights and Shadows: The Memoirs of a Hollywood Cameraman* by Charles G. Clarke (1989)

22. *I Went That-a-Way: The Memoirs of a Western Film Director* by Harry L. Fraser, edited by Wheeler Winston Dixon and Audrey Brown Fraser (1990)

23. *Order in the Universe: The Films of John Carpenter* by Robert C. Cumbow (1990)

24. *The Films of Freddie Francis* by Wheeler Winston Dixon (1991)

25. *Hollywood Be Thy Name* by William Bakewell (1991)

26. *The Charm of Evil: The Life and Films of Terence Fisher* by Wheeler Winston Dixon (1991)

27. *Lionheart in Hollywood: The Autobiography of Henry Wilcoxon*, with Katherine Orrison (1991)

28. *William Desmond Taylor: A Dossier* by Bruce Long (1991)

29. *The Films of Leni Riefenstahl* by David B. Hinton (1991)

30. *Hollywood's Holyland: The Filming and Scoring of "The Greatest Story Ever Told"* by Ken Darby (1992)

31. *The Films of Reginald LeBorg: Interviews, Essays and Filmography* by Wheeler Winston Dixon (1992)

32. *Memoirs of a Professional Cad* by George Sanders, with Tony Thomas (1992)

33. *The Holocaust in French Film* by André Pierrre Colombat (1993)

34. *Robert Goldstein and "The Spirit of '76"* edited and compiled by Anthony Slide (1993)

35. *Those Were the Days My Friend: My Life in Hollywood with David O. Selznick and Others* by Paul Macnamara (1993)

36. *The Creative Producer* by David Lewis, edited by James Curtis (1993)

37. *Rejuvenating Reality: The Art and Life of Rouben Mamoulian* by Mark Spergel (1993)

38. *Malcolm St. Clair: His Films, 1915-1948* by Ruth Anne Dwyer (1997)

39. *Beyond Hollywood's Grasp: American Filmmakers Abroad, 1914-1945* by Harry Waldman (1994)

40. *A Steady Digression to a Fixed Point* by Rose Hobart (1994)

41. *Radical Juxtaposition: The Films of Yvonne Rainer* by Shelley Green (1994)

42. *Company of Heroes: My Life as an Actor in the John Ford Stock Company* by Harry Carey, Jr. (1994)

43. *Strangers in Hollywood: A History of Scandinavian Actors in American Films from 1910 to World War Two* by Hans J. Wollstein (1994)

44. *Charlie Chaplin: Intimate Close-Ups* by Georgia Hale, edited with an introduction and notes by Heather Kiernan (1995)

45. *The World Made Flesh: Catholicism and Conflict in the Films of Martin Scorsese* by Michael Bliss (1995)

46. *W.S. Van Dyke's Journal: "White Shadows in the South Seas" (1927-1928) and Other Van Dyke on Van Dyke*, edited and annotated by Rudy Behlmer (1996)

47. *Music from the House of Hammer: Music in the Hammer Horror Films, 1950-1980* by Randall D. Larson (1996)

48. *Directing: Learn from the Masters* by Tay Garnett (1996)

49. *Featured Player: An Oral Autobiography of Mae Clarke*, edited with an introduction by James Curtis (1996)

50. *A Great Lady: A Life of the Screenwriter Sonya Levien* by Larry Ceplair (1996)

51. *A History of Horrors: The Rise and Fall of the House of Hammer* by Denis Meikle (1996)

52. *The Films of Michael Powell and the Archers* by Scott Salwolke (1997)

53. *From Oz to E.T.: Wally Worsley's Half-Century in Hollywood — A Memoir in Collaboration with Sue Dwiggins Worsley*, edited by Charles Ziarko (1997)

54. *Thorold Dickinson and the British Cinema* by Jeffrey Richards (1997)

55. *The Films of Oliver Stone*, edited by Don Kunz (1997)

56. *Before, In and After Hollywood: The Autobiography of Joseph E. Henabery*, edited by Anthony Slide (1997)

57. *Ravished Armenia and the Story of Aurora Mardiganian*, compiled by Anthony Slide (1997)

58. *Smile When the Raindrops Fall* by Brian Anthony and Andy Edmonds (1998)

59. *Joseph H. Lewis: Overview, Interview and Filmography* by Francis M. Nevins (1998)

60. *September Song: An Intimate Biography of Walter Huston* by John Weld (1998)

61. *Wife of the Life of the Party* by Lita Grey Chaplin and Jeffrey Vance (1998)

62. *Down but Not Quite Out in Holly-Weird: A Documentary in Letters of Eric Knight* by Geoff Gehman, 1998

63. *On Actors and Acting: Essays by Alexander Knox*, edited by Anthony Slide (1998)

64. *Back Lot: Growing Up with the Movies* by Maurice Rapf (1999)

65. *Mr. Bernds Goes to Hollywood: My Early life and Career in Sound Recording at Columbia with Frank Capra and Others* by Edward Bernds (1999)

66. *Hugo Friedhofer: The Best Years of His Life: A Hollywood Master of Music for the Movies*, edited by Linda Danly (1999)

67. *Actors on Red Alert: Interviews with Five Actors and Actresses Affected by the Blacklist* by Anthony Slide (1999)

68. *My Only Great Passion: The Life and Films of Carl Th. Dreyer* by Jean Drum and Dale D. Drum (1999)

69. *Ready When You Are, Mr. Coppola, Mr. Spielberg, Mr. Crowe* by Jerry Ziesmer (1999)

70. *Order in the Universe: The Films of John Carpenter* 2nd edition by Robert C. Cumbow (2000)

71. *Making Music with Charlie Chaplin* by Eric James (2000)

72. *Open Window: The Cinema of Victor Erice*, edited by Linda C. Ehrlich (2000)

73. *Satyajit Ray: In Search of the Modern* by Suranjan Ganguly (2000)

74. *Voices from the Set: The "Film Heritage" Interviews*, edited by Tony Macklin and Nick Pici (2000)

75 *Paul Landres: A Director's Stories* by Francis M. Nevins (2000)

76 *No Film in My Camera* by Bill Gibson (2000)

77 *Saved from Oblivion: An Autobiography* by Bernard Vorhaus (2000)

78. *Wolf Man's Maker: A Memoir of a Hollywood Writer* by Curt Siodmak (2001)

79. *An Actor and a Rare One: Peter Cushing as Sherlock Holmes* by Tony Earnshaw (2001)

80. *Picture Perfect* by Herbert L. Strock (2000)

81. *Peter Greenaway's Postmodern/Poststructuralist Cinema*, edited by Paula Willoquet-Maricondi and Mary Alemany Galway (2001)

82. *Member of the Crew* by Winfrid Kay Thackrey (2001)

83. *Barefoot on Barbed Wire* by Jimmy Starr (2001)

84. *Henry Hathaway: A Director's Guild of America Oral History*, edited and annotated by Rudy Behlmer (2001)

85. *The Divine Comic: The Cinema of Roberto Benigni* by Carlo Celli (2001)

86. *With or Without a Song: A Memoir* by Edward Eliscu (2001)

87. *Stuart Erwin: The Invisible Actor* by Judy Cornes (2001)

88. *Some Cutting Remarks: Seventy Years a Film Editor* by Ralph E. Winters (2001)

89. *Confessions of a Hollywood Director* by Richard L. Bare (2001)

90. *Peckinpah's Women: A Reappraisal of the Portrayal of Women in the Period Westerns of Sam Peckinpah* by Bill Mesce, Jr. (2001)

91. *Budd Schulberg: A Bio-Bibliography* by Nicholas Beck (2001)

92. *Between the Bullets: The Spiritual Cinema of John Woo* by Michael Bliss (2002)

93. *The Hollywood I Knew, 1916-1988* by Herbert Coleman (2002)

94. *The Films of Stephen Spielberg*, edited by Charles L.P. Silet (2002)

95. *Hitchcock and the Making of "Marnie"* by Tony Lee Moral (2002)

96. *White Horse, Black Hat: A Quarter Century of Hollywood's Poverty Row* by C. Jack Lewis (2002)

97. *Worms in the Winecup* by John Bright (2002)

98. *Straight from the Horse's Mouth: An Autobiography* by Ronald Neame (2003)

99. *Reach for the Top: The Turbulent Life of Laurence Harvey* by Anna Sinai (2003)

100. *Jackie Coogan, The World's Boy King: A Biography of Hollywood's Legendary Child Star* by Diana Serra Cary (2003)

101. *Rungs on a Ladder: Hammer Films Seen through a Soft Gauze* by Christopher Neame (2003)

102. *The Classically American Comedy of Larry Gelbart* by Jay Malarchar (2003)

103. *Perpetually Cool: The Many Lives of Anna May Wong (1905-1961)* by Anthony B. Chan (2003)

104. *Irene Dunne: The First Lady of Hollywood* by Wes D. Gehring (2003)

105. *Scorsese Up Close: A Study of the Films* by Ben Nyce (2004)

106. *Hitchcock and Poe: The Legacy of Delight and Terror* by Dennis R. Perry (2003)

107. *Life Is Beautiful, But Not for Jews: Another View of the Film by Begnini* by Kobi Vincent Nive, translated by Jonathan Beyrack Lev (2003)

108. *Young Man in Movieland* by Jan Read (2004)

109. *A Cast of Shadows* by Ronnie Maasz (2004)

110. *Body and Soul: The Cinematic vision of Robert Aldrich* by Tony Williams (2004)

111. *Showdown at High Noon: Witch Hunts, Critics, and the End of the Western* by Jeremy Byman (2004)

112. *Take on British TV Drama: Stories from the Golden Years* by Christopher Neame (2004)

113. *George Arliss: The Man Who Played God* by Robert M. Fells (2004)

114. *And the Stars Spoke Back: A Dialogue Coach Remembers Hollywood Players of the Sixties in Paris* by Frawley Becker (2004)

115. *Hollywood in Wide Angle* by Jack Rothman (2004)

116. *William Beaudine: From Silents to Television* by Wendy L. Marshall (2005)

117. *Leo McCarey: From Marx to McCarthy* by Wes D. Gehring (2005)

118. *From "My Three Sons" to "Major Dad": My Life as a TV Producer* by John G. Stephens (2005)

119. *3-D Filmmakers: Conversations with Creators of Stereoscopic Motion Pictures* by Ray Zone (2005)

120. *Elisabeth Welch: Soft Lights and Sweet Music* by Stephen Bourne (2005)

121. *Designing for the Movies: The Memoirs of Laurence Irving* (2005)

122. *The Lion That Lost Its Way* by Sydney Box (2005)

123. *Principal Characters: Film Players out of Frame* by Christopher Neame (2005)

124. *Huston, We Have a Problem* by Oswald Morris with Geoffrey Bull (2006)

125. *Walter Mycroft: The Time of My Life* by Walter Mycroft, introduced, edited and annotated by Vincent Porter (2006)

126. *David Lynch: Beautiful Dark* by Greg Olson (2008)

Scarecrow Press "Studies and Documentation in the History of Popular Entertainment," Edited by Anthony Slide

1. *Stage Dust: A Critic's Cultural Scrapbook from the 1990s* by Charles Marowitz (2001)

2. *The Rise of the Crooners: Gene Austin, Russ Colombo, Bing Crosby, Nick Lucas, Johnny Marvin, and Rudy Vallee* by Michael Pitts and Frank Hoffmann (2002)

3. *Thelma Who?: Almost 100 Years of Showbiz* by Thelma White, with Harry Preston (2002)

4. *Lollipop: Vaudeville Turns with a Fanchon and Marco Dancer* by Reva Howitt Clar, edited by Mimi Melnick (2002)

5. *Words at War: World War II Era Radio Drama and the Postwar Broadcasting Industry Blacklist* by Howard Blue (2002)

6. *In Hollywood with Nemirovich-Danchenko, 1926-1927: The Memoirs of Sergei Bertensson*, translated by Anna Shoulgat, edited by Paul Fryer (2004)

7. *James Agee, Omnibus, and Mr. Lincoln* by William Hughes

Scarecrow Press "Studies in Film Genres," Edited by Anthony Slide

1. *Romance vs. Screwball Comedy: Charting the Difference* by Wes D. Gehring

2. *Screening Politics: The Politician in American Movies, 1931-2001* by Harry Keyishian (2003)

3. *People Like Ourselves: Portrayals of Mental Illness in the Movies* by Jacqueline Noll Zimmermann (2003)

Other Books Edited by Anthony Slide

The Ultimate Directory of the Silent Screen Performers by Billy H. Doyle (Scarecrow Press, 1995) — "Consulting Editor"

Charles Dickens on the Screen: The Film, Television and Video Adaptations by Michael Pointer (Scarecrow Press, 1996) — "Consulting Editor"

Hollywood and the Foreign Touch: A Dictionary of Foreign Filmmakers and Their Films from America, 1910-1995 by Harry Waldman (Scarecrow Press, 1996) — "Consulting Editor"

Marihuana, Motherhood & Madness: Three Screenplays from the Exploitation Cinema of Dwain Esper, edited by Bret Wood (Scarecrow Press, 1998) — "Consulting Editor"

Paramount in Paris: 300 Films Produced at the Joinville Studios, 1930-1933, with Credits and Biographies by Harry Waldman (Scarecrow Press, 1998) — "Consulting Editor"

The Blood Poets: A Cinema of Savagery 1958-1999 by Jake Horsley (Scarecrow Press, 1999, two volumes) — "Consulting Editor"

The Ultimate Directory of Film Technicians by Billy H. Doyle (Scarecrow Press, 1999) — "Consulting Editor"

The Ultimate Directory of Silent and Sound Performers by Billy H. Doyle (Scarecrow Press, 1999) — "Consulting Editor"

Bohemian Rogue: The Life of Hollywood Artist John Decker by Stephen C. Jordan (Scarecrow Press, 2005) — "Consulting Editor"

The Badger Kid by Arthur Gardner (Trafford Publishing, 2008) — "Literary Editor" (ghostwriter)

Index

The Abominable Snowman, 104-105
Aitken, Spottiswoode, 92
All Quiet on the Western Front, 142
Anderson, Lindsay, 170-171
Are You Being Served?, 148-150, 151
Askey, Arthur, 99
Atlantic, 168

Barrymore, Lionel, 28
The Beast with Five Fingers, 47-48
Becky Sharp, 15-21
Bedlam, 48
Behind the Door, 140
Bexhill-on-Sea, 165-166
Bioscope Shows, 116-118
Birth of the Movies, 78
The Black Cat, 35
Blackhawk Films, 72-73
The Body Snatchers, 48-49
Bondi, Beulah, 22-33
Breen, Joseph I., 17, 34-53
Bride of Frankenstein, 35-37
Bride of the Regiment, 156-157

Casino Royale, 106-108
The Cat and the Canary, 159-160
Cates, George, 179-180
Champion, 69
Chaplin, Charlie, 54-58, 137, 186
Columbo, Russ, 59-62
Compson, John R., 91
Cortez, Stanley, 85-86
The Countess from Hong Kong, 57
The Crime of Dr. Crespi, 37-38
Crisp, Donald, 94

The Day the Earth Caught Fire, 106, 108
Dead of Night, 49
Death at Broadcasting House, 174
The Devil Bat, 49
Dodd, Neal, 63-64
Donaldson, Geoffrey, 65-67
Donlan, Yolande, 96-97, 101-102, 107
Douglas, Kirk, 68-71
Dracula's Daughter, 38-39

Eastenders, 150-151
Eastin, Kent D., 72-73
Éclair Company, 165-166
Edgar, Mariott, 99
Expresso Bongo, 105-106

Fawcett, George, 94
Fiddler's Three, 175
Forde, Walter, 74-76
Four Sons, 141
Frankenstein Meets the Wolf Man, 49-50

Gaye, Howard, 95
Germany, 132-143
The Ghost of Frankenstein, 50
Gish, Lillian, 77-86
Giuseppina, 87-88
Golden Dawn, 155-156
The Golden Girls, 183
Graybill, Joseph, 91
Griffith, D.W., 89-95
Guest, Val, 96-108

Haggar, William, 109-110
Hambone and Hillie, 81, 86

Hay, Will, 98-99
Hearts of the World, 137-138
Hill, George, 83-84
Hill, James, 87-88
Hitchcock, Alfred, 99
Horton, Edward Everett, 120-122
Howerd, Frankie, 102, 149
Hull, 8, 111-118

I, Mrs. Bibb, 79
I Walked with a Zombie, 50
In America, 163
The Invisible Ray, 26, 39-40
Island of Lost Souls, 40-41
Isn't Life Wonderful, 139-140

Jigsaw, 105
Johnson, Arthur, 90-91
Jones, Robert Edmond, 16, 17
Julian, Rupert, 136

The Kaiser, the Beast of Berlin, 136
Kerrigan, J. Warren, 119-120
A King in New York, 56-57

Land without Music, 74-76
The Late Christopher Bean, 77-78
Laughton, Charles, 187
Lesser, Sol, 29-30
Life with Elizabeth, 181-182
Lloyd, Norman, 9, 185-188
London Town, 100
Lonely Are the Brave, 70
Long, Walter, 93

Mad Love, 41
Make Way for Tomorrow, 27-28
Mamoulian, Rouben, 15, 17-19, 21
Mark of the Vampire, 41-42
Marshman, D.M., Jr., 124-128
The Mary Tyler Moore Show, 182
The Mask of Dijon, 51
Miller, Walter, 90
A Mormon Maid, 129-131
Morning's at Seven, 80
Morton, William, 113-115
Murder at the Windmill, 100
Murray, Mae, 129-131

My Four Years in Germany, 135
Mystery of the Wax Museum, 42-43

Neilan, Marshall, 95
Netherlands, 65-67
The Night of the Hunter, 85-86
The Nose Has It, 99
Novello, Ivor, 174

Of Human Hearts, 29
Old Heidelberg, 133
Our Town, 39-30

Paget, Alfred, 91-92
Pal Joey, 160
Panchromatic Film, 84
Paths of Glory, 70
Phantom of the Opera, 51
The Picture of Dorian Gray, 51-52
Porter, Cole, 173
Production Code, 34-53

The Quatermass Xperiment, 97, 103

Rain, 26
The Raven, 43
The Regulars, 144-146
Renoir, Jean, 9, 31-32
The Return of the Vampire, 52
Revolt of the Zombies, 43-44
Richard, Wendy, 147-152
Robeson, Paul, 174-175
Romola, 84
The Runaway Bus, 102
Rutherford, Margaret, 102-103

Segal, Vivienne, 153-16
Sheridan, Jim, 162-164
Sherlock Holmes, 165-166
Shoulder Arms, 137
Siegmann, George, 92, 93-94
Son of Frankenstein, 44
Song of Freedom, 174-175
Song of the West, 154-155
The Southerner, 31-32, 188
Street Scene, 24-25
Stewart, James 28-29
Stroheim, Erich von, 138

Strong, Porter, 94-95
Stuart, John, 167-169
Sunset Blvd., 124-128

Technicolor, 15-21, 154
Thursday's Children, 170-171
Tower of London, 44-45
Track of the Cat, 32
The Trip to Bountiful, 78-79

The Uninvited, 52-53

The Vampire's Ghost 53
Varnel, Marcel, 98
Viennese Nights, 157-159

Wales, 109-110
The Waltons, 33
Way Down East, 82-83
Webb, Clifton, 122-123
Welch, Elisabeth, 172-176
Welk, Lawrence, 177-180
Welles, Orson, 188
The Werewolf of London, 45-46
White, Betty, 181-184
White Zombie, 46
Williams, Randall, 116, 118
The Wolf Man, 53

Yesterday's Enemy, 104

www.ingramcontent.com/pod-product-compliance
Lightning Source LLC
Chambersburg PA
CBHW051053160426
43193CB00010B/1166